DEEPAK SETH

THE STORY OF A SELF-MADE ENTREPRENEUR

**The Man Who Defied All Odds,
To Become an Entrepreneurial Business
Leader and Build A Global Multinational**

By Rajendra K. Aneja

"It's a funny thing about life; if you refuse to accept anything but the best, you very often get it."

– W. Somerset Maugham

"For they conquer, who believe they can."

– John Dryden

Dedicated to

Mrs. Mina Seth and Mr. Madan Lal Seth

and

Their sons, Chand, Harish, Mahesh, Krishen and

Deepak and their families

and

All members of PDS and Pearl families.

ABOUT THE BOOK

This book is about a young man with a "Dream". His vision was to dress the world and build a global multinational enterprise. He did it.

Deepak Seth started his business with a small order for 6,000 shirts to the USA, through an importer in 1976. Now, the Deepak Seth Group (DS Group), including PDS Ltd. and Pearl Global Industries Ltd. (PGIL), ships over a million pieces of garments daily from factories across the world. On an average, the Group has supplied at least two garments to each person, in the entire world, since starting the business. The Group counts more than 200 of the top global retailers, such as Zara, GAP, Marks & Spencer, etc., as its customers.

Deepak's first order was despatched from his garage. Now, the Group has its sourcing and servicing offices across the world, in more than 20 countries including the USA, UK, Hong Kong, Dubai, etc. The business is truly an Indian multinational with global roots.

This book explores the mind and working style of this dynamic entrepreneur, Deepak Seth. Deepak's vitality has catapulted him to the top of his profession. This book lists the best practices and legacies that the company has evolved during the past five decades. The Group steadfastly adheres to the highest ethical standards in all countries. Its dedication to quality, customer satisfaction and modern business practices, has contributed to its leadership in a highly volatile industry.

Deepak's personal qualities have contributed immensely to his success and popularity. He has a pure heart. Family relations are the core of his personality. He is a fabulous husband and father. He is very close to his four brothers and their families. His values of integrity and hard work are inspired by his late father, Mr. M. L. Seth. His strong belief in family values is stimulated by his late mother, Mrs. Mina Seth. He is always there for his family and friends. Deepak is the best friend that anyone can have.

The book has a chapter on the "Best Practices of the Group". I hope that these legacies will inspire businessmen to establish responsible global organisations. The last chapter of the book is "Deepak Seth's Lessons for the Young". His dedication to work, integrity, punctuality and humaneness are inspiring.

I am grateful to Deepak Seth for the opportunity to write this book. It was an education for me, in rediscovering him and his many admirable qualities. His wife Payel and his two sons Pallak and Pulkit, gave me their time abundantly. His four brothers, Chand, Harish, Dr. Mahesh and Krishen, were also generous with their time and reminiscences.

Encompassing the journey of a multi-faceted and daring professional and a company, over 50 years requires intense homework. So, we interviewed more than 60 people for this book, involving around 250 hours of discussions and analysis of interviews. The people interviewed included Deepak's family members, colleagues, friends, classmates, government, and industry officials and even competitors. I am indebted to all of them for sharing their perspectives.

I am also grateful to my colleagues, Gnanesh Mehta, Abhishek Gupta, Prachi Pohani, Payal Waghela, Amritaa Aneja and Priyanka Singh, for their contributions. I also thank Gnanesh Mehta for the front and the back covers of the book.

I hope you enjoy reading this book, as much as I have relished writing it.

Rajendra K. Aneja

ABOUT THE AUTHOR

Rajendra Aneja is the Managing Director of a Management Consulting company providing services in Rural Marketing, Retailing, Business Strategy, Distribution, Feasibilities, Productivity, etc.

He worked with Unilever for 28 years in India, Latin America and Africa in a range of General Management, Marketing and Sales positions.

He was a Sir Dorabji Tata Scholar throughout his graduation from Sydenham College of Commerce and Economics and completed his Master's Degree in Management Studies from Jamnalal Bajaj Institute. He is an alumnus of the Harvard Business School and the Harvard Kennedy School of Government.

He has written twelve other books, including "Conquer Rural Marketing", "Agenda for a New India", "My Experiences in Modern Retail", "Slices & Spices of Life: From Rio to Manila via Mumbai, Dubai, etc.", "A Common Man writes over One Thousand Letters to the Editor, Volume 1 & 2", "Little Thoughts for a Better World", "Indian Apparel Industry" and "Covid-19: Mankind's Bitter Battle." He also writes for national and international newspapers regularly.

TABLE OF CONTENTS

Sr. No.	Chapters	Page No.
	Foreword	**23**
1	**A Song in the Heart**	**25**
2	**An Inspiring Father**	**29**
	1) Manifold Dreams	29
	2) Great Belief in Education	32
	3) Sharp Intellect	34
	4) Value of Discipline	35
3	**The Lady Who Wove the Pearls into a Necklace**	**37**
	1) Fabulous Family Builder	38
	2) Fearless and Relaxed	39
	3) Overflowing with Love	41
	4) Laying the Foundation	42
4	**Bodybuilding and Breaking Bricks: School to College**	**45**
	1) Developing the Body	46
	2) Sports and Studies	48
	3) Fourteen Trophies	49
	4) St. Stephen's College	51
	5) Protector Role	53
	6) Clear Thinker	53
5	**Learning Leadership and Harnessing MBA**	**57**
	1) Practical Faculty	58
	2) Tough Schedule	60

	3) Learning in the Markets	61
	4) Continuous Assessment	63
	5) Building Leadership Skills	65
	6) Heavy Workloads	68
	7) Friends, Forever	70
6	**First Corporate Step**	**74**
	1) Joyous First Job	75
	2) Bonding with Workers	76
7	**The Pearl Polymers Business**	**78**
	1) Giving Up the American Dream	79
	2) The Five Pearls	80
8	**Bubble Film: Tough Selling in the Streets**	**83**
9	**The First 6,000-Shirt Order**	**85**
	1) Never-Ending Challenges	86
	2) Great Learnings	88
	3) Exports, Good Business	89
	4) A Mother Goes	91
10	**The Foundation: Values First**	**95**
	1) Values: Not Pliable	96
	2) Building Brands and Relationships	98
	3) Managing Devaluations	100
	4) Fairness	100
11	**Nurturing the Seeds of Growth**	**102**
	1) Managing Quotas	102
	2) Quotas and Hills	103
	3) Global Supply Chain Business	105

4) Systems and Processes 106
5) Liberalising India 108
6) Building a MIS 109
7) Managing Risks 111
8) Happy Vendors 112
9) Assembly Line Production 113
10) Long-Term Vision 114

12 Getting Close to Customers 117

1) Sales Offices, Design Services 119
2) Building Blocks in London 120
3) Segmenting 123
4) Sourcing Offices 125
5) Finger on the Pulse 126
6) Customer Is Always Right 127
7) Moving Ahead of the Market Needle 128
8) Integrity and Partnerships 128
9) Learning from Deepak 130
10) Unique Mentoring 134

13 USA: Capturing World's Biggest Market 135

1) USA: World's Biggest Market 136
2) Building a Team 137
3) Changing Business Models 139
4) Multi-National, Multi-Product 141
5) Cordial Relations, USA and India 142
6) Success Factors 142

14 Profit Centre Concept Takes Birth 145

1) Financial Discipline 146
2) Mentoring and Training 147

15 The Entrepreneurial Model 149

1) Deep Respect for Team 150

2) Working with Entrepreneurs 151
3) Rigorous Analysis 152
4) Builder of People 152
5) Entrepreneurial Bifurcation 154
6) Sharing Insights 155
7) Pragmatic Relationships 155
8) Art of Listening 156
9) Professionalism, Family Management 157

16 Factories in India and Beyond 160

1) Overseas Production 161
2) Post-Quota World 162
3) Garments Production: Not Simple 164
4) Factory Specialisation 166
5) Aggressive Expansion: India 168
6) Formidable Presence 169
7) 400 Million Garments Annually 171
8) Nuts and Bolts of a Factory 171
9) Nine Pillars of Manufacturing Prowess 172
10) One-Stop Shop 176
11) Mentoring of Expatriate CEOs 177

17 Building the Best Teams 188

1) Best Quality Professionals 190
2) Entrepreneurial Freedom, Delegation 190
3) Geographic, Product Businesses 192
4) Compensation, Welfare, Mentoring 192
5) Employee Growth 195
6) Integrity, Timeliness and Discipline 196
7) Respect, Sensitivity for Staff 199
8) Multinational Design Professionals 200
9) Caring Forever 201
10) Leading by Personal Example 203

11) Straight to Work 204
12) Unstoppable 205
13) A Man of His Word 205

18 The Compliances Syndrome 208

1) Codes of Conduct 209
2) Adherence to Laws 210
3) Environment and Sustainability 211
4) Respect for Labour 212
5) Occupational Health 213
6) Security Concerns 213
7) Systematic Assessment 214
8) Rigorous Compliances 215
9) Transparency with Board 217
10) Environment and Sustainability 217
11) Shelf-Life of Clothes 219
12) Youth and Sustainability 220
13) Sustainability Contributions 221
14) Organic Raw Materials 221
15) Change in Industry Structure 222
16) Global Business with Ethics 223

19 Social Compliances, Sustainability and CSR 225

1) Environment and Sustainability 226
2) Green Factories 227
3) Health, Sanitation and Welfare 228
4) Faster Salaries 229
5) Aadhar Card and Digitisation 230
6) Gender Equality Training 231
7) Capability Building 232
8) Model Factory, India 233
9) Education 234
10) Happy Employees Grow 234

20	**The Public Issue 2007**	**237**
	1) Dancing on the Global Stage	238
	2) Integration of Businesses	239
	3) Post-Quota: Wings to Soar	240
	4) Strategic Advantages	241
	5) Business Strategy	243
	6) Funds for Growth	244
	7) IPO: Road Map	245
	8) A Unique Model	247
	9) Post IPO 2007: New Era	249
	10) Demerger: To Accelerate Growth	249
	11) A Global Company	251
21	**The Lady of Dignity, Payel, who Keeps it Together**	**254**
	1) Early Wedding Years	255
	2) The Dedicated Wife	258
	3) Gracious Hostess	259
	4) A Devoted Mother	260
	5) Managing an Elegant Home	262
	6) Evolving into an Entrepreneur	263
22	**Pallak: Northwestern to Norwest**	**265**
	1) Learning the Ropes in Hong Kong	266
	2) Building the Business in UK	268
	3) Entrepreneurial Model	269
	4) The Modalities	271
	5) The Platform Model	272
	6) Three Criteria for Onboarding	272
	7) Mosaic of Partners	274
	8) Platform and Financial Support	275
	9) Entrepreneurial Spirit	276
	10) A Million Garments, Daily	277

11) Operating Philosophy and Values 278
12) Free Hand to Deliver 279

23 The Harvard Experience 282

1) New Horizons 283
2) Harvard's PDS Case Study 284

24 Building Professional Partnerships 287

1) Boundaries and Risks 287
2) Managing Risks 288
3) Collaborative Model, Executive Board 289
4) Three Verticals 290
5) Levers of Influence 292
6) Factories: Sri Lanka and Bangladesh 293
7) Focus on Sustainability 295
8) Handbook: Bible of Values 295
9) PDS's Metamorphosis 296
10) Building Culture, People 296
11) Future Challenges 297
12) Lessons Learnt 298
13) Recipes for Success 301
14) Win-Win Formula 302

25 Pulkit's Entry 305

1) Building New Factories 306
2) Deepak's Plans for Continuity 307
3) Awards and Accolades 309

26 IT and Digital Revolution 330

1) Benefits of SAP 331
2) The Barcode 332
3) Chip Technology, RFID 334
4) Line Planning to Optimise Production 334

	5) Automation of Material Requirements	335
	6) Order Closure Process	336
	7) Business Intelligence Reports	337
27	**Story of Lilly & Sid: B2C and Digitisation Venture**	**339**
	1) Entering the B2C Segment	339
	2) Joining the Platform	340
	3) B2C: Impact on Margins	342
	4) Digitisation Initiative	342
28	**A Company of Entrepreneurs**	**345**
	1) Trust: The Glue	346
	2) Nursery of Entrepreneurs	347
	3) Encyclopaedia of Knowledge	349
29	**Business Is People**	**353**
	1) Transforming Lives	354
	2) Happy Employees: Assets	355
	3) Learning from Father	356
	4) Laws of Lands	357
	5) Fruit Salad and Rigorous Work	358
	6) Careers, Not Jobs	359
	7) Learning and Development Culture	359
30	**Training for Leadership and Growth**	**361**
	1) iLEAD	361
	2) SEED for Supervisors	362
	3) Global HR Management System	362
	4) Workers Engagement Platform	363
	5) Human Resource Platform	363
	6) "My Voice", Global Ethics Helpline	364
	7) "Simpliance": Online Compliance Tool	364
	8) P.A.C.E - Empowering Women	365

9) Training Rural Youth 365
10) The 5S Initiative 366
11) Insurance Benefits 366
12) "Great Place to Work" Survey 366
13) Wellness Initiatives 366
14) Fostering Self-Development 367
15) People Commitment 368
16) Pulkit's Futuristic Leadership 369
17) Inspiring Managers 370
18) "Pearlites": Alumni Network 371

31 Laxmi's Story and Developing the Hinterland 372

1) Life Changing Experience 373
2) Return to the Countryside 374
3) Make in India, 2014 376
4) Indian Leadership, Garments 376

32 Sharing and Caring for People 378

1) Open Door Policy 382

33 Battling the Covid-19 Pandemic 384

1) "Blood Bath" on Streets 385
2) Covid-19 War Room 387
3) Battling Covid-19 388
4) Hobson's Choice: Credit 390
5) Impact on Manufacturing 392
6) Steadying the Ship 392
7) Impact on Workers 393
8) Restructuring for Growth 394
9) Opportunities in Crisis 396
10) Hopes for Recoveries 398
11) Long Term Impact of Covid-19 399
12) New Retailer Strategies 400

13) Online Will Be King 400
14) Changing Customer Preferences 401
15) Harvesting the Power of 3D 401
16) New Technologies 402

34 Mr. Chairman's Role 405

1) Multiple Roles 406
2) Strategic Focus 407
3) Punctuality and Commitments 408
4) Win-Win Business 409
5) Brilliant Executor 410
6) Garments Industry: New Challenges 412
7) People: Backbone of Business 419
8) A Businessman for All Seasons 421

35 Playing a Role in the Industry 430

1) Meeting the Prime Minister 431
2) Respect in Industry 433

36 At Heart, A Family Man 436

1) Brothers: Strong Pillars, Arms 437
2) Strong Relationships 438
3) Balancing Role: Own Family 442
4) Makes You Believe in Yourself 443
5) Daughters, Not Daughters-In-Law 445
6) Sylvester Stallone to Nephews, Nieces 446
7) Student of the Grandchildren 448
8) Time for Music, Movies and Books 449
9) Time for Pets, Too 450
10) Prayer Time 450

37 A Friend's Friend 453

1) Humility 455

2) Best Adversity Friend 456
3) Fabulous Hostess and Host 459
4) Organising a Party 460
5) Best Pickles in the World 461
6) Unique Personality 463

38 Pearl Academy: An Institution in Itself 465

1) Search for Professional Staff 466
2) Practical Syllabus 467
3) Wide Range of Subjects 469
4) Global Recognition 470
5) Becoming a Star in the Industry 472
6) Success Stories of Alumni 474
7) Commitment to Excellence 476

39 "Little Pearls": Building Beautiful Minds 479

1) Goals of the School 480
2) Creative Options 481
3) A Global School 482
4) "Arpan" Initiative 483
5) Day-Care Facilities 484
6) "Peekaboo" Kids Club 485
7) Caring, Experienced Staff 486
8) Safety and Hygiene 487
9) Children as Family 488
10) Awards and Accolades 490
11) Parents' Comments 491

40 Best Business Practices and Legacies 500

1) The Values 500
   i. Integrity and Ethics in Business 500
   ii. Code of Conduct for Employees 500

iii. Transparency and Trust 501
iv. Love and Care for Employees 501
v. Philanthropy 501

2) The Business Model 502
i. Having a Vision 502
ii. Building a Brand 502
iii. Global Business, Customers 503
iv. Services at the Doorsteps 503
v. Value-Added Design Services 504
vi. Factories Across the World 504
vii. 100 Percent Compliant Factories 504
viii. Sustainable Growth 505
ix. Entrepreneurial, Profit-Sharing 505
x. Professionals to the Fore 505
xi. Company-wise Profit Centres 506
xii. Core Business: Stick to Knitting 506
xiii. Constant Addition of Customers 506
xiv. Outsourcing Model: Scalable 507
xv. Hedging Future Risks 507
xvi. Cut your Losses, Move On 507
xvii. Succession Planning 507

3) Business Practices 508
i. Ahead of the Curve 508
ii. IT Practices, Measures 508
iii. Managing Cannibalisation 509
iv. Risk Management 509
v. Zero Stock Risks 510
vi. Controlling Costs 510
vii. Keeping Employees Motivated 510
viii. Happy and Loyal Vendors 511
ix. Execution Skills 511
x. Quick Decision-Making 511

	xi. Empowered Business Heads	512
	xii. Open to Suggestions	512
	xiii. Boots on the Ground	512
	xiv. Disciplines – Punctuality	513
41	**Deepak Seth's Lessons for The Young**	**514**
	1) Sustained Work and Discipline	514
	2) Importance of Family, Relationships	514
	3) Respect for Elders	515
	4) Burning Desire to be Number One	515
	5) Never Give Up	516
	6) Health, the Real Wealth	517
	7) Fight for the Weak	517
	8) Tireless Innovations	518
	9) Will and Way	518
	10) Dedication and Commitment	519
	11) Crisp Details, No Papers	519
	12) Being Fair – A Religion	520
	13) Decision-Making Skills	520
	14) Grasping and Art of Listening	520
	15) Immediate Responses	521
	16) Thank People	521
	17) Invest to Grow Rich	521
	18) Goodwill: Best Asset in Bank of Life	521
	19) Managing Reorganisation Amicably	522
	20) Maintaining Work-Life Balance	522
	21) An Integrated Lifestyle	522
	22) "Sparkle", "Angel" and "Biscuit"	523
	23) Power of Prayer	523
42	**Poem on Mr. Deepak Seth, by Mr. Surender Dhillon**	**524**

LIST OF PHOTOGRAPHS

Sr. No.	Description	Page No.
1	Aerial view of Chennai factory	179
2	Production floor, Chennai factory	179
3	Stitching at Indonesia factory	180
4	Laying the fabrics	180
5	Typical Washing Area in the Factory	181
6	Quality checking of every garment	181
7	Deepak Seth at the Indonesia factory	182
8	Production at the Group's Indonesia factory	182
9	Finishing department	183
10	Quilting machine	183
11	Dining facilities at a Group factory	184
12	Doctor's room at the Bangladesh factory	184
13	Sewing at Group's Bangladesh factory	185
14	Solar panel roof of Group's Vietnam factory	185
15	Lunar New Year Celebration, Vietnam	186
16	Football League, Vietnam employees	186
17	Grandparents and parents of Deepak Seth	311
18	Mr. Madan Lal Seth and Mrs. Mina Seth	312
19	Mr. Madan Lal Seth, father of Deepak Seth	312
20	Mr. Madan Lal Seth meeting Prime Minister	313
21	Deepak Seth with his brothers	313
22	Young Deepak, in college, 1970	314
23	Wedding photo of Deepak and Krishen	315
24	Wedding photo of Deepak, with Family	315
25	Payel Seth, at her marriage in 1976	316

26	Payel and Deepak Seth	317
27	Payel with her parents	317
28	Deepak and Payel Seth	318
29	Deepak with his parents and sons	318
30	Deepak with Sanjay Pershad and family	319
31	Deepak and Payel with sons	319
32	Deepak with his sons, Pallak and Pulkit	320
33	Deepak and Payel with Pallak and Faiza	320
34	Deepak and Payel with Pallak and family	321
35	Deepak with his elder son, Pallak	322
36	Deepak and Payel, with Ritu and Rakesh	323
37	Deepak and Payel with Shifalli and Pulkit	323
38	Deepak and Payel with Pulkit and Family - 1	324
39	Deepak and Payel with Pulkit and Family - 2	324
40	Deepak with Sahana, granddaughter	325
41	Deepak with Vice Chancellor	325
42	Deepak with Arun Gujral and family	326
43	Deepak with Ashok Sanghi and wife	326
44	Deepak with Ashutosh Bhupatkar and wife	327
45	Deepak with Narendra and Rajendra Aneja	328
46	Deepak Seth at reunion of JBIMS	328
47	Deepak Seth with Prime Minister	329
48	Deepak Seth with Prime Minister, Mr. Modi	329
49	Achievers Award, St. Columba's School	422
50	Udyog Ratna, PHDCCI	423
51	Member of the Board of Trustees, AIT	424
52	Valuable Support, Pearl Academy of Fashion	425
53	30 Years of Service, AEMA	426
54	Guest Speaker, D. E. Society's IMDR	427
55	Member – Managing Committee, GEMA	428

56	Little Pearls School	495
57	Entrance lobby of the Little Pearls School	495
58	Deepak and Payel Seth at a School event	496
59	Science Lab at Little Pearls School	496
60	Music and Activity Room at Little Pearls	497
61	Indoor play zone at Little Pearls School	497
62	Children playing in the outdoor play zone	498
63	Playroom for girls, Little Pearls School	498
64	Happy children playing at Little Pearls School	499
65	Children at Little Pearls School	499
66	Children learning at Little Pearls School	499

FOREWORD

I have great pleasure in presenting this book, "Deepak Seth: The Story Of A Self-Made Entrepreneur".

Deepak Seth is a prodigious leader. He has put India on the garment map of the world. His garments sell across the world, through top retail chains. He has built brands and factories across the world, including in ferociously competitive markets like the USA and Europe.

Deepak has also built an entire generation of entrepreneurs, who partner with his businesses in over 22 countries. Starting from a scratch, Deepak has built a formidable global Indian multinational, the DS Group (including PDS and PGIL), with a turnover heading for USD two billion. Deepak's sons, Pallak and Pulkit, are now firmly ensconced in the business, to provide continuity.

In the garment industry, Deepak's voice is heard with respect, due to his knowledge and experience. He also advises various apparel councils, chambers of commerce and economic associations on growth and development. Deepak also founded the premier Pearl Academy of Fashion as early as 1993.

India will progress if we create more entrepreneurs, to spur growth and development. Deepak's wonderful journey, should inspire youngsters in India and across the world. Deepak and his wife Payel, are also involved with various charities like the Mina Seth Clinic, Arpan initiative for slum children and other initiatives for the underprivileged. They also manage the prestigious "Little Pearls" school ventures.

Deepak is a fabulous role model, for the young. I am therefore delighted that a book has been written on Deepak's achievements and success story. May it inspire youngsters across countries.

Rakesh Kapoor,
Former Global CEO, Reckitt Benckiser plc.

1
A Song In The Heart

Deepak waded very warily through the rain flooded road, petrified of stumbling at some open potholes. It had been pouring ceaselessly in Bombay (Mumbai, after 1995) and many streets were flooded. Bombay is a pretty and elegant city. However, it can be miserable during the monsoons. Sometimes, it rains continuously for two to four days. Then the roads are flooded, the trains cease running, the flights are cancelled and the shops are shut. Normal life comes to an abrupt halt.

The sky was overcast and grey, though it was just 3 o'clock in the afternoon, on an August day in 1972. The city was turning dark and despondent. The road in Matunga East, which Deepak was trudging, was flooded with knee-deep water. His shoes, socks and trousers were entirely soaked in the rainwater. The passing cars and double-decker public buses sprayed him with muddy water, as they drove through the flooded roads.

Deepak had to interview 200 housewives in a month on their consumption habits of Parle Glucose biscuits, as part of the Marketing Research Programme for his business management degree. His feet felt cramped as he waded through the mucky rainwater. He was wondering if any housewife would allow him to enter her apartment in his drenched condition. He was tempted to return to his hostel. However, he reasoned tomorrow may not be very different from today. The rains, thunder and lightning in Bombay would continue unabated for at least three months. So, it made sense to complete the five interviews planned for the day.

There were further hurdles to cross. He had to get past the watchman of a building, to an apartment. Then, the housewife must be in a certain income range to qualify to answer the questionnaire. Moreover, she should be ready to spare 30 to 40 minutes for answering the 50 questions on Parle Glucose biscuits. Often, Deepak faced humiliation, when the watchman refused him entry in the building or a housewife banged the door on him, saying she had no time to answer questions on biscuits. Some of the households did not even offer him a glass of water.

Deepak had no time to have lunch or a snack. He had considered visiting Mysore Café at Kings Circle, started in 1934 by the famous Rama Nayak. It is renowned for its soft "idlis" (rice cakes) and crisp "dosas" (a pancake, like a crepe, made from a fermented batter of rice and lentils). The simple, unassuming eatery had become famous because the eminent Indian actor Raj Kapoor and his family used to visit it for snacks, when they lived in its vicinity. However, there was no way Deepak could wade through the muddy rain waters and reach the restaurant. He just munched some of the biscuits from a packet in his pocket. The biscuits too, had turned damp. He had a daily target of completing five interviews. He was determined to meet the target.

Deepak was also apprehensive about how he would return to the Government Colleges Hostel at Churchgate, 16 kilometres away, where he resided. There were no taxis around, due to the flooded streets. Even if he waded across to the Matunga East railway station, the trains would have stopped running due to the flooded tracks. Then, he would have to spend the night on the platform of the railway station.

It is not easy to collect a master's degree in business management, he ruminated.

Deepak's favourite song during his school days was, "I Never Promised You A Rose Garden" by Lynn Anderson. The song was embellished in his heart. He would hum the lines to himself:

"I beg your pardon
I never promised you a rose garden
Along with the sunshine
There's gotta be a little rain sometime."

Deepak was learning that life is neither a rose garden nor a bed of roses. He knew he would have to sweat to achieve anything in life.

Whenever he felt like giving up for the day, he remembered the tenacity of Madan Lal Seth, the young chemist at DCM Chemicals.

From his grandmother, Mrs. Chand Rani Seth, Deepak learnt to always walk with self-respect. “Never bow down your head before anything unjust or wrong,” she would counsel him.

***

“My Dad used to leave on a bicycle and go to work before dawn and then return late at night. We would be asleep by the time he returned home. However, we saw how much hard effort it was taking to bring us up. He was very particular about getting us admitted to good schools for a sound education. He insisted we qualify professionally.”
- Chand Seth, eldest son of Mr. M. L. Seth

2
An Inspiring Father

The bitter, icy cold winds of Delhi blew fiercely in his face. It was 5 am on this freezing morning. His devoted wife, Mina, had hand-knitted a red woollen muffler for him. It was wrapped tightly around his head and neck. The icy breeze almost blew it away. With his left hand on the cycle handle, he used his right hand to tuck the muffler tightly around his neck. Visibility was poor due to the dense fog. He struggled to see the lights of the oncoming cars and trucks. He had just left his residence at Mint Road and was cycling to his workplace, 25 kilometres away.

He had recently commenced his career as a chemist at DCM Chemical Works Ltd., located at Najafgarh, in Delhi. He worked at the plant from 7.45 am to 5.30 pm daily. Since there was no company bus service, he cycled daily for about two hours each way. It was not easy. In the summers, the temperature would touch 40 to 45 degrees Celsius. The dust-laden winds, called "loo", would blow fiercely on his face. During the monsoons, the slush and the potholes on the roads made the cycling very hazardous.

Manifold Dreams

However, Madan Lal Seth was unmindful of the icy winds, the blazing hot summers or the miserable monsoons. He cycled with single-minded determination to his office for two hours every morning and then for two hours in the evening to return home. His eyes were on the road and his feet were on the bicycle pedals, but his mind was far away, chasing manifold dreams.

Ram Nath Seth, Madan Lal's father, addressed as "Bauji", worked for the Government of India, in Lahore, in undivided British India. He was transferred to Delhi in India in 1942, five years prior to the independence of India. Thus, "Bauji" and his family were spared of the horrors of the partition of India in 1947. In lieu of his long and distinguished services to the Government, he had been bestowed the title of "Rai Bahadur". This was a title of honour bestowed by the British Government on those individuals, who had served the country bravely and faithfully. "Bauji" lived in an apartment at Mint Road, near Connaught Circus, Delhi's prestigious shopping centre.

Madan Lal had always believed in acquiring a specialist education. He had obtained a Master's Degree in Chemistry, from Lahore's renowned Forman Christian College. On arrival in India, he had been employed by the prestigious DCM Chemicals Ltd. He lived with his parents and family at Mint Road. "Bauji's" wife, addressed as "Mataji" (mother) was reputed to be a very beautiful lady. There were no Miss India contests those days, but if they were, she would be the winner, thought her entire family. More importantly, she too agreed with them.

The beautiful Mina, from a family of doctors, was married to Madan Lal. She hailed from Amritsar. The city is renowned for the Golden Temple, an important Sikh shrine in India. Amritsar is also the holy city of the Sikh community. The three elder sons, Chand, Harish and Mahesh, were born in Delhi. Though there were a few rooms in the house, the family lived harmoniously, sharing all the household work. The youngest two sons were born in Amritsar. Deepak was born on 22 May 1951.

The four hours of cycling to and from work every day, provided Madan Lal time for reflection. He made some important decisions. He decided he would live life by the values that his father had taught him. Hard work, honesty, sincerity and fairness were the bedrocks of "Bauji's" values. Madan Lal was determined to build his own life on these cherished ideals. He also decided that his sons would study at the best of schools and colleges as they grew up.

Madan Lal was grateful that he had arrived in India, at the age of 22 years in 1942. This was before the holocaust of India's partition in 1947, when over a million people lost their lives. So, having been blessed with a safe entry into India, his challenge was how to fulfil his own professional destiny, educate his sons and help them to achieve their potential.

The mood in India was jubilant in the 1950s, as Madan Lal cycled to work. India had gained freedom in 1947, led by Mahatma Gandhi, by waging a non-violent movement. The Cambridge-educated Indian National Congress leader, Pandit Jawaharlal Nehru had been elected as the first Prime Minister of independent India. He had a scientific temper and was promoting the rapid agricultural and industrial development of India. His charm and intellect inspired the Indians. His vision of a modern India enthused the country.

Pandit Nehru's speech at the time of Independence in 1947 stirred every Indian. He declared, "Long years ago we made a tryst with destiny, and now the time comes when we shall redeem our pledge, not wholly or in full measure, but very substantially. At the stroke of the midnight hour, when the world sleeps, India will awake to life and freedom. A moment comes, which comes but rarely in history, when we step out from the old to the new, when an age ends, and when the soul of a nation, long suppressed, finds utterance." Indians could look forward to a new future. Madan Lal too, was inspired by the vision of a wonderful future in a free India.

The Delhi Cloth & General Mills Group (DCM Group), where Madan Lal worked, was one of the most respected industrial groups in India. The origin of the DCM Group dates as early as 1889, established by a pioneering businessman, Mr. Sri Ram. Now, it was managed by his sons, Dr. Bharat Ram and Mr. Charat Ram. The Group was engaged in the manufacture of diverse products like textiles, sugar, chemicals, rayon, tyre cord, fertilisers, cooking fats, sewing machines and engineering products.

Mr. Charat Ram was impressed with the diligence and application of young Madan Lal, who had joined as an Assistant Trainee. By sheer dint of his efforts and quality contributions, Madan Lal was promoted regularly and rose to the rank of Works Manager. The family moved to a larger house at Rohtak Road, where DCM had its own apartments.

Great Belief in Education

Chand Seth, the eldest son of Madan Lal, recalls, "My dad used to leave on a bicycle and go to work before dawn and then return late at night. We would be asleep by the time he returned home. However, we saw how much hard effort it was taking, to bring us up. Dad was very particular about getting us admitted to good schools, for a sound education. He insisted we should get an excellent education and qualify professionally. He was not satisfied for us to merely graduate. He himself was a specialist in technology and manufacturing. So, he was very keen that all the sons should acquire higher education in engineering, science, or management."

Chand and his brother Harish joined Delhi Public School. It was started by Mr. James Douglas Tytler, the founder of many public schools, including Summer Fields School. As the school had just started, it did not have a building. Chand reminiscences, "The classes were held in tents near Nizamuddin zoo. We spent two years there. Then my father managed to get us admitted into St. Columba's, which was considered to be one of the good missionary schools. After that, practically every year or two, there was a Seth brother passing out of St. Columba's School. I passed out in 1959, Harish passed out in 1960 and then Mahesh passed out in 1961."

Chand remembers, "I, my brothers Harish and Mahesh spent our childhood in the house at Mint Road. My father like my grandfather, was always working. Working hard was highly respected in our family. Everyone worked extremely hard. The result was that we had very little time and interaction with our father as children, because he was always away at work."

Deepak's grandfather was a very disciplined person. He followed a strict timetable daily. The Seth brothers say, "You could set your clock based on his schedule". His times to wake up, walk, breakfast, lunch, dinner, work and rest, were all pre-determined. He adhered to his daily schedule like an army officer. If the guests were expected at 7.30 pm, then everything had to be ready before 7.15 pm.

Chand says, "My grandfather, "Bauji" was a very strict person and a disciplinarian. He had a daily routine and schedule in terms of work and diet and adhered to it steadfastly." These values were to percolate down to all his grandsons. Deepak learnt punctuality and discipline from his grandfather.

The grandparents of the young Seth brothers ensured that they studied regularly and completed their daily homework, since Madan Lal was always at work.

Madan Lal's commitment, loyalty and hard work paid dividends. As his career progressed in the company, the family moved to a larger house at 14-B Gangaram Hospital Marg. This was a large one-storied independent house, with numerous bedrooms. The house had a beautiful lawn in the front and ample parking space for five cars. Madan Lal's parents continued to stay with him in this large house. His sister and her daughter also stayed in the house.

Though his work schedule was very demanding, Madan Lal ensured that his family enjoyed an annual vacation. So, every year he took his sons and wife to interesting tourist places like Agra to see the Taj Mahal or to Jaipur to see the majestic palaces of the Maharajas. Those excursions have become fond memories. The Seth brothers reminisce them even now.

Sharp Intellect

Madan Lal was an exceptionally sharp person with a keen intellect and mind. He could assess any situation or a person in a few seconds. He was a man of few words. He was feared and respected in the office and at home. He had a unique way of simply gazing at someone for a few seconds and then sizing up the person. Deepak inherited these brilliant qualities from his father.

Madan Lal had a soft and warm heart, but never showed it to anyone easily. He took a keen interest in the studies of his sons and their extra-curricular achievements. He was also a friend, to the friends of all his sons. Many of them sought his advice on their careers. He even counselled some of them on the type of life partners that they should have.

Madan Lal's sons and their wives also stayed together in this happy home, at 14-B Gangaram Hospital Marg. It is in this house that Deepak grew up, went to school and college and married Payel. His two sons Pallak and Pulkit also lived here for some years, as children.

Madan Lal's sons were great entertainers. They loved to party. Every festival like Diwali (annual Indian festival), New Year Eve, etc., was an occasion for a massive, throbbing party at the Seth home. Hundreds of relatives and friends of the Seth family would dance and dine till the wee hours of the morning. Madan Lal attended all the parties. He was always a bit reserved, but smiled generously at all the guests.

Madan Lal gradually rose to the highest position in DCM Chemicals. He was appointed as the Executive Director, reporting to the Managing Director, Mr. Charat Ram. Always dressed in a suit or a jacket and tie, he was a picture of sartorial elegance.

Madan Lal Seth now had a bunch of imported cars in the drive of his house. A massive Chevrolet, a Plymouth, etc., with liveried chauffeurs, were at his service. The years of dedication had started paying. He had arrived.

Value of Discipline

Deepak recollects that his dad taught him to lead a down-to-earth and disciplined life. As the Executive Director of DCM Chemicals, Deepak's Dad frequently entertained guests at home. DCM had many collaborations with Japanese companies, like Mitsubishi for fertilisers. The Japanese are gracious hosts and guests. They are very respectful. They bow down when they meet anybody.

Madan Lal Seth wanted to expose his sons Deepak and Krishen to foreigners and their operating styles. He would ask them to serve the drinks and meals on these occasions. Says Deepak with a smile, "Papaji used to make Krishen and me, almost like waiters, for these parties. We learnt how to serve. We went around, met the guests and looked after them."

He adds, "For me, attending to my dad's guests was very educative. I learnt how to talk to strangers and how to engage with them socially. I observed the guests, especially the foreigners. The important learnings for me came by listening to their discussions. It built my self-confidence. I was not overwhelmed by foreigners or guests. I lost my shyness. My character and outlook to life were moulded by these early exposures, provided by Papaji at our home."

Deepak learnt the value of hard work from his father, who rose all the way to the top in DCM Chemicals. From his grandmother, Mrs. Chand Rani Seth, he learnt to always walk with self-respect. "Never bow down your head before anything unjust or wrong," she would counsel him, when he was a child.

Mr. Madan Lal Seth's bicycle, which had ferried him 50 kilometres every day to work and then back home, had gone away long ago. He had kept it as a remembrance in his garage, though.

Some years later, his youngest son Deepak would enjoy racing another bicycle against the school bus, on the roads of Delhi.

3
The Lady Who Wove the Pearls into a Necklace

Mina was a fiercely energetic and busy lady. Every day at 4 am, the lights were switched on in her kitchen, in the apartment at Mint Road in Delhi. Her husband was due to leave at 5 am for work. She had to get his breakfast ready.

Later, her three sons, Chand, Harish and Mahesh had to depart for school at 7.30 am. She had to get their breakfast and lunch organised. Around 9 am she had to ensure that her father-in-law and mother-in-law received their breakfast. Her days were long. Rare was the day, when she could go to bed before midnight. Yet, a smile always adorned her face.

Mina loved working to make her family comfortable. She was delighted that she could fulfil the needs of every family member and bring happiness in their lives. The happiness of her family brought pure joy to her heart. Her entire purpose of living was to serve her family. She wanted her husband to progress in his career. She loved to see her in-laws happy. She was keen that her sons shine in their academics so that they could prosper in their lives.

She maintained a low profile and was always cheerful. Later, after Krishen and Deepak were born, she would say, "God has been kind to me. All my sons are like pearls."

It was Mina Seth who wove all the pearls together and bonded the entire family. The family had already moved to the more spacious 14-B Gangaram Marg villa. Mina continued to hold the family together with her energy, zeal and boundless affection. The five sons got married in this spacious house. Chand, Harish, Krishen and Deepak continued to stay in the same house, with their wives and children. Mahesh and his wife also stayed here whenever they visited India from the USA. Mina's in-laws also stayed with them. She loved it when the entire family bonded together at weddings and festivals like Diwali.

Fabulous Family Builder

At New Year Eve parties, she was delighted to watch her sons and their wives dance and enjoy themselves, with their children and friends. She was a magnificent hostess and ensured that every guest was attended to. She never forgot the name or face of any of the friends of her sons. She welcomed each of them personally and made time to talk to everyone.

Mina lived effortlessly with her own in-laws and her four daughters-in-law under the same roof. She wanted the entire family to be together. Reminiscing the memories of his mother, Deepak says, "My mother was all about love and sacrifice. She was always there for one and all. She was a fantastic person and got along with everyone. She did not have an enemy in the world. She always showered love and understanding on anyone she met."

On any family member's birthday or wedding anniversary, Mina would organise a "pooja" (prayers) at home. She would then visit the Birla Mandir Temple to seek the blessings of the deities. Food and gifts were distributed in the school of the blind and to the poor.

Mina also knew the importance of frequently bonding with the extended family. So, every three months, she would host a dinner where her five sons met her and her husband's siblings. All the children would also be invited. Mina remembered the name of every child. "My mother was always a very loving person, who relished having the entire family around her," recalls Krishen.

Mina Seth was instrumental in keeping the family together. She inculcated the values of love and care in everyone, whether it was the immediate family or the larger extended family.

Born and brought up in a family of doctors, hailing from Amritsar, she was a magnificent Punjabi lady. The Punjabis as a community are very gregarious, fun-loving and adore eating and dancing. They love people and partying. It is rare to find a Punjabi alone or depressed.

In Brazil, if a discussion between colleagues gets heated, they will say, "OK, let's stop. We will pause. Let's have a beer." Similarly, most Punjabis believe that any problem can be solved by having a sumptuous meal, a drink, a dance or a party. And, the Punjabis love entertaining guests.

Fearless and Relaxed

Deepak describes his mother fondly, "She was like a tigress. She was not afraid of anything. She would make light of every incident and move on. I remember, I used to go out to play and often fall down. Like all children, whenever I bled, I used to come running home. She would tell me, 'Do not worry. It is nothing, but a scratch. Apply some Iodex cream and go back to play.' That was her frame of mind. Life was about moving on, about getting on. She taught me, never to be afraid. Her message got ingrained in me. That's the reason, why business tumults and Covid-19 do not worry me too much."

Deepak recalls, "I was a very sporty person. I was always an outdoor person, playing cricket or football. I also participated in gymnastics and acrobatics. I was perpetually jumping from the ceilings or from the walls. So, I was always getting hurt. If you see my toes even now, there are lots of small wounds and scars. Mom always provided comfort. She would tell me, 'Koi gal nai beta. Kuch nai honda. Theek ho jayega.' (It is not an issue. Nothing will happen. It will be fine.)

Deepak also recollects that his mother was very relaxed when the family had meals together. The children were free to eat whatever they relished, be it spicy foods or a poppadum or pickles. In many parts of the world, modern parents are obsessed with the health of their offspring. Deepak recollects it was a pleasure eating normally on the family dining table. He is grateful to his parents for letting him have a simple, relaxed and stress-free life as a child. It made him a happy child and later, a happy person.

Deepak adds, "The first few years of your life, are the ones that really define your character and your personality. So, I think that my parents were big contributors to what my character is today. I am certainly God fearing. However, I am also fearless, which means I am not overly anxious. These are very positive strengths that I imbibed from my parents."

Mina Seth was a very social person. She was always there for her family, friends and guests. If ten people arrived suddenly for dinner, it did not flummox her. She would say, "Let us feed them and make them comfortable." She was simply unflappable. She was an amazing person.

Overflowing with Love

Deepak's dad had a taxing and stressful schedule. He departed for work at 6 am and returned around 8 pm. There was always a lot of pressure on him. So, Mina handled the home very competently. She never gave up. She was an excellent wife, mother and friend. Being a very amiable person, she had built a loyal group of friends in her neighbourhood. Everybody loved her. If she ever fell ill, all the neighbourhood friends visited her. They were always there for her, just as she was always there for them. Deepak observed all these positive characteristics in his mother as a child. Subconsciously, he imbibed all her strengths.

Santosh Gadia, a friend of Krishen, who visited him at his home to study together, recalls "I lived as a bachelor in Delhi in those youthful days. Hence, I was always looking for home-cooked food. Krishen's mother would always ensure that I was treated to a sumptuous meal. I can never forget her kindness and hospitality. There was always an abundance of love and food in that home, due to Mummy. She had lots of care and love to bestow even on me. She was always asking me about my studies and about my marriage plans. I always thought of her as my own mother."

The entire family was glued by Mina's love. Again, the love of the entire family for Mina, forged everyone together. She was the centripetal force in the family.

Santosh adds, "Deepak's dad was a very esteemed professional. He was a doyen in the chemicals industry. He was highly respected. Whenever I entered their house, I used to be awed of him. So, even if he was in the house, I would go and talk to Deepak's mother. All the brothers were very attached to their mother. Papaji (Deepak's father) was a very educated and accomplished person. So, he took pains to ensure that all his sons studied in the best educational institutions."

The professional education shepherded by the father Mr. M. L. Seth and the family values ingrained by the mother Mrs. Mina Seth, have shaped the lives of all the sons. Their sound education and the family values, laid the foundations for their future success.

Chand, the eldest son says, "Our family has stayed together with warm and friendly relationships. The main reason for this fraternity is my mother. She always wanted the family to be together. When I went to the USA to study, my mother made me promise that I would return to India. We did not have any family business for which she wanted me to return. She just wanted me to take care of all my brothers and ensure that they are well settled in their lives."

Laying the Foundation

Deepak's parents belonged to a very generous generation. Their principal purpose and joy in life was to provide a comfortable home and excellent education to their children. Salaries were low in India between the 1950s and the 2000s. India had achieved independence from the British in 1947. There was negligible private industry in the country. The government-owned public sector dominated the industrial sector. About 50 percent of the population lived below the poverty line. Wealth was considered evil, and frugality was perceived as a great virtue. It was difficult to earn and save money due to limited employment opportunities and high rates of taxation in the country. Corporate salaries in India improved only after liberalisation in the 1990s.

So, most middle-class parents realised that they could give only modest amounts of monies or properties to their children. The best gift they could bestow on their children was an excellent professional education. With a comprehensive education from a reputed institution, the children could stand on their feet and construct a future for themselves.

Thus, Deepak's father ensured that all his five sons attended St. Columba's School, which was one of the best schools in Delhi. Then, they went to the best institutes for post-graduate studies, like the prestigious Indian Institute of Technology (IIT), Jamnalal Bajaj Institute of Management Studies, etc. Three of his eldest sons, Chand, Harish and Mahesh, after graduating from the IITs were accepted by prestigious universities in the USA for their Masters in Engineering. Krishen qualified as a Chartered Accountant and Deepak acquired a Master's Degree in Management Studies.

Madan Lal and Mina focussed on providing a loving home and the best quality education to their children. They also ensured that they married very fine brides.

They had set all the five sons and their families on their success journeys, as professionals and family builders.

“God has been kind to me. All my sons are like pearls.”

- Mrs. Mina Seth, Deepak’s Mother

4
Bodybuilding and Breaking Bricks: School to College

"You will break the walls of this house," Deepak's apprehensive mother admonished him. Her warning fell on deaf ears. Deepak was always in his own world, whenever he exercised. He continued raining blows on the external wall of his house. Finally, his mother had to shake him by his shoulder and caution him, "Even if the walls do not crack, you will fracture your wrists." However, Deepak continued banging on the wall. He had to land 100 blows, with his clenched fists on the wall of the house. He wanted to have strong arms, hands, wrists and palms. His goal was to be the strongest boy in his school and in Delhi city.

Having rained a hundred blows on the walls of his house, Deepak moved to the garden. There he summoned his brother Krishen. "See how I crack an entire brick with the edge of my palm." Krishen did not believe him. So, Deepak placed a brick on a concrete ledge in the garden. He raised his palm and then brought the edge down compellingly on the red brick. The force of the blow of his palm shattered the brick. He broke a few bricks with his hand to impress Krishen.

Deepak had developed a deep passion for sports and bodybuilding. He would spend hours banging his clenched fists on the walls of his house, to strengthen his palms. He loved showing his friends how he could splinter a brick with just one blow. His brothers Chand and Harish yet recollect his passion of cracking bricks with a stinging blow of his bare hand. Harish recollects, "He broke many bricks in front of me and other people. The palms of his hands are still very hard.

You need strong muscles and fibres to break a brick. When Deepak was young, you could ask him to break a brick twice or even five times a day. He would readily oblige."

Developing the Body

Deepak was dedicated to developing his body. He would get up at 4 am daily and go to the Birla Mandir wrestling pit to practice. He developed a strong and muscular body. He was planning to compete for the "Mr. Delhi" championship title. He reshaped and muscled his body completely.

After returning from the Birla Mandir wrestling pit, Deepak would drink three or four glasses of milk, eat many eggs and then challenge his elder brother Krishen to a wrestling match in their bedroom. Being thin and strong, he would pin Krishen down. However, when Krishen got Deepak under him, Deepak would say "give up, no retaliation". Krishen was heavy and Deepak said he could not take his weight.

Deepak had made it his mission to be the strongest boy in the school and later in the college. Until he was about 40 years old, he would enthral his young nephews and nieces by shattering a brick with a single blow of his hand.

The Seth brothers also loved playing cricket, India's national passion. They have fond memories of coming home from school, having "sherbet" (frozen dessert made with fruit juice added to milk, cream and egg white) and scampering to play. The long driveway at their 14-B home was their cricket pitch. The five brothers constituted a team. So, there was a bowler, a batsman, and three fielders, enabling them to have their own game. They also played "Gilli-Danda", an Indian game played with one large stick called the "Danda" used to hit a smaller one, called the "Gilli". They went down the Gangaram Hospital Road, hitting the "Gilli" with the "Danda" and following it.

Deepak was the youngest child in the family. He would often play mischievous pranks to tease the elders in the family. His grandfather was a teetotaller. However, he did entertain his friends at home with whisky. Krishen and Deepak were responsible for serving the drinks at these parties. Deepak would surreptitiously add some drops of whisky to his grandfather's fruit juice or soft drink. If the grandfather felt relaxed and complimented him on making a good fruit cocktail, Deepak would confess that he had fortified it with some drops of whisky.

Deepak would also ferment trouble for his grandfather with his grandmother. He would snitch and tell her, "Grandfather has drunk a lot of whisky today." She abhorred alcohol and took it up with her husband. After much commotion, it would be revealed that Deepak had played a prank on everybody. After that incident, when Deepak's grandfather was agitated with anything, his grandmother would light-heartedly advise Deepak, "Serve him that special drink you make. Then, he will calm down."

Deepak, as a child, would often pull the legs of others. Sometimes, his grandmother or mother invited their friends to their house. Again, Krishen and Deepak would be responsible for serving the guests. Some of the ladies were strict vegetarians. If any lady enjoyed or praised a sandwich, cutlet or any snack, Deepak would tell her, "Auntie, you had this sandwich? It contains some chicken. It is not vegetarian!" The lady would suffer pangs of remorse until Deepak's mother would tell her, that Deepak is playing a prank.

Everyone forgave Deepak's naughtiness. He was the youngest child in the family and was forgiven all such light trespasses. A few drops of whisky in a juice or letting an aunt think that she had consumed a sliver of chicken instead of cheese, were laughable anecdotes. He was always cautioned, "Aage na karna!" (Do not do it again.) However, who can stop the wind from blowing or a child from having fun? Deepak recollects, "I had a great childhood. It was absolutely stress free."

Sports and Studies

St. Columba's School in Delhi is an institution with deep red walls and yellow arches. The school started in 1941, a few years before the independence of India in 1947. It was one of the best schools in Delhi, reputed to build character and integrity among its students. The foundation of the values of a person's character, are often cemented during their school years.

The Christian Brothers managed St. Columba's School in a very structured manner. The school taught the full range of subjects like physics, chemistry, mathematics, Hindi and English. It emphasised strict discipline and actively promoted sports. Scoring good marks in all subjects was important, as they helped to secure admission to a reputed college. The school also encouraged students to explore their athletic talents. It had compulsory swimming sessions after classes to eliminate the fear of water from the minds of students. If a person can swim, he is never frightened of the sea.

Deepak developed a hunger and passion for all forms of sports. He wanted to be the best in every game. He showed great talent in football, track and field events. He was always winning medals in his school and inter-school competitions. Deepak reminisces, "I think in my life, no one has ever beaten me in arm wrestling till today."

Deepak's physical strength made him a competitive and well-known person in his own school and also in the neighbouring schools. He became famous among all the schools of Delhi.

After studies, students from other schools used to wait at the gate to see Deepak. He was renowned as the "dada" (boss) of the school. He was always ready to smack anybody who challenged him.

In gymnastics, Deepak would dive through rings of fire. His grandmother would be very upset and counsel him, "This is very dangerous. Please do not do this."

Deepak also loved riding dangerously on the footboard of a bus, even when there were ample free seats inside. The fresh wind blew on his face and invigorated him. However, he had to abandon this hazardous habit, when his father once saw him hanging out of the school bus precariously.

Young Deepak was a daredevil. He used to ride a bicycle to school. On the road, he would race with his school bus to see who could reach the school faster. The traffic on Delhi's streets is treacherous. Yet, Deepak would race his bicycle against the school bus, to prove that he could beat it.

So, school days overflowed with athletics and swimming. Deepak was a backstroke swimmer and also played water polo. He participated actively in all field sports like cricket, hockey and football. The former Finance Minister of India, the late Mr. Arun Jaitley, was his childhood cricketing companion.

Fourteen Trophies

Deepak's crowning memory of school was in the final year. At the annual sports meet, he sprinted away with 14 trophies for various sports events. He won trophies for the 100, 200, 400 and 800 metres events, class and school relays, gymnastics, javelin throw, shot put, high jump, long jump, triple jump events, etc. He had developed a lean, strong and muscular body. He worked on it daily.

As he was a bodybuilder and weightlifter, Deepak was the strongest boy in the class. This awakened a very protective streak in him. “I always wanted to take care of the meek and the weak, whether they were girls or boys,” he affirms.

St. Columba’s was a school for boys. However, the school had a common entrance with the Convent of Jesus and Mary, an all-girls school. Sometimes, skirmishes broke out between the young boys and the girls. “I was always looking after the girls. I did not like anyone irritating them or teasing them,” says Deepak. He was always ready to expose the bullies of the school. He was the first one to pick up a fight with anyone, who troubled the younger boys or girls in a neighbouring school.

Harish recollects, “Deepak was very popular. He was liked by everyone. I do not recall anybody saying anything nasty about him. The two youngest brothers, Krishen and Deepak, were always full of pranks and like a house on fire. However, they were very respectful of the elder brothers and looked up to them with awe and pride for their achievements.”

In school, Deepak continued to score excellent grades, but his heart was clearly in sports and extracurricular activities. Deepak laboured hard as the exams drew closer. He would study through the entire night and then go to the exam in the morning. He would always be ranked amongst the first four students in the class. His elder brother, Dr. Mahesh recalls, “I taught Deepu (Deepak) basic mathematics, like addition, subtraction, division and multiplication, when he was a child.”

As he excelled in studies and sports, Deepak was amongst the four students from his school who were admitted to St. Stephen’s College, in 1967. Krishen, his elder brother, recollects, "Deepak was exceptionally sharp. We had a very strong relationship. When I have to tell him something, even before I am half-way through my sentence, he grasps and understands my point."

Deepak frequently spent his summer holidays in Amritsar, along with his mother, in his maternal grandfather's home. There he played various Indian games like "kabaddi" (contact team sport, native to India) and "Gilli-Danda". He often visited the celebrated Sikh Golden Temple. Amritsar is also famous for its street food. It was here that Deepak fell in love with Punjabi food and snacks like "dahi-papdi" (spicy yoghurt snack), "aloo-tikkis", (potato cutlets), "masala choley" (spicy chickpeas), etc. These loves would be perennial.

His classmate at school and college, Madhav Mishra, who was focussed on swimming, recalls, "Deepak was very well known in school for being extremely tough physically. He knew me and everybody in our class. He still remains a very gregarious person who wants to know everybody around him. He has had this characteristic since school."

Deepak's school felicitated him with the "Alumni Achiever's Award" for his outstanding contributions to his profession, in 2002. At the same time, the school bestowed the award on another luminary ex-student, the famous Indian actor, Shah Rukh Khan.

St. Stephen's College

After school, Deepak joined the prestigious St. Stephen's College for a degree in Economics. St. Stephen's College in Delhi is considered one of the best colleges in India. Its history can be traced back to St. Stephen's High School, founded in

1854 by the Reverend Samuel Scott Allnutt, Chaplain of Delhi. The Cambridge Brotherhood founded St. Stephen's College on 1 February 1881. The Reverend Samuel Scott Allnutt served as its first principal. Over the decades, the college has built a reputation for excellent education in the arts and sciences.

Many renowned politicians, corporate leaders, senior bureaucrats, police officers, thinkers and scientists of India, have studied at St. Stephen's College. Their fraternity continues lifelong. It is an informal club. Mr. Fakhruddin Ali Ahmed, the former President of India; Mr. Rahul Gandhi, a member of the Indian Parliament and leader of the Indian National Congress; Mr. Arun Shourie, a former Minister and journalist; Mr. Rahul Bajaj, Chairman of the Bajaj Group; actors Kabir Bedi and Roshan Seth and writer Khushwant Singh, are some of the luminaries who have passed through the portals of the college.

Performing well at college was important. Good grades led to admission in a reputed professional programme. So, Deepak started to focus more on his studies and less on sports. He continued weightlifting and played cricket whenever he had time.

However, if he ever saw some freshers getting bullied, he would be distraught. "Whenever I saw someone getting tormented, I would always stand up for the person. I was strong. My philosophy in life has always been to support the weak," asserts Deepak. He was always very energetic. He never wearied despite his multifarious sporting involvements. He always had tremendous energy.

Protector Role

Madhav recalls, "Deepak used to protect the weaker students. So, if he saw somebody being intimidated or he saw somebody misbehaving, he would put the bully in his place, even physically if necessary. This gives you an idea of his character. Deepak was bright at studies too. The Economic Honours class comprised of only 32 students. Four of us, including Deepak, from St. Columba's had made it to this coveted class."

Deepak enjoyed building his body, protecting the freshers from the bullies and ensuring he did well academically. However, he had a few more pursuits at St. Stephen's. Despite being a bodybuilder, Deepak would visit the college cafe daily. The cafeteria made delectable vegetable cutlets, sprinkled with miniscule breadcrumbs, which were a favourite of the students. Deepak fell in love with them and devoured a few daily.

There was also a snacks vendor named Sukhiya, who sold homemade "samosas" (savouries) with fillings of boiled mashed potatoes, green peas, cilantro and spices like carom seeds. Sukhiya also sold mouth-watering "gulab-jamuns" (Indian sweets made of milk and sugar, served warm). Deepak was frequently at Sukhiya's stall, enjoying the crispy hot "samosas" and letting the hot "gulab-jamun" sweets just melt in his mouth. The passion for "samosas" would become permanent.

Clear Thinker

Madhav remembers, "Deepak was a very curious person. He was very gregarious. He knew everybody in the college." The courses in economics, economic development of India and the rigorous study of the works and thoughts of economists like Paul Samuelson and John Maynard Keynes, sharpened Deepak's understanding of market dynamics. He was particularly impressed with Keynes's book, "The General Theory of Employment, Interest and Money". Though it was an economics textbook, Deepak enjoyed reading it like a novel, due to the lucid thoughts, clear writing and simple English of Keynes. "His thoughts flow like a clear, gurgling stream in the mountains," says Deepak.

At school and college, Deepak was known to be a clear thinker. He could seize the pith of any problem with lightning speed. He could separate the grain from the chaff, even before a person had finished talking. If any of his friends made an incoherent or illogical statement, Deepak would tell him, that he was not being honest with himself. He would advise his friend to think through clearly. He never let wobbly thoughts or excuses go by. This characteristic has helped Deepak to build a strong business. Even now, if he thinks somebody is making an excuse or is fuzzy in his thinking, he will instantly pinpoint it.

Another classmate who remembers Deepak, is Dr. Rajiv Kumar, the Vice-Chairman of the prestigious NITI Aayog, the policy think-tank of the Government of India. According to him, "Economics Honours was supposed to be an intellectual type of programme. The bodybuilder type of students used to be doing other courses. We were very pleasantly surprised to see somebody like Deepak walk into our class with his very broad shoulders. He was a very jovial person and always had time for a story or a joke."

Pradeep Dinodia was also a classmate of Deepak at college. He is a practising Chartered Accountant (CA) now and recalls, "Deepak and I were in the same class at St. Stephen's college. I still remember him as a very conscious bodybuilder. We used to look upon him as one of the toughies in the class. He was good at studies too and did well in college. However, he had this sheer desire to be a strong person physically. He worked on it steadfastly. Doing well at studies and sports, demands tremendous discipline and time management. Basically, Deepak always demanded more from himself. He was never satisfied with his achievements."

Throughout the school and university days, all the Seth brothers loved and supported each other under the affectionate gaze of their mother. A barefoot "Swami" (holy man), who used to visit their home sometimes, had christened the Seth brothers as the five "Pandavas". The "Pandavas" are the five brothers in a family, who fought for justice, in the epic of Mahabharata. The heroic battle is described in the holy book of the Hindus, "The Bhagavad Gita".

The affection between Deepak and his brothers was evident even in the early 1970s. Krishen was preparing for the Chartered Accountancy exams. This was a tough professional examination, with only about one or two percent of the students qualifying every year. Santosh Gadia was a senior colleague of Krishen in the accounting firm, where they were apprenticing. Santosh was bright in accountancy and would visit the Seth residence to share notes and study with Krishen. He also became friendly with Deepak.

Santosh recalls, "Deepak was keen that Krishen should qualify as a Chartered Accountant (CA). Deepak loved eating non-vegetarian food, like butter chicken. He also enjoyed his drinks. Deepak took an oath that he would not consume any non-vegetarian food or alcoholic drinks till his brother Krishen cleared the CA exams. Perhaps he prayed too, for his brother's success, though he did not tell me. Fortunately, Krishen cleared the exams. Then, Deepak could enjoy his butter chicken and drinks again. I was impressed with Deepak's love and affection for his brother."

Deepak keeps in touch with his school and college friends through various WhatsApp Groups, that he has created. So, the classmates still bond after a gap of 40 to 50 years. Every summer, he hosts a reunion party for them in London or Delhi. A classmate of Deepak says, "Everybody in our group is a high achiever. Yet, they all gravitate towards Deepak and look towards him, to glue us together due to his charisma and humility."

Charisma and humility are the very qualities, with which Deepak built the business, in the later years.

His classmates attribute his success to clear thinking, shunning excuses and unlimited energy. Deepak never gets tired. He was never tired in school, he was never tired in college and he does not tire even now. He is quite simply indefatigable at work, play or a party.

Deepak also evinced keen interest in his fellow students. He always tried to understand what motivated them. He was anxious to understand what really inspired any person. Then, he was able to stimulate the person. These qualities which characterised his youth, when he graduated in 1971, became the basic ingredients of his business success later.

5
Learning Leadership and Harnessing MBA

In his weekly "Perspective Management" session, Dr. K. S. Basu would take the class on a brisk management walk through various industries, companies, scenarios, concepts, etc. He was a walking-talking encyclopaedia of business knowledge. Through his wisdom and declamation, he transported the students into a new stratosphere. Every seat in the Institute's auditorium would be occupied. Deepak loved the Sunday 9 am lecture, delivered by Dr. Basu, Director of the prestigious Jamnalal Bajaj Institute of Management Studies, in Bombay.

There was only one issue. Dr. Basu began his class sharp at 9.00 am. At 9.05 am, he would signal to the attendant that no late comer must be allowed to enter the class. Then, the doors of the auditorium were shut. They would open only after the lecture was over at 10.30 am.

Deepak's roommate, Ashutosh Bhupatkar, recalls an incident when he and Deepak struggled to make it to the lecture: "Once we got late over breakfast in the hostel. There were just seven minutes left to reach the Institute from the hostel, a distance of 1.6 kilometres. I told Deepak, 'We are not going to make it. Let's just enjoy our breakfast.' Deepak replied, 'Nothing doing. Let's grab the breakfast, wrap it up and we will have it in the taxi.' Still, I insisted that we will not be able to make it on time. Deepak persisted that we make a run for it."

So, they wrapped some toast and omelette in a newspaper and fled. They hopped into a black and yellow Fiat taxi. It was a

Sunday, so there was little traffic on Bombay's notoriously crowded roads. The taxi sped past Eros theatre and Bombay's iconic landmark, the Oval Maidan.

The cab screeched to a halt outside the Institute. Deepak and Ashutosh jumped out and raced to the auditorium on the ground floor. They made it to the class, just 30 seconds before Dr. Basu entered. Ashutosh says, "That was very quick thinking on Deepak's part. He always insists, 'Let's work out some alternatives. We cannot give up.'"

From the late 1960s onwards, one of the best ways to build a strong professional career in the corporate sector, has been to acquire an MBA (Master of Business Administration) Degree. In the early 1970s, three institutes of management were coveted in India, the Indian Institutes of Management in Ahmedabad (IIMA) and in Calcutta (Kolkata from 2001) (IIMC) and the Jamnalal Bajaj Institute of Management Studies (JBIMS). Getting admitted to any of these three institutes was tough, but very prestigious.

Practical Faculty

"My dad had clearly told us when we were young boys, 'I do not have much money. I can only give you a good education. You will have to go out and make a life for yourself,'" recalls Krishen. Mr. M. L. Seth was the Executive Director of one of the largest chemical companies in India, but the high rates of income tax at 92 percent, put pressure on all senior corporate leaders in India. So, the Seth brothers decided very early to garner engineering, accounting and management skills among them, in case they went into business themselves.

Deepak was one of the 33 fortunate students to be admitted to JBIMS, from around 6,000 applicants in 1971. He competed in a series of entrance tests involving mathematics, vocabulary, personality profiling, group discussions and personal interviews.

Deepak's family was thrilled that he had been selected and would join the JBIMS in Bombay. They would miss him at home, but were ecstatic that he would acquire a management education and a master's degree. This would be the first time that Deepak would be staying alone, away from the comforts of his loving home. The family was keen that he should pursue a management degree. The three elder brothers were engineers, having studied at the prestigious IIT (Indian Institute of Technology). They had also completed their Masters in Engineering in the USA. Krishen had completed the Chartered Accountancy course. So, if Deepak garnered a master's degree in management, the family would have a mosaic of skills for any future business venture.

JBIMS was led by Dr. K. S. Basu, the Director, who was previously Personnel (Human Resources) Director of Hindustan Lever Ltd., (now Hindustan Unilever Ltd.). Located in Churchgate, the heart of Bombay's office district, the Institute had about 70 percent of its faculty drawn from prestigious companies. They were Chairmen, Managing Directors, Vice-Presidents of multinationals and family businesses, who enjoyed teaching over the weekends. Since these external corporate faculty members worked throughout the week, they could teach only on Saturdays and Sundays. Thus, the Institute worked full day on Saturdays and half-day on Sundays, with the weekly off on Mondays.

The Institute had built a strong reputation for churning out hands-on, practical managers. It taught its graduates to deliver results in addition to constructing conceptual models.

Deepak was always focussed on action. He had landed in the right management school.

Tough Schedule

Like all MBA programmes, JBIMS's Master of Management Studies (MMS) was a high-pressure business programme. Classes commenced daily at 9.00 am and finished by 7.30 pm. Then, there were assignments to be completed, case studies to be analysed, books to be perused, etc. So, after returning home, a student could be working on assignments till midnight. Examination times were even more painstaking. It was a luxury to be able to sleep more than four hours on any night.

The first two months of the programme comprised of a Foundation Course. The 33 selected students hailed from various disciplines like engineering, accounting, economics, mathematics, physics, chemistry and sciences. The aim of the two-month Foundation Course was to familiarise all the students with basic functional concepts, to bring them to a common platform. It included subjects like management accounting, financial accounting, economics, statistics and production management. At the conclusion of the Foundation course, all the students had to undergo an examination. The Institute then decided, whether any student was under-performing and would have to be dropped from the programme.

The students who cleared the Foundation Course examination then went through the first year of the programme. They studied the entire range of business subjects like financial management, management accounting, sales and marketing, personnel (human resources), production management, business environment and quantitative methods. The first year exposed the students to all the functions and facets of management.

The second year offered specialisation in functional areas like finance, operations research, sales and marketing and human resources. However, JBIMS's specialisation had a very wide base. When a student chose to specialise in sales and marketing, he would have five electives in this arena. However, he would yet have to take sessions in finance, quantitative methods and personnel too. If the total subjects were ten, specialisation implied five subjects in the selected arena and the other five in functional areas. The curriculum was designed to churn out a well-rounded manager.

JBIMS's philosophy was to build general managers. It did not prepare its students for pure functional roles, operating in silos. JBIMS wanted to produce generalist managers who could be specialists, but also lead corporations.

Learning in the Markets

The Institute relied on individual project work, group assignments, lectures and case studies to educate the students. A business management programme cannot be taught. It has to be learnt, on one's own. The student is responsible for what he learns, from a range of exposures and experiences.

Thus, many business schools rely on the case study method to impart learning. Case studies are typically written by professors after studying a business issue in depth for many months and even years. Then, these case studies are rigorously dissected in the class with the students. Thus, the case study brings business problems to the classroom for diagnosis.

JBIMS went a step further. It sent the students to the companies to give them real-time exposure. Students were given a brand with which they literally lived and slept for two long years. For instance, Deepak had chosen to specialise in marketing. His allotted product was Parle Glucose biscuit. He would have to study the marketing, distribution, advertising, promotions, consumer behaviour and sales trends of the biscuit. He would have to visit the company and meet the concerned managers. Then, he would conduct marketing research among 200 consumers and prepare a marketing plan for the product. So, Deepak did not learn marketing only in the classroom. He had to visit the company, the distributors, warehouses, retailers and consumers to learn marketing. This was case study learning, but in the markets and in the streets.

Deepak and the other students were guided by a slew of practising managers from various industries. Mr. Pran Choudhary, marketing director of SmithKline Beecham; Mr. Srinivasan Murthy, general manager of Hindustan Lever Ltd.; Dr. Jagdish Parikh, managing director of Lemir Group of companies; Dr. Ramu Pandit, Secretary-General of Indo-American Chamber of Commerce; Dr. Tarun Gupta, marketing director of Glaxo Pharmaceuticals; Mr. M. L. Gauba, general manager of Bajaj Electricals Ltd.; Dr. Suren Chawla, general manager of Lintas and other visiting faculty members steered the learning of the students. They brought the best business practices of the corporate sector to the classrooms. However, through the projects, they also sent the students to the companies and the markets.

Besides the visiting faculty, there were full-time Professors at the Institute. Professor Varanasi Murthy headed the finance programme, with Dr. Guruprasad Murthy teaching management accounting. Dr. P. K. Ghosh taught human resources (HR). Dr. Vimla Patil headed operations research. She was later appointed as the Director of the Indian Institute of Management in Lucknow. Dr. K. Santhanam taught quantitative methods to the students.

Continuous Assessment

The students were assessed almost continuously. There were monthly tests in addition to the quarterly examinations. The monthly test results were aggregated for the quarterly assessments, all of which congregated into the final assessment. It was a gruelling programme with very little personal time for the students.

The management programme also graded students on the basis of their class participation and contributions. A good management programme relies on sharing knowledge to foster learning. Deepak always participated judiciously in the group discussions. He would raise his hand in the class, make a point succinctly and then listen to the other students. There was an economy of words and precision in his class contributions. Deepak's friends observed that he grasped concepts very quickly and was an effective communicator.

Deepak enjoyed all the subjects, be it marketing, finance or management accounting. He attended all the classes punctiliously. His favourite sessions were sales, customer-service and marketing. However, when he was alone, he focussed on how to deploy the learning after graduation.

The class of 1973 included students with varied academic backgrounds. Some of them were IIT engineers and others were graduates in commerce, sciences or arts. Deepak got along well with all of them. His classmates at JBIMS observed that he was outgoing, fun-loving and very intelligent. His indefatigable energy, planning and risk-taking capabilities were evident even as a student.

Deepak's roommate at JBIMS, Ashok Sanghi, who knew him from the first day at the Institute, recalls, "Deepak was a real go-getter. If he decided to do something, he was unstoppable. He also ensured that whatever he had decided to do, he did successfully. That's his forte. He was dynamic from the very first day. If there was any problem, he faced it head on. He would generate innovative solutions for any challenge that emerged. He has managed his business, with the same aggressiveness and vigour."

Deepak was hard working and tenacious during those two laborious years. In the marketing research course, each student had to visit 200 unknown homes to fill a ten-page questionnaire on a product, within the span of a few weeks. Each student was given a brand to research among consumers and then prepare a marketing plan for it. A questionnaire of about 50 questions was prepared by the student and approved by the marketing professor. The random homes to be visited were earmarked by locality and based on specific statistical parameters. Each interview with the housewife took about 30 to 45 minutes. The students had to complete five to eight interviews per day.

The marketing professor believed in the rigour of the entire exercise. He insisted on 200 interviews. Moreover, even if one interview was faked, the student would be rusticated from the Institute.

Now, it is not easy to be admitted to unknown homes in Bombay. It is a challenge even to get past the watchmen of the buildings due to security concerns. Deepak recalls, "Those days, I hardly ate any food. There was no time for lunch. I carried packets of Parle biscuits in my pockets and munched them whenever I felt hungry." This single-minded dedication to any task, would be the bed-rock of his success even in later years.

The marketing research project involved visits to middle and lower-middle class homes in the bustling city of Bombay. Many parts of Bombay city are pretty and elegant. However, like all great cities in the world, many parts of the city are squalid and slummy. Deepak hailed from a privileged family from Delhi and was raised in luxury. For the marketing research project, he had to walk through the streets of the city, travel by bus and local trains and beseech unknown housewives to answer 50 questions on a biscuit. Visiting 200 homes in the middle and lower-income categories, exposed him to how middle and lower-middle class people live, behave and eat. It was an education in itself. Deepak was getting exposed to a new facet of India.

So, JBIMS was teaching its students that business strategies are born in the streets, not merely in air-conditioned offices. You have to walk the roads and sell yourself at every stage, to complete a task.

Building Leadership Skills

On the very first day at the Institute, Deepak had met another student Ashok Sanghi from Hyderabad. His family owned a bunch of theatres. The two of them decided to share a room at the Government College Hostel, on C-Road at Churchgate. The hostel was located in the swanky business and banking district of Bombay. The picturesque Nariman Point, the best five-star hotels, posh restaurants and theatres were all within walking distance. The hostel was about three minutes away from Marine Drive, the iconic seaside promenade of Bombay. It was renowned as the "Queen's necklace" among locals and tourists. The azure blue waters stretched as far as the eye could see.

The Government College Hostel where Deepak resided, became the first arena for testing and developing his leadership skills.

The hostel was managed by an elected management committee led by a Chairman. Deepak decided to stand for election for the position of Chairman, in 1972. Some of his buddies from JBIMS also stood for elections for other positions. Thus, if Deepak won, he would have a harmonious working committee of friends. It was a tense election, with round-the-clock meetings and whisperings. Everybody loves to win any election. Nobody likes to lose.

As the votes were counted, Deepak emerged victorious. However, all his friends, whom he wanted to win, were vanquished. He had won, but his dream team was rent asunder. Deepak was disappointed.

Nevertheless, Deepak resolved to find an opportunity in this dejection. He resolved to work closely with the newly elected management committee, all of whom were from the opposite camp. He had a disarming smile and made friends easily. So, he shed past rivalries and befriended the newly elected committee members. Deepak does not carry enmity or acrimony in his heart. He forgives and forgets. His concern always is, how do we make the current situation work.

Deepak noticed that the hostel service staff members like cooks, waiters, cleaners and watchmen needed some benefits. He led the committee to establish a welfare fund for the service staff. He then persuaded the committee to sponsor a film show, the proceeds of which would go to the staff welfare fund.

The tickets for the movie show had to be sold aggressively to the public. Every day after the class, Deepak would go with his friends, Ashok Sanghi and Ashutosh Bhupatkar, to prominent five-star hotels to sell the tickets. They stood outside the celebrated Taj Mahal Hotel at Colaba and sold the charity movie tickets to guests entering the hotel. Ashok recalls that Deepak sold tickets to famous Indian movie stars like Dharmendra and Amitabh Bachchan.

The charity show was a huge success. Deepak and his team were able to generate Rs. 25,000 (about USD 3,300, at the rate of Rs. 7.59 for one USD in 1972), for the staff welfare fund. They also had a surplus, which was spent to buy table tennis facilities for the hostel.

The JBIMS stint was financially comfortable for Deepak. His family supported him with a pocket money allowance of Rs. 1,500 (USD 200 in 1971) per month. Now, that was a princely sum of money in 1971. Consider, the starting salary of an MBA from the IIMs or JBIMS ranged between Rs. 900 (USD 120) and Rs. 1,000 (USD 135) per month, at that time. If any student received a salary in excess of Rs. 1,000, it was impressive. So, during his studies, Deepak was getting more pocket money, than the starting salary of an MBA.

Deepak recalls that he was never wanting for anything as a student during graduation or post-graduation. He used to drive a 1932 vintage Austin car to St. Stephen's college when he was studying in Delhi. A friend and neighbour of his, Vinod Gujral who was fond of cars, helped him to buy and recondition it.

Families are always more loving of the youngest child. Deepak's grandparents and elder brothers were always very generous to him, as he was the youngest in the family. "I never felt a shortage of anything during my student days, because of the very generous family I had," says Deepak. He recalls when he studied at JBIMS, whenever any of his elder brothers visited Bombay, he would give him a thick wad of 100-rupee currency notes to enjoy himself.

Deepak could not handle the humid weather of Bombay. He had lived in Delhi, which is known for its blazing heat in summer and bitter cold in the winters. To compound matters, his room was on the topmost floor of the hostel building. As the sun beat down directly on the roof, his room was always very warm.

Deepak wanted to study in a cooler environment. Fortunately, the five-star Oberoi Hotel had just opened in Bombay about 1.5 kilometres from the hostel. Its coffee shop "Samarkand" served a Cona coffee for about Rs. 2.50 and then gave endless free refills. So, after dinner, Deepak and his friends would carry their textbooks to the coffee shop of Oberoi Hotel. They would study there till 2 am and then return to the hostel. The manager at "Samarkand" had begun to recognise Deepak. He was moved by the sight of some students studying management textbooks till the wee hours every morning. So, he was generous to them and let them be.

Heavy Workloads

The heavy workloads and the nocturnal study sessions did take their toll occasionally. There was a quantitative method test and Deepak wanted to excel in it. So, he studied at the Oberoi Hotel coffee shop till 5 am. He returned to the hostel and told Ashok to awaken him around 8 am so that he could get ready for college. However, despite Ashok's best efforts, Deepak would not awaken. Then, Ashok decided to go to the exam alone.

In the evening when Ashok returned, he found Deepak fast asleep. When shaken, Deepak replied he wanted to sleep some more.

Deepak woke up next morning and made haste to go to the Institute. "We have a test today, hurry up," he exhorted Ashok who was asleep. Ashok was flummoxed. He explained to Deepak that the exam was already over the previous day. Only then did Deepak realised that he had slept for about 26 hours at a stretch.

Deepak's roommate Ashok Sanghi also hailed from a wealthy family. He too received Rs. 1,500 every month as pocket money from his family. So, the two of them often took taxis to the JBIMS in the mornings to make it to the class on time.

They were not entirely happy with the hostel food. So, they often dined in premium restaurants located near their hostel. They visited some of the well-known restaurants in Churchgate like Khyber, Volga, Gaylord, Quality, etc. Deepak loved food. He would devour his favourite dishes "boneless butter chicken" or "mutton Rogan-Josh" (Kashmiri mutton dish), accompanied by crisp "nans" (leavened, oven-baked Indian flatbreads) and mango pickles, at these restaurants.

To Deepak's and Ashok's credit, none of the other classmates ever knew that they received pocket-monies, higher than the salaries that MBAs garnered after graduating. Nobody in the class knew that Deepak and Ashok often took taxis to the Institute. Even though they were very affluent, they never showed their monies. At the Institute, they would lunch with their classmates in the cafeteria, eating a simple meal costing about Rs. 7-8 (one USD). They indulged in their fancies only when they were by themselves.

Deepak's desire to excel at studies created some panic situations too. Many people in India believe that the regular consumption of almonds sharpens the intellect of a person. Whenever Deepak's father Mr. M. L. Seth or his elder brother Chand Seth visited Bombay, they would bring a few kilograms of the best quality almonds for him from Delhi. His father would advise him, "Beta roj kuch badaam khaya karo. Isse takat badhegi our acchi padhai hogi," (Son, you should eat some almonds daily. They will give you mental prowess and you will study well.) So, Deepak fell in love with almonds.

One fine day, Deepak consumed about 500 grams of almonds so that he could prepare well before an exam. The result was that he had a severe headache, resulting in excruciating pain. It took about three hours and a good night's sleep, with the efforts of his roommates to manage the situation. Nobody could establish the link between migraine and almonds. However, young Deepak decided that it is best to eat a few almonds daily, rather than eating them in bulk.

Ashok Sanghi recalls, "Deepak was a gem of a personality. We had a small group of friends and moved around together. Deepak was the prime mover in our group, planning outings, movies and meals. We did not have any relatives in Bombay, so we had to amuse ourselves on our own. It was during one of our dinners that we both had a beer. Prior to this, we had never drunk beer. We drank beer about three times in a year. It was a new and unique experience. We felt grown-up!"

Friends, Forever

Deepak has kept in touch with his buddies from JBIMS over the decades. Ashok Sanghi and Ashutosh Bhupatkar have worked at various times in the Group. Both are Independent Directors in the Group companies.

Deepak continues to be the chief social motivator of his class. Every year, he galvanises the entire class of 1973, for a rendezvous in some exotic location like Goa or Jaipur for three days.

Deepak delights in organising these annual get-togethers. He telephones all the classmates personally to check their convenient dates. Then, he agrees the venue with them. Typically, the first evening is cocktails and dinner for everyone to mingle and chat. The second evening is dancing and various entertainment events. The third evening is a dinner in some exotic location. The days are full of swimming, excursions and sight-seeing. Deepak leads all the activities and frolics. He keeps everyone together. Anybody who is quiet or a recluse is roped in by Deepak's ebullience. He is the first person on the dance floor and the last to leave any party. Many of the classmates who have not met each other for three or four decades after graduating, are united by these reunions. The class bonds annually even after five decades, spurred by Deepak's organising skills and contagious enthusiasm.

MBAs were in great demand in Indian industries. Though the exams and results were in the months of April-May, job placement interviews would commence in January itself. By March, much before the exams, the entire class would have secured jobs.

The beginning of 1973 saw all the top companies visiting the Institute to interview students for placements. So, every day the students would be dressed in well-pressed, sharp suits, starched white shirts and regimental ties for formal interviews.

Deepak attended a particular interview in colourful shorts and a T-shirt. It was preposterous. A rather scandalised friend asked him the reason for this serious lapse in protocol. Deepak replied, "Everyone in the class has complained that the interviewers from this company are being nasty to the students. They just fire questions. They do not give us the time to reply. They do not even listen. I am not interested in joining this company. However, I did want to tell them that this is not the way to interview students. Hence, I attended the interview to give them a piece of my mind."

In January 1973, Deepak boarded an Indian Airlines flight to Calcutta for an interview with India Tobacco Company Limited (ITC Ltd.), a large Indian conglomerate, operating in cigarettes, hotels, agro-products, etc.

"Deepak has to have a clear vision of where he is headed.

Then, he is very determined to reach the goal."

- Chand Seth, Deepak's Eldest Brother

6
First Corporate Step

"So, the three of you represent the labour union. The other three are the company management. Labour has requested for a bonus in view of the good profits in the current year. Management is reluctant to give a bonus, due to the ambitious expansion plans. You have 45 minutes to discuss among yourself and arrive at a decision," explained the Personnel Manager of India Tobacco Company (ITC), in their distinguished Head Office in Calcutta.

It was recruitment time in early 1973. The JBIMS Management programme was about to conclude. The students were being interviewed for jobs. Hindustan Lever Ltd. (Unilever), ITC, Tatas, DCM and Pfizer were some of the top companies recruiting the management graduates.

These companies had rigorous recruitment processes to select their managers. There would be at least three interviews with senior managers, a group discussion, written tests, personality profiling and even a role-playing session, to identify the best candidates. The directors and senior managers of the companies participated in the selection process. The rigorous selection process typically lasted two or three days. So, getting a job in any of the top companies was like clearing another examination; tantamount to having an additional qualifying certificate or a degree in one's career.

In the interview room, Deepak positioned himself as the head of the personnel function in the role-playing session. Two other candidates sat with him on the management side. Three candidates posing as the labour representatives sat opposite him. The selection committee members sat at a discreet distance. They would decide who would be selected for the prized position of ITC Pupils (ITC's terminology for management trainees).

Joyous First Job

Deepak sat on the chair as if it belonged to him. He was in complete command. Points, pleas and ideas flew from both sides, but Deepak held firm, no bonus. However, he conducted the tough discussions with a smile and respect for the labour representatives. He won the day. He was selected, as a Management Pupil in the Human Resources department.

Deepak's family was overjoyed. To be selected by ITC was indeed an achievement. "The qualities he displayed at the interview, firmness, openness to listen to others, decency in the discussion, the smile on his face, told me that he would succeed wherever he worked in his life," commented another candidate.

Deepak joined ITC in Calcutta and was put through various rounds of training. Companies like ITC, Unilever and Tatas have a predetermined 12 to 18 months induction and training programme. The newly recruited trainee has to complete the stint satisfactorily, before being confirmed.

Deepak spent the first few months getting familiar with the ITC's operations and systems in the Head Office in Calcutta. Then, he was transferred to the Bangalore (Bengaluru after October 2014) factory. As is his habit, he threw himself wholeheartedly into his new assignment. His superiors were impressed with his quick grasping power, plentiful energy and his ability to take charge of any situation expeditiously.

Bonding with Workers

He would visit many of the workers at their homes to talk to them. It helped him to bond and cement relationships with them. He was enjoying the job and learning a great deal. Forty-five years later, Deepak was to reminisce, "The biggest learnings from those days was learning how to deal with the labour unions and building relationships with the workers. I used to visit the workmen at their homes, talk to their wives and children to understand their issues. If any worker fell sick, I would always visit him at home to buoy his spirits. I also observed the living conditions of the workers."

However, deep in the night when Deepak tried to sleep, there was a gnawing thought, as to where a career in a large company would take him. He had seen his own father rise from the bottom to the top of the pyramid in DCM Chemicals as Executive Director. At that level, in the 1970s, the income tax rate was 92 percent. For every Rs. 100 that his father received as salary, Rs. 92 was paid as taxes. The appointment and salaries of directors of companies had to be approved by the Government. So where would all the hard work and dedication take him in his life?

Whilst he received about Rs. 1,000 per month as salary, his family continued to support him, with a monthly allowance of Rs. 1,500 per month. Deepak was realising that without the family support, he would not be able to maintain a comfortable lifestyle on any company's salary.

He had a concrete example of business success at home. His three elder brothers, Chand, Harish and Krishen had started a polymers business. It was flourishing. Chand and Harish were engineers; Krishen was a Chartered Accountant. The family business could do with an MBA in the team. Deepak spent many nights pondering over his options.

The family was keen to grow the polymers business. His eldest brother Chand had told him, "What are you doing there? You have got enough training, now come and join us."

After some months of discussion, Deepak asked, "Fine. What will I do, what will be my role?" Chand comments that this was typical of Deepak. "He has to have a clear vision of where he is headed. Then, he is very determined to reach the goal," says Chand.

Deepak's dad was quite happy with his son continuing a corporate career with ITC. He was not sure that leaving a company like ITC is the right thing to do. A job in ITC, Tatas or Hindustan Lever Ltd., was very coveted in the 1970s.

However, Chand and his mother persisted that Deepak should return to Delhi and join the family business. Finally, Deepak gave in.

ITC was not happy with Deepak's decision to leave the company. The Personnel Director, Mr. Monu Basu, based in the Head Office in Calcutta phoned him. He told Deepak that ITC was opening a hotel in Delhi and offered him the position of a Personnel manager. "Why do you want to leave ITC? You have learnt so much here and are held in esteem," said the director. Ravi Bhoothalingam, another senior HR manager, also called Deepak and advised, "You should not leave. You are considered very highly by the company."

However, Deepak had already made up his mind to walk another path. He recollected a poem by Robert Frost:

"Two roads diverged in a wood, and
I took the one less travelled by,
And that has made all the difference."

7
The Pearl Polymers Business

"Fine, you can go to America for higher studies, but promise me, that you will return after two years. All your brothers are younger than you. They have to build careers. They have to get married and settle down," said Mrs. Mina Seth to Chand. In the 1960s, it was a momentous achievement to pursue studies in the USA after graduating from the IIT. So, the entire Seth family was delighted when Chand and later Harish went to pursue master's degrees in the USA.

Chand Seth had completed his B. Tech. in Mechanical Engineering from IIT Kharagpur in 1965. He had worked for two years as a Management Trainee in the machine building and flexible packaging divisions of Metal Box Co. of India Ltd. in Calcutta. In 1966, he went to the Illinois Institute of Technology, Chicago, to obtain a Master's degree in Mechanical Engineering.

Later, he joined Kraft Foods Inc., Chicago, makers of world-famous cheese and food products, as a Project Engineer. He was gaining valuable experience in the packaging industry.

Harish Seth had followed his elder brother's scintillating academic footsteps. After finishing studies from St. Columba's School in 1962, he was accepted by IIT Madras (Chennai, from 1996). He received his B.Tech. degree in chemical engineering in 1967. Then, he travelled to the USA to complete his Masters at Purdue University in Indiana, majoring in chemical engineering. After completing his studies, he joined the headquarters of Olin Chemicals Corporation in Stamford Connecticut.

Deepak kept pressing Chand to return home through his letters, "Why are you not coming back? Mummy is asking why are you taking so long?" Chand recalls, "I remember telling him, 'Look, I must have something to do, when I return.'" However, his mother's innumerable letters and telephone calls made him think seriously about returning home.

Giving Up the American Dream

Chand and Harish were in a dilemma. They were living the American dream, which all young Indians yearned for in the 1960s and 1970s. During those decades, the Indian economy was growing at around 3.5 percent per annum, known as the "Hindu rate of Growth," due to its static slowness. The government was promoting the public sector. The private sector was not trusted. Mrs. Indira Gandhi nationalised the private banks in 1969. At that time, South Korea was growing at 9.35 percent and Taiwan by 10 percent. Jobs were not easily available in India and salaries were low. The infrastructure in India was weak. Life was not very comfortable. So, the brightest young Indians dreamed of studying in the USA and then pursuing businesses or careers there.

Now, Chand and Harish were under family pressure to return home. At that junction, they took an important decision. They decided, "If we have to work for somebody else, as in a corporation, then we will settle down in the USA. However, if we go to live in India, then we will work for ourselves. We will start a business." Both the brothers had well-paying jobs and career paths in blue chip companies. Nevertheless, they decided to return to India. They worked in the USA until 1971, then flew home.

Chand and Harish commenced the groundwork for a packaging business on returning to India. Chand had studied a range of packaging materials like cans, glass and plastic to package foods in Kraft. India was poised for rapid growth in the packaged foods industry. The brothers thought that packaging could be a revolutionary business in India.

They were short of capital. They did not want to risk their father's savings in a new business. So, they decided to fund their business through bank loans. After the nationalisation of 14 banks in 1969, the Government of India had initiated various schemes to benefit the neglected sectors of the Indian economy. The Government had also introduced a loan scheme to enable engineers to launch their own projects. So, the two brothers got a loan from nationalised banks and started "Pearl Polymers Limited" (PPL).

The Five Pearls

As their mother thought of them as pearls, the brothers decided to incorporate the word "Pearl" in the name of the firm. They ordered the plant and machinery, rented the factory premises and commenced manufacturing in 1972. PPL was engaged in processing of thermoplastics and later pioneered the production of polyethylene terephthalate bottles (PET) in India.

Thus, the foundation of the Pearl Group was laid. The Group was to gradually diversify into several areas like garments and travel.

One of the biggest breaks for the new company came from the shoe-manufacturing multinational Bata, in India. The company launched sandals made from plastic. The division was called "Sandak", being an acronym of sandal. The sandals made from plastic were durable, clean and inexpensive. They were spongy, soft and comfortable to wear. The sandals became very popular in the villages with the farmers, as they were waterproof and very light in weight.

The new business was thriving by 1973. Chand and Harish were fully immersed in it. Krishen joined them after qualifying as a Chartered Accountant. Chand was hoping Deepak too would join the family business. However, Deepak had been selected by ITC. Chand thought that the exposure in a large corporation would be useful for Deepak at this early stage in his career.

Deepak told a friend,

"I have merely fractured my leg.

In case I had damaged my leg, I would be back at work immediately on crutches or on an artificial leg. I am unstoppable."

8
Bubble Film: Tough Selling in the Streets

When Deepak agreed to join the family business, Chand and Harish contemplated the portfolio which could interest him. Deepak had a marketing background. They had to carve a challenging role for him. They had a chemicals trading business, which was doing well. However, Chand thought that a chemicals business would not interest a marketing graduate like Deepak.

Bubble film had just been introduced in India. Pearl was representing a company and was also manufacturing for it. Deepak was given the challenge to develop the market for the bubble film and build a new vertical. Typically, bubble film is used to wrap delicate and fragile items like electronics, wrist watches and crystals. It is commonly used today, but in the early 1970s, it was a revolutionary new concept.

Deepak plunged into the project with all his energy. Harish remembers him to be unbelievably passionate about the product. He innovated usage of the film in new products. Deepak designed dining table mats from the bubble film. He sandwiched the bubble film between a polyvinyl chloride sheet below it and a transparent film above it. The mats were a novelty with the bubbles showing through. He also designed water and baby-feeding bottle covers with the bubble film.

Deepak was keen to succeed in his first venture. It was a tall order. It is always tough to sell a new product in a new market. However, selling a new concept or product which the market has not even conceived the need of, is even tougher. One has to talk, persuade and convince ceaselessly.

Bubble film was expensive compared with traditional packaging materials like tissue papers, cardboard and newspaper stuffing. This, added to the challenge of selling it.

Deepak was the first person to leave the house for work every morning and the last to return at night. He reached the distributor offices even before they had rolled up their shutters. They were all located in Sadar Bazaar, the largest wholesale market for household items in Delhi.

Deepak had fractured his leg in 1974. A plastered foot did not deter him. Every morning, he left home at 8.30 am sharp on his crutches, visiting clients, trying to sell the bubble film. Whenever Deepak took on a task, he would ensure that it was accomplished. He put in his best and wanted to succeed. He told a friend, "I have merely fractured my leg. In case I had damaged my leg and it had to be cut off, I would have done it; but I would be back at work immediately on crutches or on an artificial leg. I am unstoppable."

The bubble film business started generating cash. It looked promising. However, Deepak was not happy with the scale of the returns. He felt that bubble film was in its infancy. His keen and penetrating eyes were scanning for bigger pastures.

9
The First 6,000-Shirt Order

Deepak's salesman, Sunil Chauhan, who worked with him to sell the bubble film, had a friend in the garments business, in New York. Observing Deepak's grit and determination, he asked Deepak, "My friend is looking for some apparel vendors in India. Would we be interested in manufacturing garments for him?"

Deepak mulled over the idea. He knew that garment exports were a sunrise industry. In the early 1970s, garments from India were a rage in the Western countries. India was known for its range and styles of garments like crepe checks, hippie style apparel and bleeding Madras Checks. The garment market was on fire. In the night, Deepak discussed the proposal with his brothers. He suggested to them that they should at least explore the business potential of garment exports. They agreed.

Anup Kapur, the friend of Sunil Chauhan, came to Delhi from New York. Deepak met him. Anup said, "Look, I am an importer of garments. If you supply me garments, I can give you orders on a regular basis. To start with, I need 6,000 pieces of a checked shirt. There is also some embroidery required on the shirts. If you can give me 6,000 pieces in six weeks, then that would show me that you can deliver. Then, we can plan the business further from there."

Deepak consulted a friend in Nizamuddin in South Delhi, who produced garments for large export houses. "We have to deliver 6,000 pieces in six weeks," he told him. The friend advised him to accept the order and agreed to work with him.

Deepak was clueless about manufacturing garments. He did not know anything about yarns, fabrics, buttons, embroidery, threads or dyes. Nevertheless, he told Anup, "You just place the order. I will take it from there."

Never-Ending Challenges

Then, commenced a saga of never-ending challenges. They needed assorted checked fabrics, which were in short supply. So, Deepak ferreted the wholesale fabric Gandhi market in Chandni Chowk. Being a newcomer in the market, Deepak could not get any credit from the vendors. He had to pay cash to buy the fabric.

Deepak was able to collate 10,000 metres of the fabric. The same night, he got the pattern made for the shirts. Next, he got his fabricator friend to make the first sample of the shirt.

Then, another challenge emerged. Each shirt had to have a hand-embroidered rose on the pocket. There was no vendor who could embroider a rose flower on 6,000 shirts in six weeks.

Finally, Deepak located a vendor in Gandhi Nagar who liaised with groups of embroidery women. They hand-embroidered designs on apparel in the nights, at their homes. Deepak met them to confirm that they could deliver. The shirts had to be carried to the women every night. They embroidered the rose design through the night and returned the shirts the next morning.

Every day about 200 to 300 shirts were stitched. Deepak transported them to Gandhi Nagar in his Ambassador car every night. They would be distributed to about 150 ladies in their homes. In the mornings, Deepak collected the shirts from the ladies and transported them back to the fabrication unit. Then, the buttonholes were cut. The buttons were sewed. The shirts would undergo a rigorous inspection. They would then be washed, pressed and packed.

Towards the end of the sixth week, Deepak realised that the consignment could be delayed by a day. He telephoned Anup in New York and sought an additional 24 hours to complete the order. The buyer refused. He said that he wanted the consignment loaded on a particular flight on the appointed day for delivery to a customer the next day. "Otherwise, we will refuse the delivery," he added.

Deepak was stunned. He did not sleep for the next few nights. Chand recalls how the order was readied on the ultimate day, "It was the last date of the shipment. The factory premises were not large enough to finish the entire packing. So, Deepak brought all the shirts to our house. We galvanised all the housemaids, servants and drivers to pack the garments, in the home and in the garages."

Finally, at 2 am, Deepak transported the cartons to the airport for loading on an aircraft. The flight took off. Deepak breathed a sigh of relief. He telephoned the buyer in New York and gave him the air waybill (AWB) number.

For those six weeks, Deepak had lived, eaten and slept in his Ambassador car. He had barely slept for four hours on any night, in those 42 days.

The journey had begun. The year was 1976. The seed was sown.

Great Learnings

Executing the first order was a harrowing, but a great learning experience for Deepak. "That was our first entry into the garment business. Deepak is an amazing man in networking with people. He is fearless. He can pick up the phone and talk to anybody and everybody. He just introduces himself and talks about his work. So, he started working with the other importers also. He managed to secure orders to kick-start the garments business. Those days, even an order of Rs. 10 lakhs (USD 1,11,600 at Rs. 8.96 for a USD in 1976) was huge," summarises Chand.

It was a difficult time to start a new business venture during that period. In June 1975, a state of emergency had been declared by the then Indian Prime Minister, Mrs. Indira Gandhi. The press was censored and 1,00,000 people were imprisoned. The Prime Minister had the authority to rule by decree, elections were suspended and civil liberties were curbed. Most of Mrs. Indira Gandhi's political opponents were imprisoned. There was also a mass forced sterilisation campaign spearheaded by Sanjay Gandhi, the Prime Minister's son. The emergency was one of the most controversial periods in independent India's history. It lasted for 21 months, until 21 March 1977. Despite the pall of uncertainty in the country, Deepak marched on to establish the new business. He had to ensure that every regulatory requirement was adhered to in entirety.

The times were tumultuous in India. The first non-Congress government swept to power following Mrs. Indira Gandhi's defeat at the general elections in 1977. Mr. Morarji Desai was elected as the Prime Minister.

Exports, Good Business

Exports were a priority for India in the 1970s, as the country needed foreign exchange. The Government provided incentives to boost exports. Exporters were entitled to a refund of the excise duties paid on various materials that went into producing an export item. For instance, the exporter would have paid excise duty on the fabric, thread, buttons, polybag, carton, etc. The procedure was that the excise paid on each of these items was refunded to the exporter.

It was very complicated and time-consuming to calculate the duties paid on every element used to manufacture a shirt or skirt. So, the exporters persuaded the Government to give a flat percentage of the sales value (known as Free-On-Board value in trade parlance) as an export incentive. For instance, if a manufacturer exported shirts worth USD 100, he would get USD 10 as an export incentive, which would replace the myriad duty refunds. This reduced the complexities for exporters.

Exporters could also generate some capital for growth, as all profits from exports were tax-free. The garment export business was thus alluring. Exporters received an incentive from the government, profits were tax-free and there were attractive margins on the manufacturing and trading activities.

However, it was a tough and intricate business in terms of getting the garments designed and manufactured within eight to twelve weeks. The foreign buyers took time to confirm the order, approve the designs and determine the sizes. Then, they wanted the goods in their warehouses, a month before the new season or the commencement of floor displays. If the supplies were delayed for any reason, there were penalties or even cancellation of orders.

The sourcing of the various materials was also a challenge. If an exporter wanted to dye 10,000 meters of a fabric, it was not easy to find a large vendor to undertake the task. Many of the ancillary units were in the small-scale or unorganised sectors. They were not focussed on quality or timeliness.

The business was a logistical challenge and required rigorous attention to minutiae. According to Chand, "Deepak was prodigious at managing specifics and people. He was a great motivator. He recruited some of our best management staff and ensured delivery. He selected bright youngsters, trained them and worked with them 12 to 15 hours a day. Over the years, he developed great relationships with many of them. Some of them later branched out on their own. They are big exporters in their own right. We are friends with all of them."

The emergency years and the post-emergency years, when a new government was managing India, were complicated and confusing for Indian businessmen. They did not know where they stood vis-à-vis the government. Uncertainty and fear prevailed. Mr. George Fernandes, the symbol of resistance during emergency, was made the Industry Minister in the new opposition government. He was a firebrand. He insisted that foreign multinationals like IBM and Coca-Cola comply with the Foreign Exchange Regulation Act (FERA). The Act mandated that foreign investors could not own over 40 percent of their Indian enterprises, unless they met other conditions pertaining to technology, exports, etc. Coca-Cola shuttered its Indian operations. It exited India in 1977.

Mrs. Indira Gandhi had returned to power in 1980. She had been a rather left-leaning populist until the 1970s. However, she realised that the private sector would have to play a larger role in reviving the economy and generating jobs. India was getting poised for reforms and an open economy. Mrs. Gandhi initiated some big-ticket economic reforms to secure an

International Monetary Fund loan. The sixth five-year plan (1980-85), in essence, pledged to undertake measures to boost the economy's competitiveness. This meant the removal of price controls, initiation of fiscal reforms, a revamp of the public sector, reductions in import duties and delicensing of the domestic industry.

So, businessmen across India, were buoyed by the possibility of some economic relaxations in taxation, travel and foreign exchange regulations.

A Mother Goes

The year 1984 was tough for Deepak and his family. He was very close to his mother. She was diagnosed with cancer. She went through extensive tests and treatments at hospitals in India and abroad. Deepak and the entire family were emotionally disturbed. Mrs. Mina Seth was the cementing force that kept the entire family bound together.

Throughout the treatment at Sloan Kettering in New York and in India, Deepak and his brothers were always with their mother. Deepak made sure he was always available to serve his mother in India or abroad. Chand recalls, "This was a rough period for us. My mother was fighting cancer in New York. My grandfather was undergoing chemotherapy in Delhi. And, Payel (Deepak's wife) was in hospital delivering a child. Fortunately, the wives of all the brothers took control and we were able to tide over an exacting period."

During that time, there were young children in the house to be tended to. There were elders in the family who needed medical attention. Chand recalls, "It was stressful at times. However, we could manage because the family was together. Everyone contributed and got the job done."

Mrs. Mina Seth passed away in 1984, after a long and courageous fight with cancer, in the best hospitals. The entire family was heartbroken. Deepak was terribly hurt and upset.

A friend of Deepak called him from another town to offer condolences. All that Deepak could manage to say was, "Mummy has gone." Later Deepak told the same friend, "Sometimes I get very upset with life. Mummy was only 59 years of age. She was so young. Why did she have to go so soon? She had so much care and affection to give. Everyone loved her."

Deepak wanted to initiate some social work in his mother's name. Along with his brothers, he started a charitable medical clinic at Naraina, Delhi, in 1987. It provides free medical treatment to the economically weak. After three decades, it continues to serve people. It is called the "Mina Seth Charitable Clinic".

The year 1984 was tragic for India too. Mrs. Indira Gandhi, the Prime Minister of India was assassinated by her bodyguards in October 1984. The country went into a turmoil.

Her son, Mr. Rajiv Gandhi, an airlines pilot by training, was elected as the Prime Minister of India. He was 40 years of age and represented the aspirations of a young India. He recognised the need for economic reforms if India was to shed its reliance on foreign aid and loans. He assembled a team comprising of a squeaky-clean politician V.P. Singh, a technocrat Sam Pitroda and a pragmatist market economist, Montek Singh Ahluwalia. The 1985-86 budget lowered direct taxes for companies and raised exemption limits for income tax. Rajiv Gandhi also took the first steps to usher an information technology and telecommunication revolution in India.

Through all these vicissitudes, the Seth brothers soldiered on. On the business front, 1984 turned out to be a robust year. Pearl had already established offices in Germany and the USA. There was a latent demand for silk shirts in the USA. So, silk fabric was imported from China by Pearl to manufacture shirts for exports to the USA.

Chand reflects, "Our business model was constantly evolving. We thought, why should we confine ourselves to exporting garments from India only? If our customers like Sears or Macy's want apparel from China, lets supply it. We commenced outsourcing to other manufacturers abroad. This was a unique and scalable model."

Chand believed that the founding principle of the business should be equality among all the brothers. He ensured all the brothers had an equal share in the business. He was the eldest and had pioneered the family business. He felt that all the four brothers should have equal shares in the business. In any family enterprise with multiple businesses, some businesses prosper, some are sluggish. How a business performs does depend on the leader, but it also hinges on the market, the stage of the business, local operating environment, etc. Hence, Chand felt it is best if all the brothers shared the gains and pains equally.

Chand was a very fair, mature and balanced businessman. He was also a caring and loving brother.

“Deepak had an absolute passion to grow.

I give him credit for his approach and style of management, which seemed brash to some, but he got the job done.

Pearl became a name to reckon with, in the garments industry and grew by leaps and bounds.”

- Harish Seth, Elder Brother

10
The Foundation: Values First

Success leads to success. The orders started to flow in. Deepak and his brothers had built a reputation for quality and timely delivery in the garments industry, for their firm. Deepak started meeting more people in the industry in India and abroad to expand the garments business.

At a party in Delhi, Deepak met Rattan Chadha, owner of the company Schafersen Chads in Holland. Rattan was a pioneer in the garment import industry. He told Deepak, "You should supply exclusively to us in Holland instead of dealing with so many buyers."

With the garment export business seeming a lucrative opportunity, Deepak's elder brother Harish also focussed on it. He and Deepak worked together on the garments business from Naraina in Delhi.

The premises belonged to Lala Bhagwan Das Garotra, who owned a printing press. He had a spare area of about 5,000 square feet and was happy to rent it for the garment factory. Over the next ten years, the company would establish six additional plants in Naraina and Mayapuri. Deepak reminiscences, "Lalaji's building was very lucky for us. He was our landlord, but he was also like a father figure in business matters. I learnt a lot from him."

So, when Rattan Chadha offered an order to the Group, the Seth brothers were delighted. Rattan was an importer based in Holland and his firm was a significant player in garments. After his university studies in India, Rattan and a few friends had gone to Europe for a holiday. He fell in love with Holland.

He decided to stay back in the country. Thus, an entrepreneur was born in Holland.

Rattan Chadha also attended the "Havan" ceremony (religious prayers for the auspicious start of a new venture), when the production commenced in the factory at A-25/1 Naraina.

Rattan Chadha went on to establish an international fashion brand, Mexx in Europe in 1986, which designed apparel and accessories for men, women and children. He sold it and now owns a smart hotel chain, Citizen M. A successful businessman, Rattan now lives between Holland, UK and South of France.

Thus, Pearl garments travelled to Holland. Then, Deepak found an importer in Germany. So, Pearl garments voyaged to Germany. A restless Deepak, inspired by his initial success, found an importer in the USA. Then, the USA opened up for Pearl garments.

Harish recalls, "Deepak had an absolute passion to grow. I give him credit for his approach and style of management, which seemed brash to some, but he got the job done. Pearl became a name to reckon with, in the garments industry and grew by leaps and bounds."

Values: Not Pliable

In a nascent, sunrise industry where everyone wants to become rich rapidly, values tend to become pliable. Deepak did not fancy fly-by-night importers. During those early years, he had to deal with some opportunistic importers. He reminiscences, "I found that some of the importers were not ethical. They would place orders, but if they were unable to sell the goods, they would try to cancel the balance orders or try to find some minor defect and seek discounts."

So, Deepak started exploring the idea of opening their own import companies in foreign markets. Then, they could keep the custody of their goods at all times. Moreover, if an order got cancelled, the goods would yet be with them and could be sold to other customers. The company would thus, not be at the receiving end of the whims of importers.

At the time when Deepak was planning to open their own import companies abroad, a young man Arun Gujral, was sitting in the office of Chesebrough-Ponds in Madras, in 1978. He had completed his MBA from the Indian Institute of Management in Ahmedabad (IIMA). He was wondering what was next for him at Ponds. He was planning to take a vacation for a few weeks in Delhi and reflect on his career.

Arun met Deepak in Delhi through his cousin Vinod. Deepak briefed Arun about expanding the garment business and the need to open an import company in Germany. "What are you doing in Ponds, getting a salary of 1,500 rupees a month? Join me and I will send you to Dusseldorf!" It is not easy for youngsters like Deepak Seth or Arun Gujral working with multinationals like ITC or Ponds, to chuck up their budding careers and become risky entrepreneurs. However, inspired by Deepak's early success and passion, Arun picked up the gauntlet.

So, Arun resigned from Ponds and joined the garments business. He worked for six months in Delhi, familiarising himself with the design, commercial and manufacturing aspects of the business. Then, he boarded a Lufthansa flight to Dusseldorf. A company to import garments was to be registered in Germany. Deepak was taking charge of his destiny.

However, despite the best of intentions and plans, life is not easy. It was not smooth sailing in Germany in the early stages. Deepak and Arun had to cross many hurdles to get the business going. Arun struggled to get his work permit as two successive Indian partners let them down. Though he went to Germany in 1979, Arun was finally able to establish the company by 1983. They launched a brand for women called "Sorrel". It started doing well.

Deepak and Arun sat in a café in Dusseldorf in 1984, sipping hot coffee. "I find that the exports of men's shirts to Germany are spiralling. We should start shirts too," Deepak suggested to Arun. So, they started manufacturing and selling men's shirts in Germany, made in India, under the brand name "Lerros", which is "Sorrel" spelt backwards. The shirts flew from the shelves straightaway. Deepak and Arun were ecstatic.

Building Brands and Relationships

Brands are like children. They need to be nurtured and pampered. Over the years, "Sorrel" migrated into "Lerros" so that the Group could focus on building and sustaining just one brand instead of two. Lerros brand of menswear is now sold in Germany, Austria, Holland, Belgium, Russia, Ukraine, Ireland, Switzerland, etc.

Arun, who has been with the Group since 1979, attributes Deepak's success to very specific personal and professional qualities. He says, "One of the major reasons why I joined Deepak was because he came across as a very ambitious person. He is always driving himself and his people. He used to be very tough with his employees, but they still loved him because he was always a very fair person. He would never take no for an answer. If he wanted something, he would go after it, till he got it. This determination is the major reason for his success. Of course, he is astute. And he is a very good judge of people."

Deepak paid great attention to building a one-to-one personal relationship with all the business associates, including the customers. Then, he maintained the relationship even if the business did not materialise or faltered. Thus, Deepak always came across as a very friendly and warm person. Most people do business first, then they establish a personal relationship. Deepak was the opposite. He made friends first and then, he did business. And, if the business did not work out, he yet treasured his friendships.

Deepak also built a strong personal relationship with his entrepreneur partners like Arun. Deepak was the best friend that anyone could have. He was always there, if a friend had any problem. His partners could always count on him, to be available to fix any issue that they faced, professionally or personally.

Many entrepreneurs sometimes pause in their journeys and say, "Let's wait and see how the markets evolve." Not Deepak. His passion for achieving greater heights and bolder challenges is insatiable. Apparel is a tough business; you live by your last delivery. Buyer relationships are often based on how well you delivered the last consignment. If the importer is unable to sell the goods, he will demand a discount from the supplier. It is a tough, merciless business, where every cent counts.

Deepak established offices abroad and recruited more entrepreneurial partners to expand rapidly. These initiatives were pragmatic in the aggressive pursuit for growth. Deepak and his elegant wife, Payel, knew all the partners and their families personally. They always remembered the names of the wives and the children. Deepak would also guide the children of his partners, on their career choices.

Managing Devaluations

Managing the exports business, also meant adroit management of currencies and devaluations. The rupee was devalued for the first time by 57 percent in June 1966 to shore up exports. The move was triggered by the 1965 Indo-Pak war.

About 25 years later on 1 July 1991, the Reserve Bank of India lowered the value of the currency by nine percent and then by 11 percent, just two days later. The Indian economy was facing a crisis. The country had limited foreign exchange reserves, just enough for three weeks of imports.

The Indian Rupee exchange rate collapsed drastically in 1992. It was Rs. 20 to USD one in January 1992 and it became Rs. 30 to USD one in December 1992; a huge 50 percent depreciation.

These devaluations caused turbulences in Deepak's operations also. However, he and his team were prepared for these exigences, as they had always believed in prudent financial management.

Fairness

In dealing with the suppliers, Deepak was demanding but also very fair. If a supplier defaulted on quality or timely delivery, he was bound to get a debit note. Deepak was in a "no excuse" industry, which forgave no error in quality or timeliness. However, Deepak never gave up on any supplier even when the latter defaulted. The supplier would get a debit note, but he continued to do business with the Group. Deepak ensured that all vendors and suppliers were paid on time or before the due date. So, the Group gradually built a reputation for integrity and fairness in a tough industry.

Eve teasing is taboo and unpardonable in any Group factory or office. Deepak had established the first manufacturing facility in Naraina in 1976. The garments industry is very labour intensive with many women working on the factory floors. Whilst the cutting and sampling of garments is done by men, the stitching and embroidery is done by women.

Deepak realised that since the majority of his employees were women, it was very important to establish a clear code of conduct on the factory floors. Every lady in the factory had to be treated like a sister or a mother. From the very first day, Deepak ensured that there was no physical, mental or sexual abuse of any type in the factory.

Deepak's vision was to establish factories which were clean, ethical and respectful towards women.

Deepak and his brothers had decided to be fair and straight in a bumpy industry. "I think Deepak has followed a principle upheld by my grandfather, which is to always be fair and never cheat anybody. My father too followed the same policy. I have not heard of a single instance, when anybody in the industry or market can say that Deepak and his brothers ever short-changed anyone," concludes Krishen.

11
Nurturing the Seeds of Growth

Deepak had arrived at a winning formula: win reputed retailer-buyers as customers, establish import companies abroad, pursue excellence in quality and timeliness and have an ethical code of conduct on the factory floors. "If you harness these four elements, you can fly," says Deepak. His secret ingredient in this success formula, was to recruit capable and honest partners and employees.

The import company in Dusseldorf, managed by Arun Gujral, built a profitable wholesale cash-and-carry business. Deepak was enchanted with the success of the Dusseldorf model. So, he opened similar import companies in New York and later in London.

Deepak never waited to consolidate any operation. The day-to-day operations were left to his professional team. Once he commenced a business in a new country, he was ready for another country. Deepak was a man on fire. He established a company in Montreal in Canada. Later, he flew to Sydney in Australia to register a company. Then, he was on a flight to launch a business in Moscow.

Managing Quotas

The garments business in the 1970s and 1980s was guided by quotas. The Multi-Fibre Agreement's (MFA) Quota System, established export quotas for all textile and garment manufacturing nations, for exports to the USA and Europe. The "Quota System" was a key constraint that had to be managed.

The USA and the European Economic Community (EEC) regulated imports from developing countries through the Quota system. These limits on garment exports to the USA and Europe had two objectives. First, to protect America's and Europe's garment industries, from being swamped by cheap imports from developing countries. The second, was to enable but also regulate, the growth of the garment industry in developing countries.

The quotas enjoyed a premium in the exporting countries. They provided the opportunity to export and do business. Quotas were allocated to exporters on the basis of previous shipments or "First come, first served" (FCFS) basis by the apparel councils of their countries. In later years, quota-free countries like Nepal and UAE, started playing a significant role in exporting garments to the USA and Europe.

When an exporter could not get adequate quotas, he could work through other manufacturers or countries who had them. Thus, the aspirations of an exporter, however aggressive his marketing, were regulated and even smothered by quotas. Quotas determined how fast or how much an exporter could grow.

Quotas and Hills

Quotas for exporting countries are as old as the hills in some ways. Countries like India, which could produce cotton at lower prices than the USA and Europe because of lower labour costs, have always had some restrictions on free exports of textiles and apparel. The first such Short-Term Arrangement (STA) regarding International Trade in Cotton Textiles was made in 1961, under the General Agreement on Tariffs and Trade (GATT). It limited cotton textile imports for a period of one year (1960–61), if there were any market disruptions in the importing markets.

This was followed by a Long-Term Arrangement (LTA) regarding International Trade in Cotton Textiles in February 1962. It was negotiated among 22 major trading nations, to allow importing countries, to use quotas to avoid market disruptions in their own markets. The LTA was renewed in 1967 and 1970.

The Multi-Fibre Arrangement (MFA) was negotiated in 1974 to widen the scope of the regulations and provide a framework of protocols for imposing import restrictions. Under the MFA, India had bilateral arrangements with developed countries such as USA, European Union (EU) and Canada. Almost 70 percent of garment exports and 40 percent of textiles exports from India, have been to quota countries, like the USA, EU and Canada.

The MFA restricted free international trade. Low-cost textile-exporting countries could not export freely to the developed countries. The system protected the domestic industries of the United States and the EU. Thus, imports from competitive suppliers like India and China were circumscribed. Each developing country was assigned quotas of specified items which could be exported. The quota systems were more restrictive against cotton-based fibres, which dominated India's textile exports.

The Agreement on Textile and Clothing (ATC) replaced the Multi-Fibre Arrangement in January 1995. The ATC envisaged the dismantling of the Multi-Fibre Agreement over a ten-year period (1995-2004). It provided for progressive elimination of quotas in selected products in four phases, ending in 2005.

In addition to gradually removing quotas, the ATC improved developing countries' access to developed markets, by accelerating quota growths over the four phases.

With the termination of the Agreement on Textiles and Clothing (ATC) in December 2004, all textiles and clothing products were finally subject to multilateral disciplines under the guidelines of the World Trade Organisation (WTO). Thus, after almost four decades, the textile industry was finally unencumbered to free competition, at the international level from 1 January 2005. A new era in the textiles and apparel trade had dawned.

After quotas were abolished, there was a remarkable improvement in the export performance of Indian products. In 2004-05, the growth had been merely 2.69 percent over the previous year. However, in 2005-06, the growth was a whopping 23.14 percent. The biggest gainers in the post-quota period were manmade textiles, followed by cotton textiles and readymade garments.

The Indian textile industry faces many challenges in the post-quota era also. The costs of manufacture are low in Bangladesh. China has raw material advantages. So, it is imperative to improve the competitiveness of Indian exports. This will require technological improvements, investments and efficient supply chains.

Global Supply Chain Business

Deepak serviced customers in all the countries by establishing import companies abroad. The Group's factories in India fed these import companies. When there were excess orders, they were farmed to other local manufacturers. The business was gradually transforming itself into a global supply chain operation, based in India.

Building the business in the initial few years was an arduous task. Deepak would be in his office for about 12 to 15 hours daily, coordinating supplies from various factories. A classmate of Deepak from JBIMS, Ashutosh Bhupatkar, visited him, recalls, "I sat in front of Deepak for about 50 minutes during which he made about 30 calls. Each call was for about a minute or so. Deepak would ask about the health of the person, his family and then discuss the business. It was hectic and bizarre, but then the business needed attention to detail. A few hours later, Deepak visited the house of a Member of the Indian Parliament. He took me with him. He was absolutely relaxed. He was at ease, talking to all the political dignitaries with panache."

Systems and Processes

The growth in the business also involved streamlining operations and embedding new systems. The quota system meant that the Group had to work with 80 to 90 companies. There were about 50 people working in the accounts and finance department. Vineet Mathur had joined in 1993, as Senior Finance Manager. He observed that there were many instances of duplication of efforts in the system. He recollects, "The Group was growing rapidly and trying to do many things simultaneously. So inevitably, there was some patch work in resolving problems to keep the needle moving."

Deepak wanted to replace expediencies with processes and systems. Some of the smaller companies were closed or merged with others. The accounting and finance departments were streamlined. Operating manuals were written and circulated.

Deepak invited suggestions and proposals for improving the systems in the firm. He had one cardinal rule: is the suggestion good for the business? Who was suggesting the innovation, was not important. It could even be a clerk, a peon or a watchman. The person could be three or four levels below a director. Says Vineet Mathur, "If a recommendation was meritorious, Deepak would support the person advocating it."

There were 300 managers in the Group in 1993. During the restructuring, Vineet noticed that they were paid their salaries every month by cheques. A payroll was prepared manually every month. Then, the 300 cheques were written. After that, two senior managers had to sign these 300 cheques. These senior managers were never free simultaneously. Sometimes, they would be travelling on work. So, the process of the two managers signing the 300 cheques, sometimes took two weeks.

Finally, after their signatures, the cheques would be issued to the managers. They visited their own banks to deposit the cheques. The clearing could take two to five days. So, the salaries were always late in reaching the bank accounts of the managers. Most managers needed the salaries in the first week of the month, to disburse household payments.

Online banking or electronic clearing had not yet come to India in 1993. The only way to streamline the system, was for all managers to open their bank accounts in the company's bank. Then, based on one instruction to the bank, the salaries would be transferred to the accounts of all the 300 managers simultaneously.

This would save a few hundred man-hours in writing cheques and signing them. So, 299 of the 300 managers, opened their bank accounts in the company's bank. However, the General Manager (GM) of a unit did not want to change his bank. All implorations to him were of no avail. For almost four months, the GM refused to change his bank. When the Accounts department finally stopped his salary, he was livid and threatened to quit.

After Deepak returned to office from abroad, he spoke to the GM, "What is the problem, why are you not opening the bank account? Somebody is trying to streamline a procedure, which will benefit everybody. So, we should support him." Later, the GM opened his bank account and the issue was resolved.

So, even small changes are not easy to execute in rapidly growing organisations. Vineet reminiscences, "If you have an idea which helps the organisation, Deepak supports you, irrespective of the consequences. That, spurred me to continue working with the Group."

Liberalising India

Around the 1990s, the Government of India started undergoing a fundamental change in its thinking. There was a growing realisation that the Government by itself, could not fulfil the rising aspirations of a growing population, through controls and licences. It was gradually dawning, that the economy would have to be liberalised. The private sector would be invigorated to play a vital role in creating jobs and boosting growth.

Gradually, the Government also became pragmatically open to foreign investment. The ease of doing business in India, became a vital parameter. The process of liberalisation started with Prime Minister Rajiv Gandhi in the late 1980s. It gathered momentum during the tenure of the ninth Prime Minister of India, Mr. Narasimha Rao, between 1991 and

1996. He appointed a renowned economist Mr. Manmohan Singh, as the Finance Minister. The "Licence-Raj" (licence era) was gradually dismantled. Foreign Direct Investment (FDI) was encouraged. Large public sector undertakings, which were not delivering profits, were offered for sale to the private sector.

The favourable investment climate, propelled Deepak to invest rapidly to modernise and upgrade processes and systems in the business.

Building a MIS

Next, Deepak focussed on developing a comprehensive Management Information System (MIS), inter-twining all the operating units. He was keen to make the monthly meetings more meaningful. He wanted to get away from the traditional Excel sheets. Deepak told Vineet to introduce budgetary control systems, whereby every profit centre would have specific budgets and targets. The monthly meetings could then focus on key result areas.

Vineet Mathur recalls, "The monthly MIS was presented to Mr. Seth by each division. It comprised of a single sheet of paper, showing the profit and loss account, with monthly and year-to-date data. The MIS sheet was an extraction from the accounting statement. Since the targets, budgets or executive summary were not presented, we could not discuss the business performance evocatively. In one of the meetings, Mr. Seth dissatisfied with the MIS, asked everyone what should be done to control costs. I mentioned the need to have budgets. He grabbed the idea. He gave me the task of introducing budgets in the business."

Vineet found it a challenge to get the Business Heads to forecast the annual sales and costs. They preferred to spend time on booking and executing business, rather than fulfilling accounting or financial requirements. There was resistance to accepting the budgetary process and sharing information. So initially, Vineet made the forecasts himself, after discussions with the Business Heads. Vineet recalls preparing at least three to four iterations of the budget for each division. The budgetary exercises acted like catalysts. They underscored the importance of the budgetary process to everyone. Gradually, all the managers realised, that they could construct forecasts and budgets.

Vineet's next challenge was to develop a monthly MIS, after phasing the annual budget into monthly projections. Garment exports are a seasonal business. Hence, the splitting of the annual budget by month, is vital to managing the working capital and the cash flows.

An Executive Summary provides a bird's eye view of the financial results, whether it is monthly or annual. So, Vineet focussed on introducing the concept of an Executive Summary for each division, in the MIS meetings. The objective was to focus on key performance indicators and parameters, so that important results of each division could be reviewed.

Gradually, the Business Heads saw value in the budgetary process to manage their operations and evaluate their performance. They could use the information to initiate corrective actions in time. If the sales were below target in some months or the costs were exceeding the budgets, they could focus on the underlying causes. They could also counsel their teams to be proactive in resolving issues. Now, budgetary control is a mainstream tool, used by the Group in all the units, to monitor and assess performance.

Managing Risks

The judicious management of risks is a major strength of the DS Group. A global business is always fraught with economic and financial perils. There are multifarious risks pertaining to the political ecosystem, economic downturns, local laws regarding foreign investments, repatriation of profits, currency fluctuations, changing market preferences, labour laws, etc. Deepak is agile and travels to various countries every month. He is constantly evaluating business risks on an ongoing basis. He provides guidelines to the operating businesses, on how to manage the environmental, financial, retailing, manufacturing, credit and currency risks.

An important business quality of Deepak is that he is open to taking risks. He thinks big and can invest big too. He watches the investments very judiciously. If the investments are not delivering, say within two or three years, he pulls out of the venture. He is not afraid to own a mistake. He is bold enough to admit an investment error. "When you invest, you have to care about every penny," remarks Deepak.

The managers in the company are perpetually vigilant. They watch the productivity of investments meticulously. Managers are aware of the constant risk of a business getting folded, if it does not deliver.

As a businessman, Deepak had learnt very early that the garments business is very volatile. He had gleaned that the key ingredients of success would be high speed of response, cost consciousness and a relationship of complete trust with all constituents like employees, vendors and customers. Deepak has ensured that the high speed of response and effective management of costs, become a part of the operating culture, the very DNA of the company.

Happy Vendors

Ashutosh Bhupatkar, an independent Director, recalls a study to understand if and why vendors enjoyed dealing with the firm. The response was, "If the Group says, we will pay you on this date, they will pay you on that date. If for some reason they cannot pay on the appointed day, they will tell you. We trust the firm completely." This statement from the vendors and contractors reflects the operating philosophy of the business.

Ashok Sanghi was a classmate of Deepak at JBIMS and his roommate for two years. After graduation, he worked for some years in Thailand. When he returned to India in 1988, he joined Deepak to help in streamlining operations. He worked with the firm in two stints, first from 1988 to 1991 and then again from 1999 to 2006.

Tailors were paid on a piece rate basis in the garments industry in the 1980s. A tailor would collect all the materials required to stitch a shirt, like the fabric, buttons, threads, etc. Then, he would stitch the complete shirt and return it to the exporter. The tailor was paid a predetermined rate per shirt. So, it was easy to keep a record of the number of shirts stitched daily.

There was a major drawback in the piece rate manufacturing system. Each tailor had his own nuances and style of stitching. The number of stitches per inch would vary. Even though there was an approved pattern to guide the tailor, he would stitch the shirt according to his personal experience or style. It was difficult to get standardised apparel. All the exporters and factories in Delhi worked on the piece rate system. Deepak and Ashok were exploring how to introduce assembly line production in their factories.

Assembly Line Production

The assembly line production focussed on specialisation. Various parts of the shirt like the collars, arms, sleeves, etc., were cut methodically. These pieces would then be given to tailors to stitch a shirt, with specific norms. Deepak and Ashok both favoured the assembly line of production. They believed if a person specialises in a specific operation, then he would improve his performance and output. Standardisation automatically improves the quality, over a period of time.

The garment manufacturers in Madras (now, Chennai), used the assembly line method of production. So, Deepak and Ashok boarded a flight to Madras to visit some factories. The visit convinced them that assembly line production was the way forward. They decided to make the change in their factories.

However, Deepak and Ashok had to iron out many problems, while implementing assembly line production in the factories.

All the tailors and supervisors had to be trained in the new system of production. The tailors observed that they were earning more than they did in the previous piece rate system, due to augmented productivity. However, a few of them were concerned that their earnings would decline. They protested. Then, Deepak called a meeting of the leaders of the tailors and assured them of a minimum monthly salary. In addition, they would receive a bonus based on their productivity. Deepak had convinced them, that the new system would not reduce their earnings, but would help them to earn more. Finally, all the tailors gracefully accepted the changes.

Deepak did not leave the negotiations entirely to the HR team. He was in the thick of the discussions, as was his style. He told the leaders of the tailors, "I am coming. Let us sit down and talk." Deepak can be as tough as nails in a negotiation. However, he can also smile and be very jovial. He can make people very comfortable. This is his strength. So, the leaders relented, saying "The boss has come to explain things personally to us. Let's move forward."

At times, the business went through minor cash crunches in the early days. Surender Dhillon, senior manager, Company Secretary's department, comments "However, salaries were always paid on time. We observed many other companies would defer salaries for a period of two to six months. In all these years, there has never been an instance when salaries have been delayed. Mr. Seth is very clear that the employees should always be paid on time."

Long-Term Vision

Even in the early years, the 1970s and 1980s, Deepak was a long-term player. He viewed every project with a telescope, sometimes going down 20 to 30 years. He decides, "This project has a future. It is my project and I am going to make it succeed." However, a decision to support a project is always based on a solid, financial analysis.

Many businessmen want a business to churn money from the very first day. Deepak worked on the basis that the operation may make some losses in the beginning. He constantly identified areas which needed correction and improvement.

Visionaries like Deepak can read emerging trends and realities and stay the course. They do not give up until they achieve success. Every business has its challenges, but Deepak has the strength to absorb losses in the first few years. He trusts his skills to turnaround a business and make it profitable.

The early 1980s, were tough years to start a garments business and manage it in India. The business was entangled by a labyrinth of licences, permits and quotas. The patchy availability of power and trained manpower were serious infrastructural challenges. Foreign exchange was very scarce. The exporter had to visit the central bank, for nominal amounts of foreign exchange to travel abroad. So, for Deepak, it was a momentous journey to establish service offices and factories abroad and build a global business. He was creating a multi-product organisation, focussed on customers and operational excellence. These would be the precious seeds of future growth.

Deepak pioneered in establishing offices and warehouses abroad to service customers.
It gave the business a significant competitive advantage.
The strategy of being "At Arm's Length" of the customer,
gave Deepak's dreams wings to fly higher.

***

Deepak meets his customers and visits their stores to study their consumers.
He spends time on shop floors, studying the clothes which shoppers wear and purchase.
This keeps him grounded to market realities.

12
Getting Close to Customers

The Seth brothers - Chand, Harish, Krishen and Deepak were huddled in their conference room, at Rohit House in Connaught Place, in 1978. Deepak was keen to establish branch offices in London and New York, to improve services to their foreign customers. He thought this would also gradually reduce the role of importers, who dictated terms to the garment exporters. However, establishing offices in London or New York was expensive and entailed costs like rentals, staff salaries, overheads, etc. He explained to his brothers, "The garments business will not be managed in the future, the way it is now. The importers control the supply chain, without adding much value. We have to take charge of our customers, supply chain and logistics. Then, we will be able to grow our business."

Indian garment exporters serviced their customers in Europe and USA from their bases in India, in the 1970s and 1980s. These export businesses were owned by individuals or by families. So, every four to six weeks, the owners would fly to London or New York to meet importers or buyers. Indian exporters had not ventured to establish offices abroad. They depended on orders from importers.

The importers had contacts with factories in various Far-East countries and Asia. When an importer got an order from an overseas retailer, he would pass it on to a factory. He would source the goods from the factory and supply them to the retailer. A local inspection agent, enabled and supervised the production process in the factory.

Deepak observed that the importer did not have any infrastructure of his own, in terms of a factory, design service, inspection capability or quality control. He was dependent on other middlemen, vendors and manufacturers to execute the order. The design came from the retailer. The production, inspection and quality control, were farmed out to third parties. No importer wanted to build or own the entire infrastructure or supply chain.

Deepak was trying to look into the future. He perceived that the business would not just be about manufacturing a skirt or a pyjama. Any factory could do it. Customers would seek value addition. Incremental services like designs, would provide a competitive edge.

Deepak's marketing classes at JBIMS and his stint with ITC, had taught him that proximity to the customer is important. It is the key to any sale and establishing a long-term relationship. Quite simply, if you have an office in London or New York, it is easier to meet customers there. You can establish rapport with them, in their markets and cities. Starting an office in Germany had paid rich dividends. The customers were being serviced at their doorsteps.

The conventional garment business operated out of India. However, Deepak saw new opportunities sprouting in the UK and USA. He needed to establish offices and design houses to provide value-added services to their customers. So, gradually offices were opened in London and New York. An office commenced in Hong Kong too.

Sales Offices, Design Services

The sales offices abroad dealt daily with the large customers like Next, GAP, Primark, Marks & Spencer, etc., on a daily basis. Opening foreign offices ensured seamless communications with customers. The teams offered instant service. The customers realised that they were dealing with a Group, with resources and operations in manifold countries.

Deepak understood that the fashion supply chain had many players, who never meet the ultimate consumers. Yet, to produce contemporary designs and apparel, it was necessary to meet consumers and study what they wear and why. So, Deepak made it a point to meet his customers. He visited their stores to study their shoppers. He spent a lot of time on shop floors, studying the clothes that shoppers purchased. This kept him grounded to market realities.

Deepak realised that though the retailers had their own design teams, they were thrilled to get new ideas from the suppliers. So, the Group recruited designers to serve the large customers. The designers made presentations to the buyers on new fashion trends and ranges. The buyers were excited. Sometimes, the customer liked the fabric of a particular garment and the styling of another piece. It was thus possible to fine-tune products, to the needs of the customers. Now, the Group has in-house designers, in all its offices.

The team of designers received ideas and inputs from the customers and then got the samples made in their factories. They could also build collections based on the latest fashion trends. Customers started getting more confidence in the skills and infrastructure of the designer teams. The supplier was teaming with the retailers, to ensure the latter's success by offering value-added services. The Group was not just selling apparel. It was offering ideas for incremental sales and profits to its customers. It was a new strategic partnership.

Deepak pioneered in establishing an infrastructure of offices and warehouses abroad to service customers. The move gave the business a significant competitive advantage, since other garment exporters, continued to operate through importers. The strategy of being close to the customers, gave Deepak's dreams wings to fly higher.

Building Blocks in London

Poeticgem in London, had been established in 1991, with just five employees, by Deepak. He had sent Anuj Banaik to strengthen the organisation. Anuj had been recruited in June 1989 and had been trained in the business in Naraina, Delhi.

Initially, Poeticgem worked with catalogue companies. These are apparel companies, selling garments through their own catalogues. The channel helped to launch the business and lay the foundation.

Two years after getting its feet wet, in 1993, the London team started working with value retail clothing outlets, based in the UK. They were principally in the foods business, but were diversifying into apparel. These were modern trade players like Asda, Tesco, Sainsbury's, etc.

Poeticgem was at the right place at the right time. The company built associations with all the chains like Asda and Walmart. So, its turnover grew rapidly to about USD 40 million by 1994.

A big break came to the company, through the business of Asda in the UK. Asda was interested in buying garments at a certain price-quality equation. The Group had a presence in many countries and relationships with fabric vendors in Bangladesh, Indonesia, Hong Kong, etc. It was able to provide Asda with the garments at the requisite price and quality.

George Davies, was a product and design specialist who worked at Asda, Walmart, UK. He had an arrangement, that his apparel creations would be sold under the brand name, "George". A lady named Mrs. Kamal Kapoor who was working with the Pearl Academy of Fashion, knew him. She provided the contact to Deepak.

Deepak went and pitched to the Asda team. So, Asda became a customer. The company also had Next and River Island as customers. It also had large mail order businesses like GUS, which was previously named Chelsea Girl, as customers. Deepak started initially with five to six customers. It was a small business, to start with. The merchandise was delivered from the UK or directly from India. The UK office managed the design and logistics parts of the business. Later, when Pallak, Deepak's elder son, joined the business, he grew it exponentially. The Group had the infrastructure and a loyal customer base. Gradually Asda became one of the largest customers of the Group.

Anuj reminiscences those early days of working closely with Deepak, "He was our guiding light. His vision and quick decision making made us winners. If I wanted any quick answers or rapid decisions, I would go to him. I always got an instant answer, a very precise response. Nothing was left open ended. These qualities are the ingredients of a successful businessman. Mr. Seth studies the facts and figures. Then, he tests his analysis on the anvil of his own instincts or "gut-feel". Finally, he acts decisively. Most of the times, the decisions go his way. Business always has risks. Mr. Seth took many risks and most of them have paid off. He is a visionary and is always ahead of his times."

If any employee approached Deepak with an intractable problem, he would not shy from getting fully involved. If a customer hesitated to sign an order, Deepak would accompany the sales manager to the meeting. If a bank delayed a facilitation, Deepak would accompany the finance manager to meet the bankers. The goal was always to get the job done.

Deepak was a man possessed, in establishing the business in London. He was keen to have ABN in Switzerland as a customer. So, he told Anuj, "Let's go and sell to them." The frenzied journey in 1993 shocked Anuj. He had never seen any Chairman carry a large suitcase overflowing with samples of garments. They boarded the local tube-train, pulling the suitcases of samples. Then, they trudged through the streets of Zurich with the heavy suitcases. Deepak carried the bag of samples to the customer's office, opened it and displayed all the garments, soliciting orders. It was not a Chairman making a presentation. Deepak was selling garments, like a simple salesman.

The visit to Zurich was a revelation to young Anuj. He says, "I thought to myself, if my Chairman can sell garments like a salesman, then, no task is too small for me." Such examples of absolute dedication to building the business, shaped the attitudes of the younger team members. Deepak was setting personal examples to his team. He was leading from the front.

Segmenting

Three factors contributed to the early success of the business in London.

The first factor was identifying the right customers. The European and American markets were crowded with a plethora of modern format outlets, high-street fashion outlets, garment wholesalers and fashion boutiques. If a supplier tried to cater to all these customer-segments, he would spread his efforts too thin.

Deepak's marketing classes at JBIMS had taught him the art of segmenting markets. Deepak identified clusters of customers, based on their potential. Then, he focussed on them. He had the vision and foresight to perceive what the market needed. He could analyse market changes very quickly.

So, very early in the business, Deepak decided to target the value retailers, who could guarantee large volumes. The strategy paid rich dividends.

There were two reasons for Deepak targeting the value retailers. First, they had a huge volume potential. Deepak was establishing large sourcing and manufacturing units in India and other countries. He needed to feed these factories with orders and keep them running throughout the year. Second, even during a recession in the UK or the USA, customers would visit value retailers for food and groceries. When they visit supermarkets to buy pasta or flour, they pass through the clothing section. They would be tempted to buy some garments too.

So, Poeticgem focussed on key value-retailers like George. The relationship with a good partner like George, provided leverage with many other customers. Poeticgem was also a part of the strategic supply chain of Tesco, one of the largest food businesses in the UK. It also had a robust relationship with Sainsbury's, a renowned food chain, which also retailed apparel.

The value-retailers have continued to be important customers of Poeticgem, through the last two decades due to the quality of service. Poeticgem also supplies garments to Primark, a large value retailer in apparel. Marks & Spencer, is also an esteemed customer of the company.

The second factor contributing to the success of Poeticgem, was the emphasis on in-house design services to the clients. Deepak's vision was to have the best customers and offer them a range of services focussed on designs, quality and delivery. He realised that providing design services would add value to their product offerings.

The design section became the heart of the business. The strategy was to have a very strong design presence in London and also in the sourcing and manufacturing units. With tempting designs, it becomes much easier to sell garments to the customers. Poeticgem also maintains its own showrooms and studios, where its garments, designs and styles are displayed.

Now, about 60 percent of the orders received by the Group, emanate from designs offered by them. So, going that extra bit, helped in delighting the customers. Poeticgem was thus able to build a robust design and sourcing business.

Of the 200 staff working in Poeticgem, 75 work in the design section. The design services have become a Unique Selling

Proposition (USP) for the company. The balance 125 staff in Poeticgem, are engaged in merchandising, critical path management, quality control and technology management.

The third factor contributing to their success was the emphasis on building a process driven organisation. Poeticgem was one of the few companies to have introduced SAP as early as the year 2000.

Every process in the business was mapped and backed by software and systems. Deepak and his team gradually designed a Management Information System (MIS), to make calculated decisions for growing the business. A process driven organisation, supported by SAP, helped Poeticgem to improve their services to their customers.

Sourcing Offices

Next, Deepak started opening offices in the countries, from where the Group sourced its garments. This was another pioneering initiative and gave the business a massive thrust. The first sourcing office was established in Bangladesh in 1999. Now, the firm's own staff could interact with the local factories. The quality standards and delivery schedules specified by the retailer, were monitored by the firm's own team, not by a third party. The third parties normally had no responsibility if an order was delayed. Now, the Group had control on the production. It also opened a sourcing office in Indonesia in 2000.

The Group's cutting edge is that it can gauge future customer needs and cater to them. Deepak had sensed almost three decades ago that the market will need design and sourcing services. He recruited designers and established sourcing offices. Deepak started the firm as an export business. Gradually, he has catapulted the firm to a value-added business by focussing on fashion, design, sourcing and manufacturing.

Finger on the Pulse

Establishing sales and sourcing offices abroad enabled Deepak and his team to bond more frequently, with the buyers and suppliers. Mridul Dasgupta has experience in manufacture, retail and sourcing of garments for over 25 years. He has worked with reputed retailers like Macy's and JCPenney in the USA. He now manages the sourcing of a large retailer in Australia. According to him, "Mr. Seth is a visionary of our times. He was among the first people in India, who recognised very early the importance of multi-country diversification. He established manufacturing organisations in Bangladesh, Indonesia, etc. Another feature which sets him apart, is his clear understanding that he and his family cannot do everything. He knew he needed professionals to grow the business."

Another customer says that he enjoys talking to Deepak because every time they meet, he learns something new. He adds, "We talk about the future of the industry. He has a strong grasp of the challenges that the industry is facing globally. Every interaction with him is a learning experience. He is very accessible and reachable, even at this stage of his career. He makes the effort to keep in touch with people. He is not isolated in an ivory tower, but has his finger on the pulse of the business. Constantly."

Deepak, his sons and the management team try to keep themselves well-grounded by travelling, understanding markets and meeting key customers. They try to comprehend the thinking of their customers. The entire team is hands-on. They study ground realities. If they are planning a new office in Sao Paulo or a new factory in Vietnam, Deepak, Pallak or Pulkit will fly there for an assessment. They are not arm-chair businessmen.

Mr. Harish Ahuja, Chairman of Shahi Exports, extols the initiatives taken by Deepak. He says, "He has been very bold and aggressive. This was necessary to establish a business in the beginning. You have to take risks; which Deepak has been doing quite well. He has established businesses all over the world. They have created a great name. Many suppliers of garments and retailers in the UK and the USA depend on them. They manufacture in Bangladesh, Vietnam and other countries. They are good suppliers. Deepak has also outsourced supplies. Thus, he has established a business worldwide."

Customer Is Always Right

Pallab Banerjee worked with a leading global retailer for 21 years, before joining as Group President, PGIL. He had heard of Deepak as early as 1992, during a three-month internship at a Group factory, when the business was known as the House of Pearl Fashion Ltd. (HoPFL). His internship was a part of his graduate studies at the National Institute of Fashion Technology (NIFT). He used to hear managers and supervisors talk about Deepak's passion for his work and his rapport with the factory workers. If the factory was running extra shifts in the nights, Deepak would join his workers and guide them. Deepak Seth, had become a charismatic folk hero, among his workers.

Pallab met Deepak much later, when he started working for a global retailer in India. The Group was a strategic supplier to the retailer. Pallab recalls an incident, where a buyer had made a demand of about USD 2,00,000, on some grounds, for a Group shipment. Pallab's own deep dive into the matter, convinced him, that Deepak should not be paying the amount. So, Pallab had a frank chat with Deepak. He told him that technically the Group should not be paying the money. However, in the larger interests of building the relationship, Deepak could consider paying the amount. Deepak did not bat an eyelid. He agreed to pay. Other vendors would take days or weeks to make the payment. Deepak sent a cheque within 24 hours.

Moving Ahead of the Market Needle

The garments market was swarming with an abundance of global suppliers circa 1980. Deepak succeeds because he and his team are able to gauge how the market needle is moving. The Group has developed an uncanny ability to discern opportunities. It has a strong understanding of current and future consumer needs. This is important in a buyers' market, where there are many providers.

Deepak scans the entire value chain and identifies market opportunities. He has developed a strong ability to connect all the dots on the demand and supply side. Over the years, he has positioned the Group to move ahead of the market.

Integrity and Partnerships

Customers ferret for ethical values and integrity in their suppliers. Says a leading retailer from Australia, "There is integrity in our dealings with the Group. Deepak has underscored good customer-service and his entire team is focussed on it."

The garment business is challenging, since it is susceptible to numerous fashion whims and economic cycles. So, suppliers who understand this and enable the business of the buyer, are natural favourites. The Group's key asset is its deep understanding of customer needs. It also builds robust relationships with customers. Customers say that the senior managers of the Group always work closely with their own teams. Deepak and his team, seek constant feedback from customers, to add value to their business.

In any business, when a vendor thinks of the profits of the principal, he is automatically preferred. For instance, a movie star in India, works conscientiously to complete a movie in 120 days, instead of the budgeted 150 days. He becomes a hot favourite of the producers. He saves 30 days of production time, film and money. Producers worship such stars. Similarly, an editor is normally concerned about the quality of thought and prose in the periodical. However, a smart editor also focusses on making the newspaper profitable. The proprietors of the newspaper adore him.

Customers love doing business with the DS Group. They find that notwithstanding the pressures of business, Deepak is a very relaxed person, with a great sense of humour. They never see him taut or stressed. For any buyer and seller to do business together, they have to like each other as persons. They have to enjoy being together. Then business follows. Deepak is an immensely likable person. He can make people laugh. He never insults or hurts anyone. He has no airs about him. His customers like to buy merchandise from him.

Deepak delights even in the small and simple things in life. He may enjoy his foreign holidays and dining at Michelin-starred restaurants. However, he also relishes a coffee on the pavement in New York or a "papdi-chaat" (Indian snack) at Bengali market in Delhi, with a customer.

Learning from Deepak

Krishna Kanodia sat nervously outside Pallak Seth's cabin in the Hong Kong office, in 2003. He had cleared the first round of interviews with Rajesh Ajwani, the CEO in Indonesia. The firm was recruiting a commercial resource to be based in London. Kanodia looked at his shoes to confirm that they were shining. He tightened his tie-knot. He had heard that Pallak was just about 24 years old and was wondering what questions he could be asked.

When Kanodia was ushered into Pallak's office, he was rather dazed. Pallak sat with a team of colleagues, surrounded by samples, designs of garments and piles of apparel. The office resembled a showroom with jackets, pullovers, shirts and trousers scattered all around. Kanodia was stumped. He had expected to be interviewed in a posh office. Pallak and he had a pleasant chat. The meeting did not feel like an interview. Kanodia left the office with a job-offer in his hand.

Kanodia was tickled that the company did not have a meeting room for formal interviews. However, it slowly dawned on him, that garments are the bread and butter of the company. So, it is natural to be always surrounded by them.

Kanodia was one of the earliest recruits in the London office in 2004. His mandate was to build a team and establish a credible financial accounting and commercial function. He was new to London. He observed that the office staff would arrive and depart punctually at the scheduled times. Kanodia recalled his experience in India, where the staff always worked for a few hours daily, after the official closing time. In London, 5 pm closing time, meant 5.01 pm departure time. Kanodia was stumped.

Kanodia sought Deepak's advice, on how to ensure that the staff took more ownership of the results.

Deepak proffered him advice on working in varying cultures. It became a "mantra" for Kanodia. Deepak counselled him, "We have to operate according to the work culture of different countries. Here, when someone comes to work in the morning, you say, 'Good morning, thank you for coming today to work. How are you?' And, at the end of the day, when the person leaves, you say 'Thank you very much for working today. See you tomorrow, again. Good Bye.' So, this is how you need to deal with people." This was Kanodia's first lesson in managing work in different cultures. Work cultures, cannot be exported or imported. Work cultures are local. The employers have to adjust to them.

Now, Kanodia has worked in the London office for over 18 years. The new office has a set of meeting and conference rooms. He works as the CFO of Poeticgem and a few other companies in the Group, with a combined turnover of around USD 200 million.

Youngsters who love an adrenaline rush and look forward to challenges, find the garments industry enthralling. Kanodia says there is never a dull moment in the industry.

The garments industry mirrors the retail industry. Any changes in shopping habits, fashion, trends, weather, etc., impact the retail industry. This has a direct consequence on the garments business. So, every day is a new day, with novel challenges.

Due to the volatility in fashion and consumer preferences, managers need to keep many balls up in the air simultaneously. They need to take decisions in real time. In many industries like banking, there are standard operating procedures (SOPs) and checklists which can be applied in a range of scenarios. In the garments business, SOPs and checklists do exist. However, there are daily situations when quick judgement and personal initiative are warranted. Every day can be a roller-coaster ride. The business therefore attracts professionals, who want to work in an exhilarating environment.

Deepak endeavoured to give a free operational hand and ownership to the senior professionals and the staff. The entrepreneurial blood runs deep in the veins of all the employees.

The young team in London also learnt a great deal by watching Deepak work. A team member recalls, "I have learnt punctuality from Mr. Seth. I do not recall him being late for any meeting. Whether a meeting was in London, Delhi or anywhere in the world, Mr. Seth was always on time." Deepak makes it a point to be at work at 9 am sharp daily, in every country.

The London team also noted that Mr. Seth always cleared all his papers on the desk, before he went home. The habit of clearing all papers or issues on his desk, literally immediately, was a great lesson for youngsters. Even if Deepak returned to his office at 5 pm after a meeting, he cleared all papers on his table within the first 10 minutes. He never left a paper or an issue for the next day. He kept nothing pending. The habit continues.

If the accounts department sent the monthly financial report to Deepak, it would be cleared immediately. Any e-mail to

Deepak, was answered on the same day. A telephone call to Deepak, would be responded to immediately or the same day.

Surender Dhillon from the corporate secretariat, also admires Deepak's quick responses. He says, "Mr. Seth replies to every message very promptly. This is unique about him. It is his speciality. If I message him now, I will get a reply within two minutes."

A colleague who worked with him in London recollects, "Mr. Seth has a razor-sharp memory. He leads by example. He is our role model." Deepak's ability to read people is highly respected by his team members. Says a colleague, "An ability that stands out, is Deepak's capacity to gauge temperaments and make calculated decisions. He is able to read people in the very first meeting."

Deepak's operating style, also impressed the new team in London. Krishna Kanodia recollects, "I have always been smitten by Mr. Deepak Seth's sharpness. Whenever I go to him with an issue for guidance, he understands and assesses the situation with whirlwind speed. Then he gives us clear guidance or decisions. There are no if's or but's in his decisions. They are crystal clear. This is a remarkable and a visible quality of our Chairman."

The new buzzword in management circles is "CQ", commercial quotient. However, the term "CQ" has a different connotation for Deepak. His team members interpret "CQ" as "Compassion Quotient". Comments a colleague of Deepak, "Anyone who meets Deepak for the first time, would find him to be a very astute, swag, firm and a tough negotiator. However, once the credibility of a person is established, Deepak tends to be very considerate and compassionate. As a visionary businessman, heading businesses in many countries, he has to have the Compassion Quotient in ample measure, since the decisions of the company, touch the lives of thousands of employees."

Unique Mentoring

Over the years, Deepak has developed unique ideas to ensure that his team studies issues in depth and takes independent decisions. Whenever a manager is a bit wobbly in his understanding of some subject, he asks him to submit a project report. The subject may be margins or costs or customer analysis. After the project report is prepared, Deepak discusses it with the manager. Gradually the managers realised that Deepak did not need the report to understand the issue. He had initiated the project to ensure that the manager studied the subject in depth. The manager improves his understanding of the subject by studying it in detail and writing a report. The commissioning of the report, was just a training tool.

This was a smart way of ensuring that the manager understood the subject clearly. Deepak manages 30 to 40 diverse businesses simultaneously. He trains his young managers to understand issues in depth and take their own decisions. Thus, the organisation is perpetually in a learning mode.

Over the years, Deepak has evolved into a one-man university of ideas, learning and training, for youngsters.

13
USA: Capturing World's Biggest Market

Swet Vij loved his life in Sri Lanka. It was a peaceful country, always serene. The beaches were very clean and the sea waters were perpetually azure. The streets were never crowded. He was very comfortable living in the country. Indian spices and foods were available in plenty, since the Sri Lankans used many Indian spices. Indian cuisine and spices have flowed beyond its borders over the decades and invaded the kitchens in Nepal, Tibet, Myanmar and Sri Lanka.

Swet Vij was a happy young man, pursuing a career with a large textiles business group in Colombo, in 1987. He loved drinking the delectable teas of Sri Lanka.

Swet had just received a letter from his close buddy, Santosh Gadia, from Delhi. Deepak Seth was visiting Sri Lanka, to scout for garment manufacturers, to execute export orders from Europe. Santosh requested Swet to introduce Deepak to some garment manufacturers in Sri Lanka, who could work with the Group.

Swet had extensive experience in textiles since he had worked in Swan Mills, a textile unit in India. Subsequently, he worked for Bombay Dyeing, another large textile group in India. The company had now seconded him to Sri Lanka. Swet knew a few garment exporters in Sri Lanka and enabled Deepak's meeting with them.

Swet recalls, "We met for just one day. The rest is history."

Deepak's vision was to build a team of young professionals with sound academic backgrounds and experiences to grow the business rapidly. Deepak and Swet sipped cups of Sri Lankan tea, in the lobby of the Taj Samudra Hotel, overlooking the soothing, blue waters of the ocean. Deepak offered a position to Swet in India or abroad. They decided to meet again and talk, after a few months.

In January 1988, Swet joined Pearl Global Ltd. (PGL), as a General Manager, Sourcing, Processed Textiles, in Delhi. His job was to source fabrics to produce the garments.

Swet recalls, "Deepak and I trusted each other completely from the very first day. He believed in me, trusted my judgement and decision making. He let me manage the entire business operation. Naturally, I kept him fully briefed through reports, e-mails and phone calls."

In August 1989, Swet moved to Canada to manage the business. They had a company named Mode Mina Fashions Inc., selling women's sportswear. Swet added a men's sportswear division. The business was nascent, but it provided Swet valuable insights into apparel design, merchandising, imports and marketing.

USA: World's Biggest Market

Deepak's focus was on expanding the USA business. The USA was the largest apparel market globally. It was also the fashion epicentre of the world. Deepak wanted to energise the business in the USA. So, in April 1990, he moved Swet to New York, where the Group had a company named Montage International Inc.

They had launched a women's sportswear division called Tribes For Her. By December 1990, Swet was managing the entire company comprising of the brands, Tribes For Her and Tribes Men. He also nurtured Sub-Studio, which was a moderate to slightly higher priced sportswear brand.

Business was tough and brutal in those early days in the USA. The team was geared for large volumes and thus had a lot of overhead expenses. Moreover, due to the competitive conditions, retailers were constantly seeking markdowns. These discounts had an adverse impact on the margins of the business. In those early years, making profits was sometimes a challenge, due to the high operating costs.

There were constant efforts and promotions to boost the sales of brands like Tribes, Sub-Studio, and Tribes For Her. The business was dependent on efficient and cost-effective sourcing. It was largely a design, import and distribution led operation. Building relationships with the buying departments of retailers, was thus paramount.

Building a Team

Swet had prioritised two key tasks. First, he had to build and motivate his design, sales and finance teams. Gradually, he built a loyal staff and focussed on training. The team comprised of merchandising, design, technical, sales, sourcing, financial and logistics professionals. They were well motivated through incentives on achievement of their goals.

Second, Swet had to develop reliable supply sources in countries like China, Vietnam and Cambodia in the Far East. Having steadfast suppliers, who met their commitments, was vital to building the supply chain. The garment business was managed through a system of quotas. Countries had limited quotas, by category, for exports to the USA. As importers, the team regularly monitored the utilisation of quotas, from the data published by the US Customs.

Well-known retailers like Macy's, Merry-Go-Round, Chess King, Montgomery Ward, Sears, JCPenney, Hills Department Stores, Caldor Inc., Uptons, Kmart, etc., did business with the Group. Business was at moderate price points, around USD 7.50 to USD 12 per piece. The volumes were large and comprised of apparel for men, women and children.

In 1996, the company had a grand launch of a new women's line "DCC", with unique designs and rigorous distribution. The new brand delivered excellent results. Swet strengthened the USA team by recruiting bright designers, customer-service and logistics professionals. The business was on a roll with the new management team.

In a subsequent restructuring, a new firm, Depa International Inc., was established. It sold apparel for men and women. Depa was a new enterprise and needed financial support. Swet recalls, "Deepak never lost confidence in me. He helped me through the most problematic times." Depa did well and became a major source of supplies for top retailers like JCPenney, Kohl's, Kmart, Sears, Macy's, Mervyns, Charming Shoppe, Maurice's, etc. The company won the coveted "Vendor of the Year" Award, from most of them. The revenues spiralled from just USD five million in the year 2000, to USD 55 million by 2005.

The company also enjoyed excellent relations with its bankers. This made it easy to source working capital to manage the business. Fashion import businesses, traded in large volumes with relatively limited working capital bases. They deployed services provided by factoring companies (short-term finance providing companies), who insure and buy receivables. The importer could borrow 85 percent of the value of receivables. The factoring companies charged a fee ranging from 0.5 percent to 1.25 percent of the receivables. They also charged an interest on the advances.

The main competitors were importers like, At last Sportswear, Andrew Sports, etc. However, many retailers also imported garments directly from the producing countries.

Gradually, Deepak's firm became one of the best companies in the garments business in the USA, in terms of design and competitive prices. Around 2006, Deepak asked Dr. Mahesh Seth, his elder brother, to join the business in the USA.

Dr. Mahesh Seth, lived in Southern California, about 50 to 60 miles east of Los Angeles. After completing engineering at the IIT, he came to the University of Wisconsin, in Madison. There he completed his Masters and Doctorate studies in mechanical engineering. He specialised in automatic controls and joined Whirlpool Corporation. Later, he started his own business. Finally, he joined the USA business.

After joining, Dr. Mahesh was based in Michigan and spent some time every month in New York, managing the operations. Later, he moved to New York to work full-time in the business.

Changing Business Models

The DS Group manufactured and imported apparel, at its own cost and shipped them to the USA. It kept the apparel at its warehouses and then delivered them to the retailers like

Macy's and JCPenney. This was termed as the "Landed Duty Paid" (LDP) business model.

The problem with this model was that the Group never knew, when it would be paid, until it was paid. Even after that, the buyer could revert with some chargebacks and say, "Oh, your goods did not sell well. So, we are going to give you a chargeback and deduct it from your next bill." The buyers chose the design, the style, the garment. They placed the order. However, if the style did not sell, they told the vendor, "We could not earn the margins we had planned on your merchandise. So, if you want the next order, give us a chargeback or at least give us some refund."

Thus, in the LDP model, there was a huge risk. The Group would never know if it was going to earn or retain the planned margin, due to chargebacks. Sometimes, the buyer cancelled the order at the last minute. Then, the supplier was stuck with the apparel. The clothes had the brand labels of the retailers on them. Then, the team had to change every label, on every garment and hunt for other customers. It was problematic to make a good margin, after all the tumult.

Deepak and Dr. Mahesh then decided to change the business model. Instead of bringing goods to the USA at their risk, they decided to sell the goods to the buyer at their factory gates. It was then the buyer's responsibility to transport the goods to the USA and sell them. This was the "Free-on-Board" (FOB) model.

After the customer placed an order, it would be his responsibility to inspect the garments in the factory. The DS Group would pack the goods and give them to the buyer's agent. The agent arranged the transport to the USA. The Group had fewer risks in the FOB business model. Its exposure was circumscribed.

The business has now worked with the FOB Model for the last decade. Some of the company's major customers, who gradually converted to FOB buying are JCPenney, Kohl's, Macy's, etc.

Multi-National, Multi-Product

The Group has prospered in the USA, since it has built a multi-national, multi-product business. It has sourcing and manufacturing operations in many countries. So, the Group offers jeans from Bangladesh, embellished ladies' blouses from India and synthetic fabric dresses from Indonesia. These varied offerings have given the business a cutting edge. There are very few companies in the garment business, based on this model.

Executing an order from a USA buyer, involves a multiplicity of the Deepak Seth Group's offices in India and abroad. Retailers like Kohl's visit the DS Group office in New York, to see the designs and styles in the showroom. They place orders through their agent Li & Fung, directly with the office in India. The commercial relationships are handled by the DS Group's office in Hong Kong. Many large retailers like GAP have offices in India. They deal directly with the Group in India.

The Group office in USA gets involved again, if there are any facilitations required to execute the order like sample approvals, trim issues, delayed deliveries, etc. It ensures speedy responses to customers, so that issues can be resolved expeditiously and do not escalate. The office in the USA maintains a showroom to exhibit their styles and designs. The negotiations, purchase orders and invoicing are handled from the offices in India or in Hong Kong. Dr. Mahesh manages the USA operation and also ensures that all government laws and regulations are adhered to.

The USA team continues to have major retailers like Macy's, Kohl's and GAP as its customers. Sears, Kmart and JCPenney, were also their customers. The USA team also does some business with discount brands like Walmart, Target, etc. Furthermore, the business is active among the middle tier retailers, focussing on women's and kids wear.

Cordial Relations, USA and India

The cordial relationship between the USA and India provided a supporting environment to the development of business between the two countries. Dr. Manmohan Singh, India's Prime Minister visited the USA in July 2005 to initiate negotiations over the Indo-US civilian nuclear agreement. This was followed by President George W. Bush's visit to India in March 2006. A nuclear agreement was signed, giving India access to American nuclear fuel and technology.

Success Factors

Swet says, "Our business association spanned 21 years, from 1988 to 2009. Working with Deepak was the best period of my career. It was professionally satisfying and financially rewarding. We are friends now, since we worked beautifully, while we were together in business. We value our mutual trust. It is my privilege to have been associated with Deepak. I am fortunate to have him as a friend."

Deepak has a great talent for building relationships with everyone he meets, including customers. He has a cardinal rule, which is, if he is meeting a client outside the office, he does not discuss work. Deepak discusses work only in the office. He builds personal and social relationships. So, over the decades, Deepak has built a massive armoury of healthy relationships with a range of people. For Deepak, building friendships, is as important as designing, marketing, production or IT.

Deepak's early start in the USA with a sourcing office helped to sow the seeds of success. The DS Group could offer products at competitive prices with timely deliveries, since it had its own factories. Adapting to the needs of varied customers, has provided strong roots to the business.

Deepak's team forged robust relationships with large customers and built the business. It focussed on being ethical, transparent and honest with customers. Over the last five decades, the managers and management structures have changed in many retailers. Yet, the brands continue to be customers of the DS Group. Their relationships have blossomed.

Introducing the profit centre concept gave ownership for results to the CEOs of various businesses.
The CEOs manage the business, as if it belonged to them.
They become entrepreneurs.

14
Profit Centre Concept Takes Birth

Every business has to stand on its own feet. It has to generate profits to pay for its expenses and also create a surplus.

With the multiplicity of import offices and factories across countries, Deepak took an important decision. He decided that each business unit would have to fund itself. Every company, whether an import operation or a factory, had to be financially viable. Thus, each company would become a profit centre. Any Group company making a loss, had to present a plan on how it proposed to become profitable.

The sales and import companies established abroad by Deepak, now had the freedom to buy from any manufacturer across the globe and not merely from the DS Group factories. The business heads abroad had more flexibility and autonomy in sourcing. However, they also had the responsibility to make their businesses profitable. The Group factories in India, had become like any other factories, for the sourcing businesses abroad.

This policy stimulated many improvements in the overseas sales offices and the manufacturing units. Each business had to deliver independently. The overseas sales office could not depend on the DS Group manufacturing units to mollycoddle them with low prices. Nor could the Group factories depend on captive orders from the overseas offices. The Indian manufacturing units had to compete on quality, delivery, service and pricing, with vendors in every country.

The policy ignited healthy competition within the entire Group. It encouraged efficiencies and cost-effectiveness. Each business unit was responsible for its own performance, profits and growth. Every country and factory manager, started combing every cost, to weed out any wasteful expenditure.

The "Be Profitable Independently" movement also led to a significant improvement in customer service. Every country manager was responsible for his top-line and bottom-line delivery. Hence, orders and customers became very important. Every cent of every cost, was reviewed granularly.

Financial Discipline

The focus on the profit centre concept, also led to an improvement in financial disciplines. Omprakash Makam, CFO, PDS, comments, "The financial disciplines and the practice to review the business with utmost rigour, are keys to excellence. In the garment and the retailing businesses, you have to be on top of many factors that impact the business. Hence financial astuteness is paramount."

A financial loss is acceptable in the business. However, a lack of integrity, is entirely unacceptable. If a person makes a mistake, Deepak will overlook it, if the person has learnt a lesson from it. However, lapses in integrity are never excused.

Sanjay Sarkar, who heads the Bangladesh business, has been with the Group for the last 12 years. He is the son of an Indian army doctor, who retired as the director of the Army Hospital in Delhi. According to him, the company has grown, since the senior managers are given a lot of responsibility and authority to take decisions.

Introducing the profit centre concept gave ownership for results to the CEOs of various countries and factories. The

CEOs manage the business, as if it belonged to them. The CEOs, thus become entrepreneurs. Nevertheless, they have complete access to Deepak in case they need any guidance.

This financial empowerment of senior managers, has fostered growth of the DS Group. The profit centre heads are not handed down targets. They prepare their own annual plans and discuss them with Deepak, Pallak or Pulkit. Then they are on their own, to manage their operations. If a business does run into a problem, a team from the central office steps in to assist.

Mentoring and Training

Sanjay Sarkar says that, "Mr. Seth visits Bangladesh every two months. When he is with us he reviews our plans, progress and we get valuable advice from him. He has a knack or instinct for quickly identifying the areas of improvement. The discussions are always friendly. He uses them to mentor the entire team."

The policy of making each unit into a profit centre empowered the business heads. Many of them have worked for over twenty to thirty years in the DS Group. They perceive Deepak to be an establishment by himself, in grooming and training them. Says Sarkar, "I have actually grown up with him. I joined the company when I was just 24 years of age. Now I am 55 years old. Today, I am not just handling a business in Bangladesh. I am managing the government, bankers and buyers. I have learnt when to be tough and when to be flexible. We joined the company very early, when we were very young. So, we worked closely with Mr. Seth. We were trained directly by him. So, it has been a journey of learning for many of us. Today, we can manage independent businesses."

The Bangladesh business comprises of three factories, employing 8,500 staff and the turnover has grown from USD five million in 2003, to about USD 120 million plus. It is always very challenging to grow exponentially, especially in foreign countries. The team has prepared a roadmap, to augment the turnover to over USD 200 million.

Initiatives like the Profit Centre Concept, have helped the business to achieve its goals and stay focussed on the bottom line.

Deepak started the business, as a family venture. However, he was keen to build a strong professional management team to manage it. Making each unit responsible for its financial performance was another step in this direction. All the overseas factories and offices are managed by professional managers, who have the autonomy to deliver. They have clear and well-defined goals, plans, budgets and quarterly reviews. The empowerment of professional managers, has contributed to the growth of the business.

15
The Entrepreneurial Model

Deepak's vision from the very first day was to establish a global business across countries, to become a major player in the garments business. This was his dream, when he commenced his business journey. Hence, as early as 1979, he took the initiative to enter into a partnership with Arun Gujral and open an office in Germany.

The apparel business continued to be a part of the Seth family business. Deepak and Harish had divided the tasks in the business amongst themselves. Around 1988, the four brothers restructured the family business amicably. Deepak received a part of the garments business. He named the business, "Pearl Agencies Pvt. Ltd." The German business had come to him in the reorganisation.

When Deepak started managing the business, he capitalised on his knowledge and experience. He entered into numerous new client relationships. His brothers sought his involvement whenever it was needed. Deepak was extremely well networked and connected. So, if anybody in the family sought his assistance, he contributed until the issue was fully resolved. If there was any dispute with a customer or a vendor, Deepak would help to resolve it. He was a skilled negotiator. He would listen to every side of the issue. He was very fair in arriving at a consensus, which would be acceptable to all.

Deepak decided to expand the business aggressively. He started building the apparel business with vigour. Within two years, he had established offices in New York and London. Talking of his foreign sourcing offices, Mr. Harish Ahuja, Managing Director of Shahi Exports Pvt. Ltd., comments,

"Deepak is a far-sighted business person. This is commendable."

Deepak had realised that people contribute their best when they have a stake in the business. Employees have to be incentivised to deliver their best. They work with more dedication, when they have ownership of the business. Deepak was clear that whilst the company would be a global business, it would be locally managed. Deepak had garnered this lesson in delegation, while working with the personnel department of ITC.

Deepak innovated an entrepreneurial model to empower the business heads. He worked out a stake in the equity or a share in the profits for each CEO. The business heads were no longer just employees. They became partners. They drove the businesses independently as if they owned them. According to Deepak, the sharing of profits accelerated the growth of the Group.

The essence of the entrepreneurial business model, is trusting the business heads and building lasting relationships with them. Deepak gives lucid overall directions. Then, he does not micromanage. He steps back on operational matters. This operating philosophy comes from respecting the competence of his CEOs.

Deep Respect for Team

Pankaj Bhasin, CEO of the woven business, is from the first batch of the Pearl Academy of Fashion. He has worked with the Group for around 25 years. He says, "Mr. Seth takes personal and professional care of all his employees. His vision of the entrepreneurship model has given many of us, the opportunity to run the businesses as our own. We work on a policy of earn, to earn. He is a role model for many of us. His long hours of work, dedication and leadership qualities are inspiring. To me personally, he is a fatherly figure. I have great regards for him, for giving me an entrepreneurial opportunity and recognition in this industry."

Deepak also ensured that all his business relationships were crystal clear. He had agreements with all his partner entrepreneurs. Whenever Deepak invested or partnered with anyone, everything was lucidly defined. There was nothing vague which could create any misunderstanding at any stage.

Working with Entrepreneurs

Rajesh Ajwani was interviewing for a position in London in 2003. During the meeting in Jakarta, he made a strong case for the Group to invest in a factory in Indonesia. Deepak and his son Pallak, who had also joined the business by then, heard him out. They did some financial calculations and agreed to invest in a factory in Indonesia. Rajesh was impressed by the speed of decision-making.

Deepak relies on his instincts to take decisions. However, he also does his mathematics. Then, he tests the numbers, with his gut-feel of the markets. He takes quick decisions and initiates rapid action. Rajesh did not relocate to London. He stayed on in Indonesia to start the new factory as Deepak's entrepreneurial partner. Based on his long association with the DS Group, Rajesh observes, "Deepak moves very fast once he takes a decision."

Rigorous Analysis

Though Deepak appears to take quick decisions, they are backed by solid homework, behind the scenes. He studies each market or location meticulously, along with detailed homework and financial projections. For instance, the Group was planning to tap the Brazilian markets. So, it commissioned a management consultant to study the market. He visited all the large retailers, wholesalers and fashion boutiques, to understand Brazilian customers and their apparel shopping habits. After the report was submitted, Deepak and Pulkit visited Sao Paulo and Rio de Janeiro, for seven days with the consultant. They had personal meetings with all major retailers like Lojas Renner, Lojas Marisa, Walmart and Carrefour.

Similarly, when the Group was planning a factory in Myanmar they sent an advance team to scout for suitable parties. The team also studied the availability of power, water, land, labour laws, minimum wages, local rules, etc. Again, Deepak and Pulkit visited Myanmar for a week to meet various vendors, accounting and legal firms.

Builder of People

The qualities that endear Deepak to his entrepreneurial partners are his openness to any suggestions that strengthen the organisation. Deepak is a very aggressive and impatient businessman. These are highly desirable qualities in a businessman, who is a catalyst in delivering growth. Deepak wanted to change the growth trajectory of the Group. If he asks a person to do something, he wants it done yesterday. A manager has to be sharp in dealing with Deepak. "You cannot give Deepak Seth a frivolous excuse for not delivering," comments a colleague.

New managers who joined the business, could not understand Deepak's demanding style. It took them some time to realise, that it was this very trait, that was driving growth. Garments is a tough industry. Buyers give repeat orders, only if a supplier is sharp and able to deliver on time.

Deepak has a very robust grasping power. A finance man could be briefing him about taxation, corporate laws or governances; Deepak grasps the nuances and complexities easily. A senior financial colleague says, "If a manager is talking to Deepak on a tax or legal matter, he will understand the issue better than the manager. He can gauge what the manager is going to say. His capability to process information mentally is phenomenal."

Over the years, Deepak has developed the flair for getting along with all kinds of people. This skill was observed very early by his classmates at the JBIMS. Deepak's philosophy in dealing with people is very simple: "This is the person. I have to work with him." He looks for the unique strengths in every person. Then, he builds on them.

Over the years, Deepak has evolved into a versatile businessman and a strategy-thinking Chairman. Though he leads the billion-dollar plus DS Group, he continues to be lithe and moves fast. Sprightliness, propensity for quick action and fierce proactiveness in the market are the hallmarks of Deepak's operating style. This action-orientation, has propelled him from being an exporter with a few tailors, to a global operation. Hence, he enjoys the respect of his entrepreneurial CEO partners.

If Deepak asks for a monthly or a quarterly report, he wants it on time. Now, when there are over 200 CEOs, vice-presidents and senior managers in the business, he insists that all reporting should be accurate and timely.

Entrepreneurial Bifurcation of the Business

Deepak understood the challenges in leading a professionally managed family business. He ensured that the professional managers had the freedom to deliver. He also provided avenues to fulfil the aspirations of the family members who worked in the business.

Deepak sensed that it was time to step forcefully on the growth accelerator, when he observed that the Indian economy was gathering momentum. The process of liberalising the Indian economy was receiving incremental impetus, during the tenure of the thirteenth Prime Minister of India, Mr. Manmohan Singh. He opened the doors of the Indian economy and restructured it.

Deepak thought it would be wise to bifurcate the business into two companies in 2014. The first company would concentrate on imports, trading and customer service. The second company would focus on manufacturing and exports.

Deepak then restructured the business. He asked Pallak to lead the import company from London. This arm of the DS Group is known as PDS Ltd. Pulkit would head the manufacturing business, known as Pearl Global Industries Ltd. (PGIL). Deepak continues as the Chairman of both the companies, guiding their growth and mentoring them. Deepak ensured that his sons, Pallak and Pulkit would continue the entrepreneurial spirit and the quest for growth.

Thus, the import and trading business and the manufacturing business, both flourished like Siamese twins.

Sharing Insights

Deepak keeps a sharp eye on the global economic situation and how it will impact the businesses across continents. He consults with his CEOs regularly and briefs them.

Deepak has an uncanny ability to analyse underlying changes in every market very quickly. He has the vision and foresight to perceive what the market needs and shares his perspectives with the CEOs. Every time the business goes through a difficult time, Deepak finds a way to unlock opportunities.

Pragmatic Relationships

When confronted with a problem, Deepak does not paint abstract scenarios in the sky. He is a practical leader. He tells himself, "This is where I am now. This is the problem, I have. How do I best deal with it, now?" This is the pragmatism, that is embedded in the senior management of the Group.

Some entrepreneurs and businessmen get emotionally attached to ventures, if they have invested in them. They do not want to let go, even if the business does not yield profits for years. They keep hoping for a miraculous turnaround. Deepak did break bricks with his palms as a young student; however, in business, he does not beat his head against the wall. He is practical. Trying to make a bleeding business yield some profits or getting emotionally attached to it, is like beating the heart with a stone.

This pragmatism does not merely apply to a business. If some business relationship is not working out as expected, Deepak pulls out cordially and moves on. He can let businesses and people go, effectively and quickly, but cordially. Deepak does not lose his friends.

Arun Gujral, Deepak Seth's first overseas recruit and entrepreneurial partner, says, "You always have two relationships with Deepak. One is at the personal level. You can never have a better friend. He will always be there, if you have a problem. You can always count on him. He will do whatever he can to help you. He is a very lovable, affectionate and a charming personality. I have been in close contact with him for almost 40 years now. We have never had any kind of a dissonance all these years. Basically, he always tries to be fair even on a professional level. At the professional level, he talks professionally."

Santosh Gadia says, "Those partners who agreed with Deepak's vision and have stayed with him, have prospered. Deepak is always there to help and provide all the strengths of the Group in finance, logistics, and design to the subsidiaries. If you work with Deepak, you cannot have a short-term gain mindset. The business and the various entrepreneurial partners have prospered, since Deepak strongly believes in sharing the fruits of growth."

Art of Listening

Deepak is a business leader who is open to learning from his CEOs. He is a great listener and open to ideas. He is very patient, in every meeting, when others talk. His mindset is, "I am competent, but others are competent in their domains too. I do not have the time to think through everything. Nor do I have the time, to impose my directions and thinking on everybody. So, let me listen to others and see what they can contribute. Then, I will know what is happening."

Deepak keeps learning as he believes that his team and business heads can contribute through their perspectives. He is confident that they have some valuable ideas which could benefit the business.

As he listens to the senior managers, he develops relationships with them and trusts them. Eventually, trust builds trust. When a leader trusts his people, they trust him too. This builds loyalty. Hence, many CEOs have worked in the company for over three decades or more. If any of them leaves or retires, he continues to maintain cordial relationships with Deepak and the business. Deepak has perfected the art of blending excellent business practices with lasting relationships.

Many business leaders stop listening to their teams as they garner success. Then, they falter. Deepak maintains a steady growth trajectory, as he always learns by listening. He is always trying to build something different, something better.

Many of the country heads miss their chats with Deepak, as the business grows and they have to operate autonomously. Sunny Malhotra is the Managing Director of Simple Approach Ltd., based in Hong Kong, a part of the Group. He asked Deepak why he was spending less time with him. Deepak replied, "Everything is going well. There is nothing to talk about."

Professionalism and Family Management

By 2000, Deepak had built a robust business with the help of his family and his team of professional managers. Leading a successful family business, managed by professional managers is a significant achievement. It requires dexterity to manage a business through professional managers and simultaneously keep the family members involved, with their independence.

To ensure professional management, Deepak ensured that the Board of Directors comprised of all industry professionals. Mr. C. R. Dua, an independent director and also the Chairman of Procter & Gamble, India, comments, "Over the years, Deepak has made very dedicated and determined efforts to professionalise the business. He has always emphasised compliance and adherence to all laws and regulations."

The DS Group (including PDS and PGIL), is now an entrepreneurially driven organisation. The business heads and senior management teams take operating decisions independently. There is commitment and trust among them. To achieve this fraternity, the Group has fostered a policy of treating people with dignity and compassion. The synthesis of a humane approach and the entrepreneurial drive, has propelled the organisation.

Whenever a customer wants any garment from anywhere, the DS Group (Deepak Seth Group, including PDS and PGIL), is able to offer it.

Diversifying the production base was a far-sighted strategic move. It required visionary understanding of the market, three decades ago, when Deepak first blueprinted the bold strategy.

16
Factories in India and Beyond

Steve Jobs wanted to "dent the world" with his creativity, technology and products. Deepak Seth's vision was to "clothe the world". During the 45 years from 1976 to 2020, the DS Group (Deepak Seth Group, including PDS and PGIL), is estimated to have produced 15 billion garments like skirts, shirts, blazers, dresses, trousers, T-shirts and pyjamas. This translates to at least two garments per person on this planet.

Many of the CEOs say that they joined the company after hearing about Deepak's vision, passion and astonishing energy.

In the 1980s, it was a standard practice to get an order from a foreign buyer and then outsource the production to smaller factories. Deepak and his team realised that getting production only through other factories, was not a long-term business option. They wanted direct control on the quality and delivery schedules. To achieve this goal, they had to have their own factories and staff.

Pearl was amongst the first few companies to commence complete in-house manufacturing in Naraina and later in Gurgaon (Gurugram after 2016). A factory was established in 1990, with 250 machines, manufacturing men's shirts for its Lerros brand in Germany. The factory was also a pioneer in establishing the first assembly line production operation in Delhi. Many of the staff and workers in the team were from Sri Lanka, as they had experience in assembly line production.

Two years later, another factory with 200 machines was started in Gurgaon. These were comprehensive garment production factories, with all in-house processes.

Overseas Production

Deepak sat in his office in 1994 and reflected on how to grow faster. He realised that as long as the business depended on production in India, growth would be limited by quotas. To grow the business, Deepak realised he would have to establish factories in quota-free countries.

There were no quotas on exports from Dubai. So, Deepak took an early morning Emirates flight from Delhi to Dubai. Throughout the 2 hours and 20 minutes flight, he was busy with a pad and a calculator. He was working through the costs and benefits of establishing a factory in Dubai. He liked Dubai for its surgical cleanliness and orderliness. After exploring the town for two days, his mind was made up. He would establish a factory in the UAE.

Deepak bought a factory from the Al Maya Group in Jebel Ali Free Zone and started manufacturing and exporting garments from there. The Group was the first Indian company to establish a production base in Dubai.

Deepak's thirst for growth was not quenched. He established a factory in Nepal, another quota-free country. While manufacturing Lerros shirts, he always preferred to establish factories in countries which were quota free. Deepak was amongst the first to go to Nepal to establish a factory in Kathmandu.

A few years later, during a review meeting, Deepak noticed that the margins from the Dubai factory were consistently under pressure. This was due to the fact that almost everything that was used to produce any garment was imported. Even the labour in the factory had to be imported from Sri Lanka, Philippines, India, etc. Hence, margins were always depressed.

Deepak had a penchant for taking quick decisions. He decided to shift the Dubai factory to Bangladesh. Bangladesh was becoming the new haven for garments manufacturers because of lower costs of production. Gradually, it became a major production hub for the business.

Later in 2004, Deepak teamed with Rajesh Ajwani, as a partner to establish a factory in Indonesia. Now, the Indonesian operation comprises of three factories. Two factories are located in Semarang in Central Java. They have an employee strength of 1,885, with about 1,000 sewing machines. The third factory is in Bawen, also in Central Java, with an employee strength of 950, with about 500 sewing machines. The office is in Jakarta, with a staff strength of 35. The Indonesia business has about 3,000 employees.

Post-Quota World

Quotas were finally abolished from 1st January 2005 by the World Trade Organisation (WTO). There had been incremental phase-outs over a 10-year period. The developing nations had sought the removal of the quotas. They argued that developed countries used them to protect their local industries. With the abolishing of the quota system, developing countries could boost their exports. The immediate beneficiaries were China and India, who had installed substantial production capacities.

With the ending of the quota system, the DS Group was poised for a giant leap into the future. There were no middlemen with quotas or export restrictions. The Group could now sell millions of pieces of garments to the USA or to Europe. It had established sales and sourcing offices in key markets, built design teams, created an infrastructure and had operational teams in place. Deepak and his teams, were finally unfettered.

In a few years, Deepak had established six factories in Delhi with 250 to 300 machines each. He had also diversified into the manufacture of knits like T-shirts. The business now had its own manufacturing facilities in India and had established the Lerros brand in Germany. The Group had also developed wholesale brands in the USA like Tribes Men, Tribe For Her and Sub-Studio.

Deepak had also anticipated that customers would decrease their dependence on importers and source garments on their own, in the post-quota era. They would diversify their sourcing and buy from multiple countries.

Every country has its own competitive advantages, in terms of availability of raw materials, processes or manpower specialisation. So, Deepak ensured that the Group had production bases in Indonesia, Bangladesh, India, Vietnam, Sri Lanka, etc. Now, whenever a customer wants anything from anywhere, the DS Group is able to offer it. Diversifying the production base was a far-sighted strategic move. However, it required visionary understanding of the market, three decades ago, when Deepak first blueprinted the bold strategy.

The five years from 1999 to 2004 were years of growth for India. India's GDP growth continued, inflation was tamed and foreign exchange reserves improved. Efforts were made to galvanise the Indian economy through privatisation and investments in infrastructure and road networks. So, the DS Group too, blossomed in the fresh winds of liberalisation blowing through India.

Garments Production: Not Simple

Production of garments in a factory is a time consuming and complicated process. Many processes are manual. Every garment starts with a sketch using a CAD (Computer-Aided Design). This is a preproduction step to produce a technical drawing and a specification sheet. Converting a piece of fabric into a shirt or a skirt involves many processes, such as:

1. Preparing the patterns – Paper vs Digital: The paper patterns of the shirt are digitised to make a sample. A pattern-making specialist takes the paper patterns and places them on a large board, called the digitiser. It enables the pattern maker to input the paper patterns into a software system. Each pattern part is tracked with a hand-held device. It takes snapshots of the position of the pattern. This is a time-consuming process, as some garments have over 10 panels or parts. For instance, in a shirt, each part like the sleeve, collar and pocket constitutes a panel.

2. Sorting patterns after digitising: The pattern maker works with the digital patterns with surgical precision. All the measurements and adjustments are recorded.

3. Lay planning, getting patterns ready for production: All the patterns have to be arranged in a specific order, considering the fabric length, roll width and number of shirts to be produced, along with a breakdown of sizes. The software used for this lay plan suggests the optimal

layout of these geometrical shapes or patterns. The objective is to optimise fabric usage. The software undertakes the task, but a good specialist can improve on it. The fabric usage can be optimised, with a higher variation of sizes and a larger number of small pattern parts.

4. Fabric cutting: The patterns are printed from the plan and the fabric is cut. Patterns are printed on a special paper that adheres firmly to the fabric. This ensures that the paper does not slide on the fabric during the cutting. Samples are cut with scissors; the finer bits are trimmed with special equipment.

5. Whilst samples are often cut manually, bulk production items are cut by machines. Similar types of fabrics are layered on top of each other for cutting in bulk. The composition and thickness of the fabrics, determines if they can be cut together. For example, cotton and viscose cannot be cut together. Various fabrics react differently to bulk cutting. Some fabrics distort more than others. The result can be uneven pieces.

6. Sets for seamstresses/tailors: After cutting, all the pieces are placed in sets. To maximise production efficiencies, similar operations are grouped together. The tailors work with speed when they undertake the same task repeatedly.

7. Finalising the colours and trims: The colours of threads and buttons, etc., have to be selected to match the fabric's colour. This is complex. There are many options; sometimes the shade differences are barely noticeable. Zips and other accessories also need to be finalised.

8. Adjusting the sewing machinery: The sewing machine has to be adjusted for different types of fabrics. The tailor has to load the new reels of thread on the sewing machine. He may test the seam on a piece of fabric, to ensure that the tension is set and adjusted appropriately.

9. Finally, at last, sewing: The tailor sews the various pieces together. The original paper design comes to life, in a fabric form.

10. Quality control: After completion, the garments are checked thoroughly for any quality issues.

11. Finishing and packing: After quality checks, the garments are washed, pressed and then packed for despatch.

Factory Specialisation

When a customer buys a shirt, a jacket or a pair of jeans, he buys it for its appearance, fashion, durability or pricing. However, producing that shirt or skirt is a rigorous process. Apparel is a vast category. There are regions, workmen and machines which specialise in manufacturing various types of garments.

Walk into any apparel store in the USA or UK and buy a blazer. There is a label inside which tells the customer where it was made. Many jackets and blazers hail from Vietnam. For a company wanting to manufacture jackets, it means that Vietnam has the specialisation to produce jackets. The specialisation of a region in a particular type of garment, is known as its handwriting. The manufacturer will head to

Vietnam to deploy available trained resources to manufacture jackets, instead of reinventing the wheel.

The manufacture of jackets requires raw materials from China. So, it is logical to produce jackets in Vietnam, as only seven days are required to sail them from China. So, jackets are the handwriting of Vietnam, which it has developed over many years.

A factory which is manufacturing shirts cannot shift easily to manufacturing blazers. This would mean changing the machines, managers and workmen and developing a new handwriting. Pressing jackets and suits requires precision. To produce jeans, a factory needs a special laundry to wash them. So even if a factory can stitch denim jeans, unless it has the appropriate laundry, it will not be able to manufacture them. Workers also acquire specialisation in producing specific types of garments over a period of time. A workman who has produced shirts for 10 years, will find it difficult to work in a factory producing skirts or blouses.

The Group has been constantly adopting technologies to ensure cost reductions, higher efficiencies and productivities. In addition, it has moved production to low-cost countries like Bangladesh, Vietnam and Indonesia.

Deepak explains the manufacturing strategy as, "We have gone to every country which had some production advantage. Vietnam and China have strengths in outerwear jackets. So, we went there to manufacture jackets. Indonesia makes very fine blouses with expensive fabrics. So, we make blouses in Indonesia. We have entered each country, due to its distinct specialisation in some garment. India cannot produce what Bangladesh produces. Bangladesh cannot produce what China does. Each country has a uniqueness, which we had the vision and foresight to see. Then, we established factories in these countries, to produce specific garments."

Deepak and his teams understood the specialisations of various regions and countries, in producing specific types of garments. This understanding was critical in deciding the location of its factories in India and abroad.

Thus, the DS Group is now able to offer multiple products from multiple locations. This is a unique global strength.

Aggressive Expansion: India

Customers prefer buying from suppliers, who have their own manufacturing plants. The large suppliers, established in-house production units and adhered to compliances and governances. They have survived and prospered. Gradually, in-house production has become the norm.

Deepak also realised that for the business to grow, it needs a presence in the fashion and core categories of apparel. Fashion garments are determined by current trends, tastes or whims. Core products are basics like T-shirts, shorts and nightwear, which people need on an ongoing basis. As fashion products are a status symbol, customers are willing to pay higher prices for them. Profit margins are lower on everyday core products. So, core product factories, are ideally located in regions where labour costs are relatively low.

As the business grew, the Group diversified its production base, spreading its wings to other parts of India. In 2008, the first plant started in Chennai, South India. Soon, there were four factories in Chennai.

The labour force in each part of India also has its own nuances. About 90 percent of the workforce in the factories comprises of local women. Women workers in South India adhere steadfastly to the factory timings. They want to complete their targets on schedule, to earn their incentives. They are keen to go home after working hours, as they have to cook dinner for their families. They do not like working overtime. So, salary costs are relatively lower in South India.

In Delhi city, about 90 percentage of the workforce comprises of migrant men from surrounding states. They stay away from their families. At the time of festivals, they go on leave for long periods, impacting production schedules adversely.

Pearl Global Industries Ltd. (PGIL) started manufacturing knits like T-shirts and polo shirts in Gurugram. The factories of 300 machines, had given way to 700 to 800 machines. Compliances and the need for efficiencies had given impetus to in-house production. In 2014, another production facility was established in Bengaluru, enhancing the total capacity of PGIL to 5,000 machines.

Formidable Presence

The Group also bought a factory in Vietnam in 2016. It is located in Bac Giang, next to the capital city of Hanoi. The office is in Hanoi. The factory (Pearl Global Vietnam Company Ltd.) has 750 machines. It produces garments like jackets, blazers and high-stretch sportswear. The business has a highly skilled work force of 1,100 in the Vietnam factory.

The establishment of factories in foreign countries provided strategic flexibilities to the Group. Over a period of time, its factories have acquired their own specialisation. The

Bangladesh factory specialises in knits and trousers, with denim and non-denim fabrics for men and women. The Vietnam factory specialises in jackets and outers for men and women. The Indian factories specialise in fashion garments like tops, skirts and dresses.

Deepak will establish a factory in Indonesia, Vietnam, Sri Lanka, etc., wherever needed. He only knows growth. He reviews the costs of raw materials, labour and availability of trained resources in any country. Then, he ensures the production of the best quality shirt or blazer. The Group's rapid growth is substantially due to its factories abroad. It is now a business without national boundaries.

In planning the establishment of new factories, the business is guided closely by its order book. An ever-expanding customer base is fundamental to the growth of any business. The DS Group builds its capacities in line with customer needs. It maintains a regular dialogue with all its key customers to assess their growth plans and needs. In addition, the team is constantly tapping new customers. It is smart business to build a strong reputation and branding in the market to allure new customers.

Deepak's production journey has evolved over the last four decades, depending on the needs of its customers and markets. With sourcing offices and teams across countries, the Group could get orders executed by its own factories, with direct supervision. It is also networked with factories globally to produce for the Group on a third-party basis. Its local offices and managers supervise the supplier factories tightly.

The DS Group (Deepak Seth Group, including PDS and PGIL) manufacturing units garner orders from the largest global customers. They are located in many countries and can produce a range of garments. The factories can produce millions of jackets, pyjamas, trousers or skirts. This strategic advantage fused with the reputation of being reliable and trustworthy, makes the Group a formidable supplier.

400 Million Garments Annually

The DS Group (Deepak Seth Group, including PDS and PGIL), can supply around 400 million garments per annum, which is over a million pieces daily, working at full capacity.

The journey from 200 machines in a small workshop in 1976, to a million pieces daily and 30,000 employees, has been a challenging experience. Deepak's vision and drive have propelled the business into the future. From six factories in Gurugram, India, the DS Group now has 22 factories in India and abroad.

The young Deepak, who did not even have a factory in 1976 when he started with an order for 6,000 shirts, was now defining the industry, by building modern, innovative factories.

Nuts and Bolts of a Factory

Mr. Sundeep Chatrath, the CEO of the Knits Division, was in deep thought. A serious challenge was confronting him. One of his factories was making a loss of about USD two million every year. He was very keen to make it profitable.

A year later, he was a delighted manager. He was able to turnaround the business and generate profits of USD three million. He achieved this milestone through a winning formula of five points.

First, he wove his people into a strong team. Second, he improved the coordination with people in other departments, to ensure seamless operations. Third, he ensured that there were no rejections from clients or air freighting of goods, which helped to control costs. Fourth, he reviewed the costs of all the materials used in the garments. He was able to reduce overtime and the cost of producing garments significantly. Fifth, he ensured that he had the strong support of Deepak and Pulkit, Deepak's younger son, in making management changes.

Chatrath says he was motivated to turnaround the loss-making unit, as he was inspired by the strong leadership of Deepak and Pulkit. According to him, "Deepak is a very visionary person. When anyone interacts with Deepak, he understands the person very quickly. Deepak also comes to conclusions swiftly and takes decisions. Every dialogue or meeting with him, results in action. There are never any loose ends to be ironed out later. He listens a lot to people and somehow always manages to take the right decisions."

Nine Pillars of Manufacturing Prowess

There are nine pillars, which have contributed to the DS Group's manufacturing prowess in a highly competitive industry.

One, the Group had the funds to expand production through investments in its own factories in India and abroad. The Group's sales were growing by 25 to 30 percent every year. So, the business was generating adequate cash for investing in factories and expansion.

Two, the Group could grow due to a strong, debt free balance sheet. According to Vineet Mathur, "A key characteristic of Mr. Seth is that he is not in business just to make money. There are businesses, where the owner only wants to make money for himself. However, Mr. Seth did not pull money out for himself; the profits were retained in the business for building factories."

The reserves in the business were deployed to fund the new projects. The business had a strong balance sheet. There was no long-term debt. When a retailer is assessing a potential supplier, he derives confidence in dealing with a vendor with a debt free balance sheet. The bankers were delighted that the owners were ploughing their profits back into the business.

Three, the Group enjoys excellent relations with its bankers. It does not take any stock risks. It does not buy fabrics and materials in anticipation of orders. It buys materials only when a customer confirms an order. This policy was leveraged with the banks to procure working capital required to fuel growth.

The policy of zero stock risk helped the business to build trust with the banks. In the 1990s and 2000s, banks were slightly diffident to lend money to garment exporters. If a garment manufacturer sought a loan, the typical banking response was, "Garments? You will produce. You will hold stocks and they will go out of fashion. Then, you will have the clothes and we will be left high and dry, with no money. How will we recover our money?"

The business convinced its bankers that it buys materials only after a confirmed customer order. So, there are no stock risk. Bankers were also assured that withdrawals towards the loan, would commence after the customer's order had been processed. These practices helped the Group to solidify its relationships with the banks.

Four, the Group enjoys credibility due to its large size. With the abolition of the quota system, the large retailers in the USA and Europe, wanted to deal with established and organised suppliers. They did not want to manage hundreds of small vendors, without an adequate organisation to support them. Customers started consolidating their vendors and identifying key suppliers. They were keen to establish partnership with strategic vendors. A strategic vendor could provide design inputs and manufacturing facilities. A strategic vendor would also be financially strong to execute large orders. The Group was robust on all these parameters.

Five, the Group has access to unlimited production capacities, due to its outsourcing model. The DS Group evolved a business model whereby it could get an order from anywhere and execute it through a basket of partner factories.

A pure brick and mortar model of growth, cannot be expanded indefinitely. The unique selling proposition of the outsourcing model is its scalability. The Group could add customers and factories and grow indefinitely. The significant advantage of the outsourcing model is its scalability and flexibility. "The sky is the limit in this model because the Group could add any number of partner factories to its portfolio. We boosted our production capabilities immensely, by teaming with well-managed factories," says Deepak.

Six, the Group developed new partnerships with its retailers. This became a pillar of strength for the business. It had sales offices in all key markets. It could meet its customers daily to talk to them and service them. The Group had also established sourcing offices in the supplying countries, to monitor quality and delivery schedules. All this needed people and money. The Group had them.

If the retailer wanted some design inputs or had a very large order, he would first approach a strategic partner-vendor like the DS Group.

Seven, Deepak is intense in his focus on garments. He is very faithful to the core business of garments. He did venture into leather exports and even retailing garments. However, when he realised that they were not his cup of tea, he shut them. Deepak understands, smells, sleeps and lives garments. Some entrepreneurs diversify into too many ventures. Frequently, they face disappointment and seek help from venture capitalists. Then, they lose control of their businesses, started and built so fondly.

Deepak believes that he should engage in businesses, which he understands thoroughly. He has stayed with garments, so that he can shine in the business. He made it a mission in his life, to clothe the world in elegant and fashionable clothes.

Eight, the Group's strategy has been to build a global business, with production footprints across the world. This is necessary to manage the seasonality factor in the garments industry. Seasonality is a very important variable in the business. When it is winter in Britain, it is summer in Brazil. To ensure that all production units run throughout the year, it is important to have customers worldwide. For instance, if a factory manufactures T-shirts, it could cater to Europe in the summers. Latin America has summer in December-January, when it is winter in Europe. Then, the factory could supply T-shirts to Latin America.

Finally, the Group has ceaselessly modernised its factories and improved its technical efficiencies. It has invested ceaselessly to introduce new technologies and ensure total compliances in all the production units. Manufacturers use the Standard Minute Value (SMV) to estimate the costing of a garment and the time it takes to produce it. The time taken to stitch every element of the garment is calculated and then aggregated. For instance, in stitching a shirt, the time taken to stitch the collar, cuff and sleeves is calculated in seconds and minutes. These times are then added to arrive at the SMV of the garment. A shirt could be a 15-minute garment. A T-shirt could be a three-minute garment. A cargo pant which may have 10 pockets and flaps could be a 50-minute garment. An outerwear jacket, with a number of components like inner layer, outer layer, inside pockets, outside pockets, zips and buttons could be a 100-minute garment. So, focus on reducing the time to produce a garment through productivities, gives the business a cutting edge.

The DS Group's best production practices also lure professionals. The improvements that it initiates in every manufacturing process, are disseminated widely across all the factories. A more efficient way of cutting the fabric or stitching the collar, is dispersed to all the factories. The initiatives in worker engagement, community welfare, supporting sustainability and SAP implementation, all contribute to building a learning organisation.

One-Stop Shop

The DS Group has positioned itself as a One-Stop Shop for its customers. It has evolved into a multi-geographical sourcing business. It has a factory in Indonesia to manufacture high-end fabric garments for any customer. The customer can also order jackets from Vietnam. Another customer can order embellished dresses from India. Bangladesh can supply core volume items like T-shirts. The customer prefers an entity like the DS Group, which can meet its varied requirements from across the world.

Mentoring of Expatriate CEOs

Managing operations abroad, creates a new genre of expatriate managers. The DS Group has around 210 expatriate staff working in its operations abroad. Their training and morale are very important. An expatriate CEO, working in a foreign country on a new project, sometimes feels lonely. The business goes through various phases. He has to negotiate the foreign environment, new vendors, employees, local regulations, tough deadlines, etc. Despite all the uncertainties, he needs to hold firm to his vision and the strategy, in unchartered waters. Deepak's tremendous experience in the industry, makes him an empathic mentor for his senior management team. His mind is like a hot cauldron, boiling constantly with new ideas.

The country CEOs respect Deepak for his energy and vision. Guru Moorthy, heads the business in Hong Kong and Vietnam. He has worked with prestigious organisations like La Perla, the Italian luxury lifestyle business. It is owned by the German entrepreneur Lars Windhorst, through the Sapinda Group and the Busana Apparel Group of Indonesia. He recalls, "During the meetings, Mr. Seth stays focussed on key topics and closes them with actionable conclusions. He has an aggressive travel schedule, yet he brings immense depth and energy to each discussion. He has a fabulous work ethic. I had a call scheduled with him before I joined the Group, at 12 pm London time. I got the call exactly at 12 pm. This is incredible. Now, I run my business with the same punctuality." Guru Moorthy recalls that he had heard of Deepak as a visionary leader as early as 1988, when he was a student at the NIFT.

Senior expatriate professionals are also delighted with the way the Group empowers them by giving them responsibility and the freedom to operate. The business heads have a clear vision and a path to get to their goal. They are also happy that Deepak has inducted his two sons Pallak and Pulkit into the business, to ensure continuity.

Deepak has mastered the art of seeing the big picture and simultaneously being comfortable with microscopic details. Many leaders only see the big picture, others get lost in detail. Deepak can juggle smoothly between overall perspective and detail.

Many best practices in organisations are definable and quantifiable. They are cloneable and even taught in business schools. However, the core strength of any organisation, is its basic DNA or its generic characteristic. In the DS Group, the inherent strength, is its vision to serve its customers selflessly and steadfastly.

PHOTOGRAPHS

1. Aerial view of Chennai factory.

2. Production floor, Chennai factory.

3. Stitching at Indonesia factory.

4. Laying the fabrics.

5. Typical washing area in a Group factory.

6. Quality checking of every garment at a Group factory.

7. Deepak Seth with the employees at the Indonesia factory.

8. Production at the Group's Indonesia factory.

9. Finishing department.

10. Quilting machine.

11. Dining facilities at a Group factory.

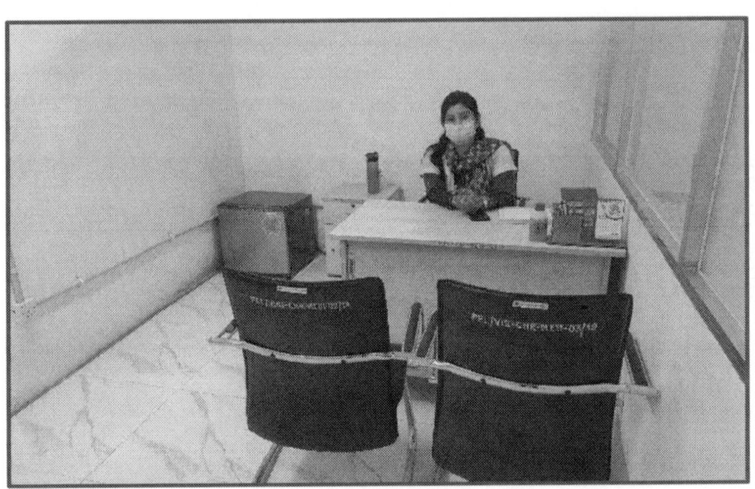

12. Doctor's room at the Group's Bangladesh Factory.

13. Sewing at Group's Bangladesh factory.

14. Solar panel roof of Group's Vietnam factory.

15. Lunar New Year Celebration at Vietnam factory.

16. Football League, Vietnam employees.

"Business Is People"

Deepak makes it clear that integrity, timeliness and discipline are critical to progress, for every employee.

Integrity is fundamental.
Timeliness is crucial in an export-oriented industry.
Discipline is a Must, for delivery.

17
Building the Best Teams

As a student at the JBIMS, Deepak often visited the room of the Director, Dr. K. S. Basu. During the two years at the Institute, he noticed a book which was always on the Director's table. The name of the book was "Business Is People".

The message that eventually, business is all about people, got deeply embedded in everyone's psyche who visited Dr. K. S. Basu's room. Deepak never forgot the learning.

The years at the personnel department of ITC, had also taught him the importance of forging good teams. He realised that the success of his business would depend on the quality of the people, who worked in the organisation.

The DS Group (Deepak Seth Group, including PDS and PGIL), now employs about 30,000 people across the world. It also employs 1,000 managers, from various nationalities, in about 22 plus countries. Building multinational teams is painstaking. It is tough to build teams of foreign nationals across countries. Building multinational and multilingual teams requires sensitivities to foreign cultures, traditions and nuances.

In assembling teams for the business, Deepak was cognisant of the unique features of the garments business. First, garment production is a nitty-gritty, hands-on business. It requires a keen eye for detail. Despite some automation and digitisation, garment manufacturing remains a labour-intensive industry. Are the button holes the right size? Does the colour of the button need to contrast or match with the colour of the fabric? Every pocket has to be stitched manually to every shirt. Every skirt has to be washed before it leaves the factory. Each blouse has to be pressed individually. Each shirt has to be packed in a box.

Second, fashion is a highly personalised business. Fabrics are soft materials. Fashion garments involve embroidery, beading, etc. They are prone to slipping. Hence, automation and standardisation in the garments industry, are constrained substantially due to the nature of the raw materials. Some shirts and suits, which are made with stiffer or thicker fabrics, do lend themselves to standardisation.

Third, garment production is a manual process, requiring skills at every stage. Embroidery, stitching buttons and pressing have to be done manually. Buttons have to be stitched by hands. Pressing has to be done by hands.

During the first few years into the business, Deepak would review every miniscule detail personally. He wanted to learn everything about the manufacturing and marketing of garments. The more he knew personally, the more he would be able to delegate to others later. He also knew that delegation is not abdication.

"Deepak wants to get into the depths of the minutest thing to understand it. He wants to keep on expanding," explains his brother Krishen. "His mind is always working on some project. He enjoys what he does. He does take an annual holiday with his family. But, it's always work, work, work, even on a holiday," he adds.

As the business grew, Deepak let his managers run the businesses. He focussed on the top-line sales and the bottom-line profits. If a business head or manager was delivering results, Deepak left him alone. He got immersed in detail, only if a unit did not deliver results.

Best Quality Professionals

Deepak built a strong team because he hired the best professionals. This was one of his key best practices. He believed in getting the right professionals and then empowering them to deliver. The garment business in India had been hitherto managed by families, typically by the founders, their relatives and close friends.

Deepak wanted to build a global business. He knew he could not be present everywhere himself. He would have to rely on information and reports. He wanted the entire operation to be on auto-pilot, without his daily interventions. He reasoned, that the company would need top-class professionals.

Pradeep Dinodia, a college classmate of Deepak says, "The DS Group makes top payments for the best talent. It pays high salaries and incentives to country heads and factory managers who deliver. Many of the senior staff work on a profit-sharing basis. So, the team stays loyal. Deepak brought Arun Gujral as a profit-sharing partner 40 years ago. Nobody in the industry was sharing profits at that time. Deepak has the instinct to recruit the right people. Then, he provides them with adequate incentives. He also gives them the freedom to operate and deliver. Even now, not many businessmen share profits as Deepak does."

Entrepreneurial Freedom and Delegation

Deepak gives his senior managers ample room to operate. He applies a simple principle in guiding his CEOs and senior managers. He never takes decisions for them. He only shares his views with them. Deepak's managers have to take their own decisions. Moreover, if a manager does not heed his advice and makes a mistake, Deepak never reminds him that he had counselled him otherwise. He lets his managers learn.

At the time of the Annual Plans, Deepak and his sons Pallak and Pulkit, are fully involved in finalising the strategy and business goals of each unit. They have predetermined parameters to assess each business unit. Businesses which meet the financial goals and clear governance audits, get augmented autonomy.

Deepak visits Indonesia about once every two years. The business services prestigious brands like Ann Taylor, Banana Republic, Talbots, Brook Brothers and Ralph Lauren. The Group's Indonesian factories produce 4.5 to 5 million garments every year, comprising of blouses, dresses and jackets. Rajesh Ajwani, the business head, enjoys operational independence to manage the business.

Deepak takes risks and gives everybody a long rope to succeed. Anil Nayar, a member of the Board of PGIL, says, "He tells a person, give me a viable idea. Here is the money. Now, start a new business, division or subsidiary." As a result, Deepak has built a team of entrepreneurs. Anil adds, "Deepak tells them, you are the boss, you run this business and your team. These are your goals. I will share the profits with you."

Being a very keen observer of people, Deepak has become a good judge of character. His high levels of energy are also due to his enthusiasm for his work. His childlike eagerness for new ideas and projects is infectious. He keeps an open mind and is always experimenting. A business colleague comments, "He is very young at heart. So, he surrounds himself with young people. That keeps him going. Also, he is very generous. He is large-hearted and hospitable with everyone." His keen eye has helped him to select high-quality, entrepreneurial business leaders.

Geographic, Product Businesses

Deepak ensured that every business was geographic or product specific. If he found five entrepreneurial candidates in Hong Kong, he would give each of them, a different geographic or product market to work in. Thus, the various subsidiaries do not compete with each other. The DS Group's organisation was built gradually, brick by brick. Like Rome, the DS Group too, was not built in a day.

Deepak had a business management education and exposure to working in a multinational like ITC. He was widely travelled and ardently believed in processes and systems. He was a champion of computerisation and digitisation. Deepak was friendly, warm and always fair. So, he was able to build teams of managers, staff and workers very effectively.

Santosh Gadia became a close family friend of the Seth brothers. He worked with them in the business at various times, in operational and advisory roles. He says that Deepak is an exceptional professional. "First, I have never seen a guy take such quick decisions. Second, he never hesitates to address any problem. He never side-tracks an issue, nor does he lock it in a cupboard. You can call him in the middle of the night with a problem and get a decision. Third, he gives a lot of freedom to people like me and others to perform and do whatever we think is right. The amount of delegation is unbelievable. Fourth, he motivates people, not merely financially, but also by looking after them personally."

Compensation, Welfare, Mentoring

Deepak believes in attractive compensation and welfare schemes for the staff. The goal is to have human resources practices, which motivate and retain the right people. Deepak does not create bureaucratic organisation structures. He selects the right leaders. Then, he helps them to build competent teams.

Selecting the appropriate people, ensures that managers work for decades with the Group. Many of the CEOs and senior managers have been with the DS Group for the last three decades. Their careers have progressed with the growth of their business units. The Group rewards the best performers generously through increments and promotions. Deepak has enabled the growth of various people from the bottom of the ladder to the top. Deepak's formula is simple. He establishes whether a person can deliver and is trustworthy. Then, he goes out of the way to propel the person's career.

The interaction and learning process between Deepak and his senior management team is a continuous process. Sunny Malhotra says, "Even, after 15 years in the company, I understand that it is very important for me to keep learning in my career. Every time I sit with Deepak, I learn something new. He is very inspirational. I admire him."

The Hong Kong operation was going through a lean phase around 1993. The business had not made any profits for three years. It was losing money. Sunny and his team were upbeat and hoped to make some profit in 1994. However, due to some unexpected exigencies, the business made a loss again.

Sunny and his colleagues were devastated. They expected a reprimand from Deepak. He recollects Deepak's call to him, "You did nothing wrong. Now, go and do what you are good at. Go out and sell and rebuild the business. We will make profits next year. Relax."

The day was a milestone in Sunny's career. Through a few words, Deepak had instilled confidence in him. Managers respect Deepak for believing in them, during their bumpy patches.

Sunny recollects that when a unit in Bangladesh was going through a tough phase, Deepak provided him with a lot of support. He adds, "In life, you do not always remember the good times. You do remember the tough times. That's when you need support. Those are the times when Deepak steps in to help. He is tough, but very clear. He can guide you adroitly in a crisis, due to his tremendous experience."

The CEOs respect Deepak for his balanced approach. Deepak can be demanding on results, but is very supportive in a crisis. He is very composed during the hard patches, ensuring stability in clamour.

Shankar Jha manages the administration and travel desk, in Delhi. He is responsible for Deepak's travel arrangements across the world and is on the phone 24 by 7. He has worked for the business for 30 years and says he has never looked for a job outside the firm. He adds, "The company always takes care of its employees. The salaries, bonuses, increments are always on schedule."

The quiet, sober and dedicated Prem Singh, has worked on Deepak's personal staff from 1991 onwards. He says that dedication and honesty are the keys to progressing in the Group.

Employee Growth: Climbing the Ladder

The growth of the employees through internal promotions is encouraged in the firm, on the basis of performance, application and skills. Many managers have progressed to leadership positions in foreign postings, with profit sharing plans. The managers who deliver results, respect time and value punctuality, progress in the DS Group.

Deepak had briefed the Finance Advisor, Mrs. Anita Gadia in 1989, to review the allocation of work among the staff. So, all the employees were interviewed to identify their key strengths and weaknesses. Many of them were assigned new roles and tasks. Surinder Sharma, who had joined in 1989, as an Accounts Assistant, was selected to clear some outstanding accounting matters. It was a breakthrough moment for Surinder. From then onwards, he proved his mettle in various assignments, in his meteoric rise to the position of Assistant General Manager.

Describing his journey, he says, "Just after clearing my 12th exams, I started my career in the accounting field with a Chartered Accountant firm, named Ved Gupta and Associates. I worked as an intern for three years. After that, I got an opportunity to join the Group as an Accounts Assistant. From the beginning I was very hard working and dedicated to my work. I never hesitated from any challenging work given to me by my superiors. They started having confidence in me and encouraged me. In 1997, I got my first promotion as an Accountant. Since then, more responsibilities were given to me by the management.

Gradually I started climbing the corporate ladder from an Accountant to Assistant Manager, Manager, Senior Manager and then Assistant General Manager (AGM). During my journey from an Accounts Assistant to an AGM, I had the opportunity to work in all the departments like payables, receivables, materials accounting, annual accounts, monthly MIS, etc. I also led the team to manage the audits. My goal is to always meet all my commitments to my seniors on schedule. In return, the management has been very responsive. It has promoted me from time to time. This has given me a morale boost and inspired me to keep working with the same zeal.

Everything that I have achieved in my career so far, is due to the supportive nature of my superiors and most important, of Mr. Deepak Seth. He has always encouraged and guided me from time to time. He taught me to overcome difficulties and achieve results. Mr. Seth has always played a very important and inspirational role in my journey. His aura is so charismatic and positive, that his sheer presence is a morale booster for all of us, who are in constant touch with him.

I have always respected and followed Mr. Seth's mantra to 'Grow with the Company'. This has made me the man, I am today. I have the deepest gratitude for Mr. Seth. He has been a very important and a fatherly figure who has helped us to progress in our careers. His contribution has always energised my role at every stage, in my professional career and personal life.

It gives me great pleasure to have the opportunity to work under such a positive person. He has taken me and the company to great heights, with his personal knowledge, leadership skills and his sheer presence."

Integrity, Timeliness and Discipline

Surinder adds that one of the biggest lessons he has learnt from Deepak, is timeliness. He says, "If you have to deliver something, it has to be always on time. This requires planning. There is always the pressure of submitting the MIS reports by the 15th day of each month. Then, we have to call the auditors for the quarterly closings and they need 20 to 30 days for a review. We also have to prepare papers for the board meetings. I have learnt to deliver on all my commitments on schedule."

Deepak makes it clear that integrity, timeliness and discipline are critical to progress for every employee. Integrity is fundamental. Timeliness is crucial in an export-oriented industry. Discipline not only covers macro factors like adhering to government regulations, but also micro situations like reporting on time for work and appropriate behaviour in the office.

Deepak does not set stringent deadlines for tasks which do not impact revenues directly. He tells the manager to give a target date and then he expects delivery.

Ashish Khatri who has worked in the firm since 1995, says that a sterling quality of Deepak is that you can disagree freely with him. "He is not a 'Yes Boss' man. If you express a view on any business issue which is contrary to his, he listens to you. You can also question him. If he is convinced about what you are telling him, he will change his decision."

Deepak is also very result oriented. He agrees the targets and the time to deliver them, with every new business unit. The first year is for establishing the business. The second year is for getting the business going. By the third year, the company expects results. Deepak provides enough time to build the organisation. If some elements are not synchronising, he gives more rope to the business unit to deliver. Finally, if there is no hope, the business unit could be shut.

Deepak does not fret if he takes a financial beating. If he loses a million dollars in a business, he takes the hit. He does not procrastinate to shut down operations, which do not deliver results.

If a business is not delivering and the businessman takes a decision to shut it, he comes out stronger. Just taking the decision, makes the businessman more mature. Next time, he is confident of taking a bigger risk because he has handled a closure in the past.

The Lerros retail business in India is a case study of decision-making in the Group. India was on a retail picnic in the early 2000s. Groceries, dairy products, garments and electronics were all selling in swanky retail outlets. New malls were mushrooming even in towns like Chandigarh, Lucknow, Nagpur and Patna. Deepak also entered the retail arena with exclusive retail outlets selling Lerros garments. About 40 Lerros retail outlets sprang-up in Bengaluru, Chennai, Chandigarh, Delhi, Noida, etc. The stores were established on a franchisee basis and the business was managed by a CEO who had excellent academic credentials, being a graduate from the Indian Institute of Technology (IIT) and the Indian Institute of Management (IIM).

Launching Lerros in India required a host of permissions from the government. Sandeep Sabharwal had just joined the firm in May 2008 as the Company Secretary. He was charged with the responsibility of getting approvals from the Government of India, as the project involved a foreign collaboration. As a fresh entrant, Sandeep was surprised at the freedom he enjoyed from the first day.

The Lerros stores were launched. After the second year, Deepak started worrying about the business. In an unwritten rule of his, a business should start delivering some profits after three years. He observed at the end of the third year, that the business was not breaking even. So, he took the tough decision to shut down the retail business.

Respect, Sensitivity for Staff

Deepak does not spare any expense to look after his team members. In 1988, Santosh Gadia who helped Deepak with financial matters was in Dusseldorf, Germany on work. It was a weekend and he was wondering how to spend it, as his family was in Delhi. His phone rang and Deepak asked him, "What are you doing in Dusseldorf?" Santosh replied, "I am chilling and wondering how to spend the weekend." Deepak immediately responded, "No, no, you come to Zurich. We are having dinner with a buyer. I want you to join us".

Santosh rushed to the airport to catch a flight to Zurich. After the dinner, Santosh realised that the bill for five persons was about USD 10,000. Now, being a finance person, Santosh was baffled. "Why did you have to fly me and invite me for such an expensive dinner? It is a lot of money," he told Deepak. "It does not matter. I wanted you to meet the buyers. And, you were all alone in Dusseldorf," replied Deepak.

Young Santosh could not fathom why Deepak had flown him to Zurich for such an expensive meal. However, he was fired with zeal, because he felt that Deepak really cared for him.

Santosh recollects that the firm did not do much business with the Zurich party. However, he learnt how Deepak built a personal rapport with the buyers and how he cared for people working with him. Deepak goes beyond immediate business interests and relationships. He builds long-terms associations with people.

Deepak trusts his team members implicitly. After a review of a USA business in 1992, Santosh concluded that it may have to be restructured radically. Since the matter was urgent, he called Deepak from New York, though it was midnight in India. He told Deepak, "We may have to take a hit of about USD 7 to 8 million. We have to restructure the teams too."

After listening to Santosh patiently for 30 minutes in the middle of the night, Deepak's only query was, "Can you handle it or do you want me to come there?" Santosh replied, "I can take care of it." Next morning, Deepak wrote off the business loss and the entire operation was restructured.

Sanjay Sarkar had a son studying accounting and finance at the Kent Business school in England. Brexit was being hotly debated in 2019. The young student was unsure of his career, as the implications of Brexit were unclear. When Deepak heard about it, he invited Sarkar's son to meet him at his home in London. Deepak spent a few hours over lunch with the youngster, understanding his career goals and then guided him appropriately. Sarkar was delighted and says, "My family was thrilled that Mr. Seth, despite his busy schedule, had kept the entire afternoon free for my son. He also went out of his way to help him in the UK."

Multinational Design Professionals

Deepak hires the best design professionals, since he believes that designing is the fulcrum of the business. The company recruits talented multinational designing teams from Britain,

Canada, Germany, etc. They are supported by design teams in India.

Though the Group sources professionals from many countries like the USA, Germany and Britain, many of them are inducted in India. These professionals from different nationalities are given exposure to the factories in India. The training of foreign recruits in the local factories, provides the youngsters with practical lessons.

The Pearl Academy of Fashion pioneered by Deepak, helped to source the right talent, in an industry desperately short of professionally trained staff. Many of the youngsters who graduated from the Institute, joined the company and built careers.

Caring Forever

Deepak's care for his core staff goes beyond their work tenures at the firm. In 1994, Santosh Gadia told Deepak that he wanted to take a career break. Santosh realised that he was travelling almost eight months a year to the offices abroad. In addition, he was managing the back office in Delhi, handling banking, IT systems, accounting, etc. Deepak asked him, "What do you want to do?" Santosh replied, "I really do not know. I just need a break from the hectic international travel."

Deepak took Santosh for lunch. They had dined together many times, but always with the families or business associates. This was the first time they were having a meal by themselves.

During the meeting, Deepak told Santosh three things. First, he did not want him to work with another exporter. Santosh replied that if he had to work with an exporter, he would work with Deepak and the Group as they were the best in class.

Second, Deepak told Santosh that even after he left, he would have to be available to him 24 by 7. Again, Santosh readily agreed. He would be available to Deepak round the clock due to their mutual affection.

Deepak's third point staggered Santosh completely. He told Santosh, "After you leave us, I want you to make the same money, that you are making with us now. Never, less. If it is less, you will get back to me." Santosh was flabbergasted. Deepak then gave his granite and travel agency businesses to Santosh.

Now, Santosh was a minority partner in the granite business, with about twelve and a half percent profit participation. He had helped Deepak to start the venture. It was making a lot of money. Deepak also gave him the travel business. Deepak told him, "You take the entire businesses. You run them. Manage them. In case you are short of money, talk to me. You can earn and pay back to me, whatever I had invested at cost. And, if you earn less than what you get now from us, talk to me." Santosh was stunned. Deepak could have knocked him down with a feather. Who could be so generous, he thought to himself.

Santosh adds, "Whatever I am today, is due to Deepak. He gets embarrassed when I say this. I tell him it is a fact and I say it from my heart. I do not mind saying this in front of thousands of people. My own experience is that Deepak is a smart businessman, but he is also a wonderful human being."

Leading by Personal Example

Deepak leads by example. His cardinal principle is to be at his work desk at 9 am every morning, irrespective of which country he is in. He may have worked until midnight; however, he is at work at 9 am the next morning.

Deepak noticed that some of the managers in the factory habitually came late to work. One day, he told the office guard, "Shut the building gate at 9 am. If anyone arrives after that, do not let them in. Call me." Now it is very embarrassing, if some senior managers are stopped at the gate by the guard. Deepak would personally go to the gate and ask the guard why the manager had been stopped. The guard would reply, "Sir you yourself had told me to shut the gate at 9 am." Everyone in the business got the message and reported for work before 9 am daily.

At other times, Deepak would call the habitual late comers on the intercom between 9 and 9.15 am. When there was no response, he would tell the manager later, "I was trying to speak to you at 9.10 am. There was no response. What's the problem?" Again, the message percolated to everyone, be at your desk by 9 am daily.

Deepak would often communicate to his staff that in the garments industry, time is of essence. He counselled his staff, "If you do not commence work on time, we will never be able to compete with the other manufacturers. Managers and supervisors should be very particular, about reaching the factory on schedule. The workers cannot commence their duties, till the managers and supervisors brief them on the production priorities for the day. So, if the manager is late, all the work gets delayed. We are dealing with foreign importers and brands. We have to satisfy them with our deliveries. They are very particular about timeliness. If there is a production delay, then we have to fly the goods to London or New York, instead of sending them by ship. Then, we incur a loss on that consignment. In a year, if we are compelled to send 10 to 15 consignments by air instead of by ship, then the business makes a loss."

The lesson on timeliness and punctuality was very important, more so in the 1970s and 1980s, when many workers had scant respect for time. Deepak works fast; he never delays or procrastinates. If there is a problem or an issue, Deepak's habit is to solve it immediately.

Deepak's management team admires him for respecting time. Says an HR manager, "Sometimes, Mr. Seth calls me for a meeting, but the previous meeting is not finished. Then, he texts me to come after 15 minutes. He ensures that I do not waste my time sitting outside his room."

Straight to Work

Deepak is so dedicated to his work, that whenever he visits a city for work, he goes straight to the office from the airport. Even when he returns to India after a long flight from New York or London, he visits his office before going home. He starts telephoning people for meetings from the airport itself. He works the entire day and returns home only in the evening.

If Deepak is travelling abroad from India, he works and briefs his team until he leaves for the airport. He does not waste a minute. If he is departing for the airport at midnight, the meetings at his house commence from 9 pm onwards.

Unstoppable

Deepak keeps walking, unmindful of the obstacles that emerge. Captain Vinod Vaish, Vice President, Administration and Procurement, recollects a symbolic incident, "We were reviewing a new property. As we were examining the plot of land, a sandal which Deepak was wearing slipped off. He did not waste any time to stop to put it back. He kept walking with one sandal. A staff member collected the sandal and offered it to Deepak, who replied, 'I am walking. How does it matter if I have only one sandal? Keep it in the car. I shall wear it on the way to the office.'"

In keeping with his style of working, Deepak walks fast. In any group on a factory or market visit, he stands out by being the fastest walker. Every morning, he walks alone for about three to five kilometres in the lawns of his house.

Deepak and the Group, have thus become a training ground for managers in the garment industry. Some of his managers have departed for leadership positions in other companies. They continue to maintain cordial relations with the Group. The DS Group, has thus become a factory, producing good-quality leaders and managers for the entire industry.

A Man of His Word

Employees work in the company for decades, due to the family atmosphere in the organisation. The salaries, statutory dues, increments and festival bonuses of all the employees are paid on schedule. This provides stability to all employees. Employees also have the time to spend with their families and look after them.

Surinder Sharma says, "Any commitment made by Mr. Seth is always delivered. I have seen this during my career of 30 years with the Group."

Deepak Seth, the youngster, who started his business journey in 1976, travelling on a Lambretta scooter with samples for clients, has travelled far.

Deepak insists on rigorous corporate governance. He told his team, "I want every rule and regulation to be followed. I do not care about the costs."

Deepak made it a cornerstone of the business, to have absolute ethical governance.

18
The Compliances Syndrome

The world was horrified. A fire had killed 117 workers and injured 200 in Bangladesh. The disaster in a garment factory near Dhaka in 2012, sent shock waves in the retail industry. Some factory supervisors were arrested. The accident rang alarm bells worldwide. The global media carried gruesome stories of how unsafe working conditions were, in many garment factories in the developing countries.

A year later in 2013, another garment factory in Dhaka collapsed. It killed more than 1,100 people and injured more than 2,500. This was the last straw on the camel's back. The world roared with disapproval. The spotlight was on low-cost developing countries like China, Bangladesh and India, to review the working conditions of workers in garment factories. Many activists launched litigations against the local companies in Bangladesh.

After the Bangladesh factory fire, foreign customers became very stringent about the operating conditions of the workers in manufacturing countries. They strengthened existing compliances and added new stipulations to ensure worker safety.

The working conditions of workers in Bangladesh were enhanced through two agreements. The first was the "Accord on Fire and Building Safety in Bangladesh" established by European Retailers, International Labour Organisations and NGOs. The second was the "Alliance for Bangladesh Worker Safety" (ABWS), established by North American retailers.

Reputed garment retailers like Marks & Spencer and GAP already had rigorous requirements, regarding the working conditions in the factories of their vendors. For instance, many buyers checked the toilets and dining facilities of the workers, before initiating any business discussions with the vendors.

Increased awareness of the environment and climate warming have made buyers fiercely conscious of their responsibilities as global citizens. Many buyers like Marks & Spencer, Ralph Lauren, Zara, etc., are global players. They are keen to be perceived as socially responsible organisations. Hence, they insist on compliances concerning worker safety, labour relations, health conditions, etc., among their vendors.

There are some basic compliances that all buyers insist on. For instance, no customer wants child labour deployed in any vendor factory. Minimum wages have to be paid to all workers. Bribery and corruption are taboo. The provident fund, social security, statutory dues, etc., of workers, should be paid regularly. Health and safety standards have to be sustained.

Global buyers are keen to ensure that their compliances are being adhered to. They prefer to deal with vendors who have their own factories. Indian exporters started investing in larger and modern factories. This, made it possible for Indian exporters to ensure that all compliances are being met.

Codes of Conduct

There are four major areas in which customers monitor their suppliers. They are adherence to government laws, environment protection, treatment of labour and occupational health and safety.

Adherence to Laws

Buyers want to work with compliant factories, which adhere religiously to all the domestic and international laws. Respecting the local national laws is an axiom. This basic condition has to be fulfilled. The DS Group ensures that all government stipulations are followed.

Buyers insist that vendors abide by the laws of the land and the prevailing rules and regulations. Many of these conditions are prescribed in the "Code of Conduct" which they have. Furthermore, buyers insist that whichever requirements are more stringent, i.e. the law of the land or their Code of Conduct, will apply. Buyers also ensure that the vendor signs an undertaking to abide by the Code of Conduct, before commencing any business. Bribes, kickbacks and improper payments are unacceptable.

Ensuring that all the statutory compliances are adhered to, has also contributed to making the operations efficient. The government has provided the option to make many statutory payments online. For instance, payments like the Provident Fund and Employees' State Insurance can now be paid online. If a company delays payments, there is an additional interest cost.

A typical factory in India needs about 78 permissions, licences and clearance certificates to operate. These permissions pertain to registration, fire regulations, energy, pollution, etc. The list is long and cumbersome, augmenting the administrative work in a factory. Many of these certifications can now be availed digitally. This enables timely compliance of many regulatory processes.

The DS Group ensures that global standards in law and ethics, are adhered to in all its units. Deepak always tells his teams that he wants the best corporate governance. Every rule, has to be followed. In the initial years, the business evolved and grew based on Deepak's personal drive. Now, the Group is managed by professional managers and teams. Deepak has ensured that they are fastidious about corporate governance. The Group avoids any issues with the government or the bankers.

The DS Group has 100 percent compliant factories. It delivers on all regulations and quality assurance standards like ISO (International Organisation for Standardisation) and 5S (Japanese Management and Strategy Institute). The Group factories have received certifications from third party inspection and quality-check companies, like Intertek (British multinational) and SGS (Swiss multinational).

Environment and Sustainability

Buyers also insist on environmental compliances and sustainability. They have a comprehensive set of checkpoints to evaluate and select a vendor.

Buyers review a range of sustainability factors with a toothcomb. They measure the quantum of electricity a vendor is consuming, greenhouse gases being emitted, chemicals management, waste handling, carbon footprint, etc. The compliance team studies granular minutiae like the source of the water being used in the factory and its treatment. If the water is extracted from the ground, they want to see the necessary permissions. The quantum of water being extracted and the recycling process are also reviewed.

Environmental compliances are measured on an electronic platform, called the HIGG Index. It is a tool used in the apparel and footwear industry to assess sustainability. It covers the product's entire life cycle, from the raw material stage to the time of discarding it after use. The Index was developed by the Sustainable Apparel Coalition. This is a non-profit organisation, formed by a group of fashion companies and the Environment Protection Agency of the US Government.

Respect for Labour

Buyers have labour Codes of Conduct which the vendors need to respect. The Codes of Conduct are based on internationally accepted labour standards. They are derived from the International Labour Organisation's (ILO) core conventions, Universal Declaration of Human Rights and the United Nations (UN) Guiding Principles for Business and Human Rights.

Many compliances are focussed on the treatment of labour and their working conditions. A person below the age of 18 years cannot be employed for any hazardous work. Any type of discrimination on the basis of race, religion, belief, colour, sex, etc., is taboo. The use of bonded labour, prison labour or forced labour is sternly forbidden. Workers should work voluntarily. Foreign workers have to be treated on par with local labour. Workers should not face any harassment or abuse of any type.

Every worker should be treated with respect and dignity. Workers should have the freedom of association. They should be free to join organisations or unions of their choice. Wages should be paid to the workers according to the minimum wage rate or the standard industry rate, whichever is higher. The number of working hours should be as per the local laws. The weekly working hours should be between 48 to 60 hours. A weekly holiday is also provided for.

Women workers have to be treated on par with men. Women should also be entitled to maternity leave. They should be able to return to their jobs at the same level, after maternity leave.

Buyers have stringent requirements about separate toilet facilities for women, kitchen and dining area hygiene, cleanliness of dormitories, etc.

Occupational Health

Employers are also required to focus on occupational health and safety measures for their staff. Workers have to be provided with a clean, safe and healthy workplace, to prevent injuries or accidents.

Factories have to comply with local occupational laws or those prescribed by the buyers, whichever are more stringent. The manufacturers have to maintain high ethical standards in their operations.

Security Concerns

After the 9/11 attacks in 2001, the USA wanted to ensure rigorous control on all types of materials entering the country. Thus, the C-TPAT (Customs Trade Partnership Against Terrorism) was introduced in 2001, to confirm that all shipments entering the USA are safe. It ensures that the entire supply chain of the private companies is secure and no undesirable or dangerous goods enter the USA.

The physical sanitisation and security of goods moving to the USA, is ensured through a three-stage process. First, every person entering the supplier's factory should have security clearance and be monitored. Second, the warehouses where the goods are stored have to be secured. This is to ensure that nobody can place anything in any carton, being exported to the USA.

Finally, the entire transportation link has to be monitored. As the shipment has to be exported, goods travel by trucks to the dockyard. The truck drivers have to be scrutinised and their backgrounds have to be checked and verified. The exporters have to ensure that the consignment is sealed in the presence of responsible staff.

Systematic Assessment

Some of the buyers have their own compliance teams which visit and evaluate their vendor factories. Others like Marks & Spencer rely on third parties like the French company Sodexo, to undertake the assessment for them. Sodexo has a rating scale for assessing factory compliances, with green being the best and red being the worst. An orange rating signals that improvements are needed.

Retailers use Score Cards to evaluate their vendors on an ongoing basis. For decades, the deciding factors in placing an order were price, quality and delivery. Now, customers also attach weightage to compliances. Consequently, suppliers are revamping their factories to ensure that they adhere to compliances.

Typically, all the factories of the DS Group, fill the required forms online and submit them to the retailers or their agencies. Sodexo grades all the factories and the buyers can access their ratings online. The buyers get a complete picture about the vendor's sustainability score, covering parameters like electrical energy, chemicals usage and water and waste management.

Buyers are investing in technologies and digital platforms to monitor the compliances of their vendors. These platforms measure social compliances, sustainability and even address security concerns.

Rigorous Compliances

Deepak always insists on rigorous corporate governance. He underscores to his teams, "I want every rule and regulation to be followed. I do not care about the costs."

Deepak made it a cornerstone of the business to have absolute ethical governance across the Group, including PDS and PGIL. Irrespective of whether the factory is in Bangladesh or Vietnam or India, it had to adhere to global governances and standards. Deepak was convinced that in the long run, compliance and transparency would enable the business to grow. He had perceived early, that buyers would review the environmental certifications of a manufacturer and the investments to conserve the environment.

Deepak knew that if the Group had to compete in the evolving environmental ecosystem, adherence to all compliances was a must. So, he took the lead in it. He ensured that all the factories met all the new compliances or surpassed them.

A new corporate leadership role was created, to manage compliances and ensure that governance norms were respected. The new manager was tasked to ensure that all the factories were compliant, as required by the buyers. He had the central responsibility for ensuring compliance globally in all the Group factories. The manager would also ensure dissemination of the best practices across all the units. He also dealt with customer queries and became the repository of governance information.

"This role did not exist before I joined," says Manoj Arora, Sustainability and CSR Head, who was recruited for this important task. "Mr. Seth wanted me to ensure hundred percent compliances, in all our factories and be answerable to all the buyers," he adds. Manoj received full support from Pulkit also.

To ensure compliance, the Group has also pioneered new technologies in the factories. For instance, new processing machines, economising on electricity consumption and water usage were pioneered, in the Bangladesh factory specialising in denim jeans.

Compliant factories generate ample credibility and goodwill for the organisation, which generates more business. The DS Group's philosophy is simple: spend any amount of money that you have to, but ensure that the factory is complaint. Says Captain Vinod Vaish, "We had to upgrade all the factories in Gurugram. We revamped the processes, the machines and the existing compliances to ensure high standards. There was constant pressure from the Chairman and Pulkit Seth. They wanted complete professionalism in our operations."

Transparency with Board

The DS Group maintains a very transparent relationship with its Board of Directors. Deepak and his senior managers share the performances of all the units, with the Board members at regular meetings. Says Anil Nayar, "Starting as a small tightly-knit family business, the DS Group (Deepak Seth Group, including PDS and PGIL), has blossomed into a multi-country international conglomerate. Deepak has shown a lot of foresight and determination." The board meetings provide a forum for the directors to interact with the senior managers.

It gives the Board members a lot of confidence to hear Deepak say, "We follow all laws, rules and regulations. We want to ensure nobody can point a finger at us." He adds, "As the business grew, we had to spend more time on governmental regulations and customer compliances. These are critical, as far as I am concerned. We want 100 percent compliance and zero tolerance for non-compliance. This is important to build a solid business. If you take shortcuts, then 90 percent of your time later, goes into negative work. So, it is our policy that whatever you have to do, do it the right way. Sometimes, this takes longer or even costs more. However, it is sustainable." Deepak believed that honesty in compliances is not merely the best policy, it is also a wise and efficient policy.

Environment and Sustainability

Maggie Taylor works as the marketing director of a multinational corporation marketing soaps and deodorants, based in New York. She is 34 years old and is always impeccably dressed in formal suits and jackets. She likes to revamp her wardrobe every season. She gives away her older clothes, many of which have been worn about half a dozen times, to her maid or to charity. Fashion conscious youngsters, like Maggie may use a blazer or a trouser for a few months or a year. Consumers from comparatively richer countries like the USA or Europe, wear their clothes for a season or two until the next collection arrives. Most affluent consumers in the West buy new clothes every season.

Rajesh Mehta is an upcoming business professional, working as production manager in a large textile mill in Mumbai, India. He is a graduate of the prestigious IIT and IIM. So, he is an electrical engineer and an MBA. At the age of 34 years, he is considered a shining star in his company. He revamps his wardrobe every two to three years. He does not follow seasonal offerings. He changes his clothes when he gets bored with them. Consumers in developing countries could wear the same garments even for three or four years. Middle class Indians tend to be frugal. So, if a young manager buys a formal suit, he could use it for three years or more.

Husseini works as an administration manager in a tea plantation in Kenya. He looks forwards to his monthly visits to Nairobi. He visits the second-hand clothes market to shop for trousers, shirts and shoes. He also buys a suit every two years, to attend weddings and the Sunday morning Church services. Husseini has never purchased any new garments. He says, "The used clothes I buy are all imported from USA and Europe. They are in excellent condition. Some of them have been barely used. They are very fashionable. They cost me around 20 to 30 percent of the price of new clothes. So, it makes a lot of sense to me, to buy these second-hand clothes from Europe and wear them. I think, I look very smart in them. Like a gentleman. My wife also loves them."

There is a growing market for second-hand or used garments. About 70 percent of the people in the world wear used garments. The US is the largest exporter of second-hand clothing followed by the UK, Germany and Netherlands. These worn clothes are transported to countries in Africa and South Asia. The spending power and discretionary incomes of people are relatively low in these continents. The clothes given away by the consumers in the USA and Europe, are sold in the local markets. Africa is one of the largest markets for used apparel. This contributes to sustainability, for the clothes are reused.

Shelf-Life of Clothes

The length of time for which someone uses a garment like a shirt or a skirt, depends on the person's fascination with fashion, economic status and the country. Many consumers give old clothes to charity. However, donated clothes comprise only 30 percent of the clothes discarded annually.

The recycling of garments does not absorb all the clothes discarded by the more affluent and middle-class consumers. It is estimated that an average consumer discards 31.75 kilograms of old clothing every year. At the global level, 13 million tons of textile waste is generated every year, 95 percent of which can be recycled, according to The Pretty Planeteer.

The majority of worn and discarded clothes go to waste bins. From the bins, they go to landfills. These discarded or old clothes are just buried in the earth. They are used to fill low-lying land areas across the world. Landfills are sites for the disposal of solid wastes. The refuse is buried between layers of earth to raise the height of low-lying lands. The clothes take years to decay and crumble. Synthetic apparel can take 30 to 40 years to decompose.

"Every second, the equivalent of one garbage truck of textiles is landfilled or burned. An estimated USD 500 billion value is lost every year due to clothing that's barely worn and rarely recycled," according to the Ellen MacArthur Foundation's report "A new textiles economy: Redesigning fashion's future". This UK registered charity aims to inspire people to re-think, re-design and build a positive future through the framework of a circular economy, designed to reduce wastages.

Retailers do realise that fast-fashion trends, puts pressure on the suppliers to produce garments rapidly. This can impact the environment adversely and sometimes, also lead to labour violations. Hence, large retailers like Marks & Spencer, Zara and Hennes & Mauritz (H&M), have corporate policies embracing sustainability, recycling of products and carbon footprints. They are the retail industry's torchbearers.

Youth and Sustainability

There is growing consciousness, especially among the youngsters, that wastage of clothes should be avoided by recycling apparel. Technology has linked the younger generation in the world, especially in the developed countries like the USA and UK. Networking tools have sensitised the young to social issues. Now, environment conscious consumers want to use their clothes for longer periods of time.

The younger generation is increasingly preoccupied with saving the planet and climate change. Youngsters are coming to grips with the impact of fashion on the environment. This has led to focus on the sustainability factor. The trend of fast fashion renders clothes redundant after a few months. These clothes are used for landfilling. So, many activists have been flagging the role of the fast-fashion industry, as detrimental to sustainability.

Younger consumers have been thinking, do we really need so many clothes? How much should we be spending on apparel and accessories? "Younger consumers think that if they spend less on clothes, they contribute to sustainability, since less clothes will go into landfills. Many trailers of old clothes go to landfill daily in the UK. Then, it could take decades for some of these garments to decompose," says Periwal, CEO of NorLanka, a Group company in Sri Lanka. The younger generation is evolving strategies and technologies to recycle used apparel.

Sustainability Contributions

The business has an association with reGAIN, a UK organisation which recycles old clothes. When a person donates his used garments to "reGAIN recyclables", it helps to raise money for charity. A person has to merely download the "reGAIN" application and donate worn apparel. Clothes can also be donated at a charity shop or at any of their 25,000 drop-off points in the UK. The organisation even arranges home pick-ups at a time convenient to the donor. The reGAIN initiative rewards donors with discount coupons, to save money on purchases of new clothes and footwear. The reGAIN initiative thus enables a person to undertake charity, contribute to preserving the planet and also refresh his wardrobe.

Organic Raw Materials

The DS Group is also evaluating the sustainability of the basic raw material, the fabrics that are used to stitch garments. The drive for sustainability, journeys all the way back to selecting the raw materials and how they are grown.

For instance, NorLanka has launched an initiative to buy more organic cotton. No child labour is used on the farms to grow this cotton. The labourers deployed on the farm are ethical labourers, which means all the farm labourers are adults and are paid their dues on time. Growing organic cotton requires less water and fertiliser as compared to growing the normal cotton. This organically grown cotton is perceived as the "better cotton".

NorLanka is focussed on producing apparel, which is 100 percent sustainable, organic and certified by the Global Organic Textile Standard (GOTS). NorLanka endeavours to maximise the use of organic fabrics in the garments it manufactures.

Change in Industry Structure

The focus of buyers on compliances has changed the structure of the apparel export industry significantly. Typically, in the 1980s, when a large exporter got an order, he would execute a major part of the apparel in his own factory. A part of the production was outsourced to small third-party factories.

The smaller exporters operated in cramped factories. They could not afford to modernise to ensure the new compliances. Many of them have gradually folded their businesses. Only the garment exporters who could invest in modern factories, technology, computerisation and environmental compliances, have survived over the decades. Thus, of the 15,000 garments exporters in India about three decades ago, only about 500 have survived.

According to Manoj, "Buyers are paying less for garments than they did some years ago. Some buying prices have declined by as much as 30 percent." Thus, the revenue per garment is declining. However, manufacturing costs are increasing due to inflation, augmented labour costs and investments to ensure compliances. The larger players have survived. The small players lacked the capital to invest.

The result of these stringent compliances is that the small exporters faded out. The bigger players like the DS Group could understand the logic and logistics of the new compliances. They invested in new systems and processes.

Global Business with Ethics

Dr. A. Sakthivel, Chairman of the Apparel Exports Promotion Council (AEPC), opines that Deepak is very sincere about his work and the quality of products. He adds, "His entire team from top to bottom knows that quality is a matter of life. That is the clear message from the Chairman when he talks to his employees, even at the lowest rung."

No businessman can really grow his business or build a global business, without ethical practices. Business has to respect the laws of the land to grow. Buyers always reviewed the quality of the garments, but now they also assess the operating practices of the vendor factories.

Pradeep Dinodia, a former statutory auditor of the business, comments, "Whenever the customers or any institution undertakes an audit of the Group, it comes out on the top. The Group does not try to save money by cutting corners. They follow the best global practices." The adherence to governances and ethical standards in every country, has contributed to its success.

Dinodia adds, "On tax matters, Deepak's dictum has always been to pay the right tax, not the maximum tax, not the minimum tax. As a tax man, I have been his advisor for all these years. He has always paid the right tax and there has never been any serious litigation. He has no tax appeals pending in any court. He is the first person to pay his taxes."

Over the years, the business has won the respect of its customers for its adherence to compliances. A senior manager adds, "We are very strict in terms of compliance, be it environmental, financial or social. We are also a learning organisation. We learn every day. We get better by the day. We introduce new norms and protocols every day."

Prior to the focus on compliances, most garment export businesses were sales-number driven. Get an order, execute it, make a profit and everyone's happy. After the focus on compliances, businesses have to be process driven.

Adherence to compliances, has become a religion in the Deepak Seth Group.

19
Social Compliances, Sustainability and CSR

Omvati had recently lost her husband. She had three children to raise. She had a kerosene stove and four utensils in her home. They were her only possessions. She was in deep financial trouble. Omvati desperately needed to work. She was relieved when the DS Group offered her a job. After working for two and half years in the company, she met with an accident and had to take long leave. She re-joined after her wounds had healed.

Now, she has worked with the PGIL for 21 years. She has been promoted twice due to her diligence and dedication. Her manager discerned her potential and she was elevated as a Finishing Supervisor.

Omvati has educated her three children. Two of them are financially independent, married and well settled. Her daughter is a yoga teacher in Singapore and her elder son is an electrician. The youngest son is studying. She talks with pride about the achievements of her children.

About 1,900 kilometres away, Parveen Aktar had joined PGIL Bangladesh in 2010, as a sewing machine operator in the production department. She was a diligent and smart worker. She was promoted from an operator to senior operator in 2014. By virtue of her good performance, she was promoted as a supervisor in 2017. This was a significant achievement in a society, where women do not easily attain supervisory or leadership roles. She was promoted to mid-level management in 2018. She has proved to be a trailblazer. Parveen continues to deliver and progress.

Social compliance is a key principle that drives the Group. It also contributes to sustainability, for it invests in people and their capabilities.

The DS Group has created five pillars for achieving its sustainable development goals. These are (1) Environment and sustainability, (2) Health, welfare and sanitation, (3) Gender equality, (4) Capability building and (5) Education. Buyers have their governances about the environment, sustainability and treatment of labour. The PGIL business, with Pulkit's leadership has pioneered multifarious initiatives, in its conviction that sustainability and labour welfare are vital for any business to flourish.

Environment and Sustainability

There is growing awareness about how rapid unbridled industrialisation and urbanisation can damage the environment. Pulkit is committed to reducing wastage and bringing sustainable changes in the garment manufacturing business. He has launched several initiatives to become a sustainable business.

Solar Panels: PGIL has installed 755 solar panels as an alternative source of energy, at its Chennai facility, thereby reducing its carbon footprint.

Effluent Treatment Plants (ETPs): The Group's manufacturing units across the globe, are equipped to process wastewater and effluents. The contaminants are removed from wastewater, so that it can be recycled.

Platinum Certification: PGIL has received a platinum certification from the US Green Building Council for its Kanchipuram (Tamil Nadu state, South India) plant. A platinum rating signifies that the unit has a green building design and makes optimal use of sustainable renewable energy. Moreover, it has water efficiency, has improved indoor environment quality and deploys sustainable practices.

Green Factories

Customers rate their supplier factories based on how environment friendly they are. A green factory is an all-inclusive concept, wherein all aspects of the unit like its design, construction and operations are harmonised to achieve sustainable performance. An environment friendly design at the architecture stage, ensures the eco-friendliness of the building when the factory commences operations.

A green factory is characterised by an eco-friendly design, use of renewable energy like solar energy and efficient usage of resources like water and energy. It has pollution control technologies in place, recycles waste and uses non-toxic raw materials.

The Gurugram Model factory has been rated as "Green" by GAP, Kohl's and Marks & Spencer, due to its high sustainability and social compliances. Kohl's has exempted the factory from audits for two years. The factory is equipped with Effluent Treatment Plants (ETPs) to treat wastewater. It has taken proactive steps to reduce the carbon footprint.

Manoj Arora says with a glow on his face, "The demand from the buyers is for high technology green factories. Our compliances have been appreciated. Our Chennai factory has been rated as a Platinum Factory, on fulfilling the requirements of LEED (Leadership in Energy and Environmental Design). This is a Green Building rating system certification, established by the US Green Building Council. The rating system covers the design, construction, operations and maintenance of the factory, for environmental responsibility and efficient resource utilisation."

Health, Sanitation and Welfare

The DS Group strongly believes in access to basic healthcare for its employees. It trains its staff to manage diseases caused by common viruses and bacteria. Pulkit has initiated various projects to improve the health of the employees and provide them with sanitised operating conditions.

Awareness and Screening of Cancer: Globally, cervical and breast cancer are common among women at certain ages. PGIL has collaborated with CAPED India (Cancer Awareness, Prevention and Early Detection), to generate awareness about cervical and breast cancer amongst women. The business also provides free cancer screenings to needy women.

HERhealth Programme: The programme aims to raise health awareness among women employees. Launched in the Bengaluru factory, the HERhealth programme has trained 60 women. Prior to the programme, 65 percent of the women felt positive about their health. After the programme, 95 percent of the women feel healthy. The programme has made women aware of various diseases and their symptoms. Attendance has improved in the factory after the programme was introduced.

Health Camps for Workers: The Group organises health camps at regular intervals in all its factories in India, in partnership with Employees State Insurance Corporation (ESIC). These health camps include general check-ups, eye tests and blood tests. Free medicines are also provided to employees at these camps. The Group arranges tests for Tuberculosis for its workers. In association with WaterAid (International non-governmental organisation, focussed on water, sanitation and hygiene), the business has implemented the WASH programme (water, sanitation and hygiene) at its Bengaluru facility.

Drug-Free India Campaign: In partnership with the State Government of Haryana, in India, PGIL participates in the "Art of Living" programme, to address the problem of drug abuse among youngsters.

Installation of Sanitary Napkin Vending Machine: PGIL has installed sanitary napkin vending machines to provide free napkins to all female workers. It also conducts workshops and sessions to spread awareness about menstrual hygiene. The Group expects 76 percent of the women workers to use the vending machines in the factory.

Through the "Mina Seth Charitable Clinic" in Delhi, the Group provides free medical consultation to the underprivileged. About 50 people benefit daily from this facility. The clinic also distributes free medicines to patients with low incomes.

Faster Salaries

The Group factories revamped the system of paying salaries to the employees in 2009. It established a Biometric Attendance System, whereby the fingerprint of a worker was linked to his attendance and the calculation of his salary. The units have finger punching machines and facial recognition machines, to record the attendance of staff. The system was rolled out in all the factories.

Deepak has revised the salaries of senior staff members, to ensure that their salaries are in line with the prevailing market scales. He realised that new and young professionals begin with higher salaries, due to competition in the market for fresh talent. Deepak and Pulkit value the contributions of employees who have worked steadfastly in the company for decades.

Aadhaar Card and Digitisation

The Government of India had launched the "Aadhaar" identification scheme in 2009. It provided a unique 12-digit individual identification number to every citizen. This number would serve as a proof of identity and address anywhere. It could be used to open bank accounts, file tax returns and avail welfare schemes. The scheme gave a fillip to digitisation in worker welfare schemes.

Later, the Government of India launched a Financial Inclusion Mission. It enabled workmen to access financial services, like banking, insurance and pensions in a user-friendly manner. The Guinness World Records recognised the opening of 15 million bank accounts on the first day of the Mission.

The scheme provided an opportunity to workmen across the country, including those in the Group, to open bank accounts expeditiously.

The Government of India had also initiated a scheme called "Jan Dhan Yojna" which permitted the opening of new bank accounts, with a zero cash balance. PGIL opened bank accounts of all their workers. So, salaries could be paid every month directly into their bank accounts.

Prior to the opening of bank accounts, the salaries of all the 10,000 workers were paid in cash every month. This created serious issues in cash handling, security and disbursements. Workers in many of the factories were migrants from various states. Many of them did not have bank accounts. The banks found it difficult to undertake the "Know Your Customer" (KYC) formalities for thousands of workers. The new schemes made it possible to open bank accounts for all the workers.

Gender Equality Training

As a part of CSR initiatives, the Group has endeavoured to increase awareness about gender equality. This empowers skilled women workers and fosters their growth.

A pioneering project started by GAP Inc., called P.A.C.E. (Personal Advancement and Career Enhancement), aims to empower women through training and capability building. PGIL has launched P.A.C.E. in all its units across the globe. Women workers of Vietnam and Bengaluru factories have benefited from the programme, as evident from the increase in the number of women supervisors. The Group plans to empower more than 5,000 women workers under this programme.

"We tell the workers that men and women can do everything. Men can also work in the kitchen and bathe the children. Women can go out to work," says Kavita Devi from the production department.

In association with Marks & Spencer, Pulkit has introduced rigorous gender awareness trainings in its factories in Gurugram. The project aims to promote gender equality at the workplace, educate workers about PoSH (Prevention of Sexual Harassment) and manage gender-related grievances at the workplace. "First, we learnt about gender equality ourselves. Then, we went to every department to speak and coach everyone. I also talk about this with my family and neighbours. It has changed how I think about women and men," comments Amit from the Fabric Store.

Twenty peer leaders were trained in gender awareness and equality. They became pioneers in raising awareness among more than 1,200 people in the factory. Training is organised in the form of role playing, dramatic plays, interactive and fun-learning activities, etc., to spread awareness about the PoSH law. "The workers really enjoyed the gender awareness training sessions. The interactive activities helped them to understand their own biases," says Madhu, a Senior Welfare Officer.

Women constitute a major part of the work force in garment factories. The Group plans to recruit more women workers in its factories. There is a zero-tolerance policy for any sexual misconduct at the workplace. "I feel safer here in the factory after this project (PoSH). The environment has become better," concludes Mamta, who works on the finishing line.

Capability Building

The Gender Equality Training programmes in partnership with Marks & Spencer, have promoted gender equality in the workplaces. These programmes have made the women workers feel safe and respected in the factory. The initiative has created more opportunities for women and contributed to their capability building.

P.A.C.E. trainings include modules on communication, time and stress management, financial planning, problem solving, decision-making, sanitation and hygiene. GAP's Workplace Cooperation Programme has helped the Group to strengthen relationships and cooperation, between the management and the workers.

PGIL has also partnered with the Ralph Lauren IMPACT programme to review its production capacities. It has led to capability building in the HR function and the production teams. It has reduced worker turnover and absenteeism.

Model Factory, India

PGIL has created a model factory in Gurugram, India. Manifold activities were initiated to boost the morale of the employees and promote their welfare. This has contributed to strengthening workplace relations and has led to zero industrial issues.

The Group has developed induction programmes for new staff recruits. The initiative informs the workers about their rights and the services available to them. Employees are appreciated and rewarded for regular attendance and exemplary performance. The Supervisory Skills Training Programme sharpens the managerial skills of the supervisors.

There is zero tolerance policy for any misconduct in any DS Group factory. The Group organises interactive sessions, workshops, plays, etc., on a regular basis to spread awareness about the PoSH law. It also invites external speakers to impart knowledge and discuss various subjects freely with the workers.

Education

The Group has pioneered to make quality education accessible to children from low-income families. Every year, it grants scholarships to more than 200 deserving primary and middle school children, to fund their education.

"Arpan", an NGO, provides quality education to underprivileged children. It acts as a tuition and vocational training centre for the development of children. Arpan also arranges recreational and extra-curricular activities for the all-round development of the students.

PGIL has also partnered with Sasakawa-India Leprosy Foundation (S-ILF) a charitable organisation. Together, they organise after school skill development programmes for unemployed youth in leprosy-impacted colonies. The Group has forged alliances with three schools in leprosy colonies in Indore, Ujjain and Barwani in Madhya Pradesh state, India.

Happy Employees Grow

PGIL is planning to collaborate with NEXT and AIDER to improve worker empowerment even further. AIDER is a charitable institute committed towards sustainable development. It focusses on social justice, eradication of poverty and welfare of socially and economically underprivileged sections in the textile industry. The project with AIDER will spread awareness about worker rights and improve workplace practices, with a focus on capability enhancement.

The DS Group (including PDS and PGIL) respects all religions and nationalities. All the important festivals are celebrated in the offices and factories across the world. The Group is also planning to organise creative competitions to develop the talents of the children of the employees.

Uma works in Bengaluru, India. She hails from a small town in Karnataka called Maddur, with a population of around 30,000. She lives with her husband and daughter. Her husband works as a security guard in a company. Her daughter is studying engineering. She is currently working as a supervisor and believes that her quality of life has improved after joining the Group. She focusses on increasing production, maintaining product quality and ensuring worker welfare. She believes that her knowledge and experience have grown significantly in the company.

Uma's goal is to continue growing further in the business.

"Deepak really worked very hard; he has also built a very good team. He deserves every bit of the praise, recognition and glory that he is getting.

He has emerged as one of the largest Indian garment exporters, working in many countries."

- Dr. Rajiv Kumar, Vice-Chairman,
NITI Aayog, Government of India

20
The Public Issue 2007

Deepak, Pallak and Vineet Mathur, the Financial Controller, sat at the pub Carpenter's Arms in London in 2003, ruminating how to expand the business. Deepak was keen to grow faster. They were determined to hammer out a strategy to boost the business.

Deepak had boosted its business by exporting to non-quota countries like Switzerland and Australia. It was also proposing to tap other non-quota markets. Growth had been steady, as the company was eligible for quotas under Past Performance Entitlement, Manufacturers Export Entitlement and Non-quota Exporters Entitlement systems. However, the company's aggressive dynamism was being dampened by the constraints of quotas in many countries.

Deepak had sensed that the quotas would gradually be phased out. He was able to foresee the future of the garments industry clearly. He realised that in the post-quota era, suppliers would have to add value to their offerings to the retailers. They would have to offer design services and warehousing and be close to the buyers. He also perceived that in the quota-free world, the buyers would buy from suppliers from any country, which offered them the best prices and quality.

To be successful, the Group would have to provide innovative designs and services to the retailers, from the best global sources. To ensure this, Deepak had already started establishing companies abroad. He had operations in the USA, UK, Hong Kong and Germany. Deepak and his team were keen to acquire businesses abroad. The challenge in acquiring new companies abroad, was to determine the right financial valuation and cultural fit. So, the process was not easy. Nevertheless, Deepak and Vineet were able to successfully accomplish the mission.

Vineet opined that the business was a bit fragmented and needed to be welded together. He felt that there were multiple Group entities operating in different parts of the world. Some of them were owned by Deepak and his family and others were in partnership with associates. Vineet advocated bringing all the units under one umbrella. He found a great ally in Pallak, who had moved from Hong Kong to London.

Dancing on the Global Stage

Pallak had ambitious plans for the business. However, he comprehended that for the business to grow, it was necessary to consolidate the entire Group. This would contribute to positioning the business as a larger and versatile entity to the customers. It was thus necessary to project the various Group businesses as a single entity, to the retailers and the banks. Deepak ruminated bringing all the companies under one umbrella.

The global retail industry was enjoying a great ride in 2003. Retailers wanted to deal with large groups, which were managed like corporations, to ensure quality and service. So, there was merit in bringing the various businesses together. Deepak asked Vineet to prepare a blueprint.

Vineet spent about six weeks preparing a strategy document to transform the Group. The strategy involved bringing the assorted businesses that the Group had under one parasol, with augmented customer services. The buyer would deal with a single business entity for designing, sourcing, manufacturing, etc.

Pallak was enthusiastic with the proposed restructuring. Deepak, as was his habit, understood the plan in about 15 to 20 minutes and bought it. He realised that the new strategy would be the catalyst, for projecting their Group on the global stage. Then, the business could dance.

Integration of Businesses

Then, began a period of sustained discussions and work to transform the strategy into a detailed action plan. The team got busy in tying various elements together. This is never easy, whenever you merge or bifurcate businesses. Business involves people. So, everyone is apprehensive. The employees reflect, "How will this restructuring impact me? Will I retain my job, my status, my salary?" So, Deepak and his leadership team had to convince employees, that the new structure would accelerate business growth. Vineet and his team commenced the integration of all the international and domestic operations in late 2003.

The restructuring process took about two years. The various businesses were brought under one company, House of Pearl Fashions Limited (HoPFL). The new, united business, was now poised for growth.

HoPFL was a ready-to-wear apparel multinational company, operating in three business streams, manufacturing, marketing plus distribution and sourcing of garments. It provided total supply chain solutions to its customers. The customers included value retailers and high-end fashion brand retailers in the United States and Europe. Some of its major customers were prestigious brands like JCPenney, TESCO, ASDA Walmart, GAP, Next and Esprit.

The Group manufactured a wide range of apparel, including knits like T-shirts, sweaters and leggings. It also churned out woven garments like shirts, trousers, jeans and denim jackets. Due to its multi-stream business model, it could supply its products across the world. Moreover, Deepak had always focussed on building long-term relationships with the customers. So, HoPFL's customers were its key assets.

Post-Quota: Wings to Soar

The quotas were a constraining factor in the aggressive growth plans of the company, ever since it started doing business. It bought a few tradable quotas from the market. However, they too were inadequate. The customers, comprising of retailers, were compelled to buy from a multitude of suppliers and countries, due to the quota system. The retailers had to place orders on the basis of quotas, instead of quality and price. The system was basically inefficient for the buyers and the suppliers.

Quotas were finally abolished in January 2005. It was a deliverance for the customers, who could now buy from the most efficient suppliers. It also liberated the suppliers, who could now export to their heart's content, to any country. The inefficient suppliers who were in the game, purely because they possessed the prized quotas for exports, were marginalised. The apparel industry was now unfettered.

The seagull could soar now. The Group was free of the quota fetters. Deepak could pursue his dreams. His vision was clear. The business would expand overseas to serve its customers. It would also establish more offices in the sourcing countries, to provide value added and efficient services to the customers. The Group would also diversify from the pure brick and mortar factory model of business. It would boost its outsourced production portfolio to achieve scalability. Outsourcing basically meant sourcing goods from third party factories in various countries, to achieve growth without investing in own factories.

After the quotas were abolished, the enormous opportunity in the market became apparent. The Group was already supplying garments from its factories and outsourced factories. Buyers were keen to consolidate their supply chains. They wanted to work with suppliers who had the financial strength and scale, to service large orders from multiple countries.

Strategic Advantages

The DS Group had evolved a unique integrated and scalable business model with eight strategic thrusts.

First, it had a global footprint. It operated in strategic countries like the UK, USA, Canada and Spain to be close to important customers. The sourcing offices were located in the countries, with the largest customers. The factories were based in countries, which offered advantages in costs, raw materials availability or labour specialisation. Each location had a competitive locational advantage. The Group leveraged these strengths to provide service at the doorstep to its customers.

Second, the Group had developed multiple-product capabilities. Its product portfolio included a wide range of woven and knit garments for men, women and children. The massive assortment of garments attracted large customers. They could source multiple products from a single vendor.

Third, though all large customers did have their own designers, the Group provided them with design ideas. It presented them with seasonal collections, from which customers chose designs, styles, colours and placed orders. This was a significant contribution of the band of dedicated designers.

Fourth, the Group had developed diverse capabilities. It could supply garments to its customers, either through its own manufacturing facilities or through the outsourced units. It had factories in India, Indonesia, Bangladesh, etc. It had relationships with 150 factories, who could supply garments to it. They were located in China, Bangladesh, India, etc. These manufacturers were selected, monitored and coordinated by the Group's staff, to ensure quality, cost and delivery parameters. The company staff, supervised the quality in these units. This sourcing strategy provided massive scalability to the business. No order was too large for the Group.

Fifth, the Group also had sourcing offices and operations in Bangladesh, Indonesia, China and Hong Kong, so it could offer multiple sourcing options to the buyers.

Sixth, the company had fortified a track record of delivery, with leading international customers. The world's leading value retailers, like JCPenney, Asda Walmart and high-end fashion brands like GAP, Next and Esprit were its customers. By 2003, global customers like JCPenney had been working with the DS Group for over a decade.

Seventh, the Group had built an experienced management team, supported by skilled designers and employees. Deepak had concentrated on hiring the best talent in the business.

Eighth, Deepak had established warehousing facilities in the USA, where it offered "Landed Duty Paid" (LDP) stocks. The Group imported the merchandise, paid the duties and warehoused them. It then supplied the goods to the customer, as required and invoiced them. It could also offer goods on a "Free-on-Board" (FOB) basis. In the FOB option, the merchandise was handed over to the customer's agent or forwarder in the country of production.

Thus, the DS Group's assets were a network of marketing offices, design capabilities, dedicated factories, outsourcing arrangements, LDP and FOB options of ordering merchandise, financial prudence, etc. The company had the unique positioning of a "One-Stop-Shop" for customers, offering every possible service in the apparel supply chain. Not many other companies could offer such a varied, customer-friendly bouquet of services.

Business Strategy

The Group's strategy was to expand its manufacturing capabilities. It had a production capacity of 20 million pieces of garments per annum in 2006. It wanted to double the production to 40 million pieces per annum by 2010. All its factories were already producing at full throttle.

Next, Deepak was keen to penetrate more markets and expand the customer base. The Group offered quality services and on-time deliveries. It had added 40 new customers. The company had leading retailers in the US and Europe as its customers, including Esprit, S. Oliver, VF Corporation, Sears, Next, Bonton and Gordmans. The Group had been selected as a strategic vendor by JCPenney and Asda Walmart. However, Deepak was eager to augment the depth and width of coverage of global markets.

Deepak's strategy was to develop markets in new product categories and geographies. He was planning to manufacture formal trousers, a new product line. He also proposed to expand its network of third-party factories in India, Bangladesh and China. His goal was to improve operating efficiencies and harvest the economies of scale.

The growing middle classes and the mall culture, were giving a fillip to modern retailing in India. So, the Group was actively exploring retailing opportunities. The entry into the retail apparel market in India was a natural forward integration. The business had in-house designers and factories in India. The plan was to sell its garments to Indian customers, manufactured in its own factories. It already had its own brands abroad, like Lerros in Germany, and DCC and Kool Hearts in the USA.

The Group was also considering acquisitions of apparel companies or brands. It was open to strategic partnerships or joint ventures with leading manufacturers or distributors of apparel in selected markets.

Funds for Growth

Consolidating the business had opened new avenues of growth for the Group. Now, it needed funds to grow and expand its manufacturing capacities. The DS Group did have its own factories, but it also outsourced production. The Group was keen to expand its own production facilities. Retail was also growing globally. Most export businesses do not have asset-intensive balance sheets. They do have their factories, but also depend on third party production. Banks and financial institutions are generally shy to lend moneys to companies, which do not have a substantial asset register.

Deepak, Pallak and Vineet pondered whether a fresh share issue could provide the financial fuel for the Group's ambitions. Deepak had launched the Initial Public Offering (IPO) in 1994 to raise funds for diversifications to manufacture leather items, synthetic, cotton and wool sweaters. The IPO was in the name of "Pearl Global Limited." It had offered about two million shares to the public, after keeping 70 percent for the promoters. Though the shares were offered at a premium, the issue was oversubscribed. The share price in the markets was Rs. 35 against the face value of Rs. 10. The 1994 IPO was a milestone in Deepak's entrepreneurial journey.

Another IPO could fund the capital expenditure of the new projects and boost the working capital. The Group was making profits and had established itself in many markets abroad. Its turnover had grown by around 50 percent during the previous three years.

IPO: Road Map

Deepak, Pallak and Vineet had many coffees, brainstorming over how to raise the moneys to expand rapidly. The business had now been christened as "House of Pearl Fashions Ltd." (HoPFL). Finally, they agreed that they would go to the public for money, through an Initial Public Offering (IPO) for HoPFL. It appeared to be the best option. The business needed funds for acquisitions and for expansions. They commenced planning an IPO, which was announced in January 2007.

A road map was prepared which Deepak studied in rigorous detail. It was a unique proposition. The IPO would be floated for the Indian entity, which would own all the businesses of the Group. About 85 percent of the Group business was overseas with the balance 15 percent in India. The Indian entity was basically an investment holding company. An Indian multinational, with businesses across the world, was taking birth.

Very few Indian businesses had gone to the market with such a unique offering. It was a new concept, a company based in India, with overseas operations.

Deepak and Vineet had a series of discussions with JM Morgan Stanley Private Limited and other financial institutions. JM Morgan Stanley was engaged as advisors to the issue. In the initial meeting, Vineet made the full presentation. As the company prepared for the presentations at the road shows, JM Morgan Stanley advised that investors, especially institutional investors, prefer to hear the business story, growth prospects and the future plans directly from the owner. Keeping this in mind, during the road shows, the business presentation was made by Deepak and the financials were presented by Vineet.

Deepak displayed another latent and uncanny talent, which many people were not aware of. Before any meeting, Deepak always tries to understand the minds of the others in the room. What are they thinking? What are their real concerns? What are their agendas? Then, he is ready with the answers.

During the IPO presentations to the bankers and financial institutions, Deepak focussed on understanding their motivations. He would mould the presentation to address the concerns of the investors in the room. He spoke of the potential of the business, future prospects, returns, etc. Every meeting involved intensive prior homework. The result was that a potential investor received replies to his queries, even before he had asked them.

A Unique Model

In his presentation, Deepak explained the Group's unique model of doing business. It involved offering design services to customers and then supplying garments, through its own factories or outsourcing partners.

The kernel of Deepak's presentation was that the growth model was unique and scalable. Other companies have to invest in new factories, infrastructure and keep adding workers, if they wish to grow. His business model was to build a robust manufacturing base and then grow through outsourcing partners. This was an asset light model.

Growing constantly entails investing in new factories and hiring people. This strategy adds to costs. Says Deepak, "Let's take the example of an Indian exporter. To achieve a turnover of about USD 700 to 750 million, he would need a manpower of about 50,000 people. We could achieve the same turnover with one-third the labour force."

The business model made sense to the investors. The second prong of the strategy, which appealed to the investors was the entrepreneurial model. Deepak had minority partners with equity, to drive the front ends of the various businesses. The two elements, an asset-light production strategy and equity-driven partners, propelled the IPO success.

Deepak, Pallak and Vineet spent many long days briefing bankers, lawyers and government officials on the proposed IPO. It was a challenge to sell an investment holding company, which had no assets of its own in India, but had investments in overseas companies. The three of them were constantly on flights covering India, UK, USA, UAE, etc. Vineet accompanied Deepak on his visits to Mumbai, London, New York, Singapore, UAE and Hong Kong, to meet investors and bankers to promote the IPO.

Deepak's elder brother Chand advised him that if the business went public, it meant getting investments from shareholders regularly and rewarding them with good dividends, bonuses and share value appreciation.

Chand told Deepak, "The valuation of the share capital does not depend entirely on the performance of the business in a particular quarter or year. Trust is built over years, if not decades, of sound performance. Through professional management and good corporate governance, an organisation can rise to the top 10 percent of the business. Then, its share price can surge in multiples." Deepak also selected a Board of Directors with varying functional expertise.

Deepak envisaged investing in manufacturing facilities. They would establish their own factories in China, Indonesia or Vietnam. Their teams would be involved right from buying the fabric till the finished shirt or jacket was delivered to the store. It was a comprehensive responsibility.

The range of services offered to customers and the business model, were unparalleled in the Indian and the overseas garment industry. So, the investors saw the potential in the IPO.

Post IPO 2007: New Era

The Group issued about six million shares at a face value of Rs. 10 per share. The issue opened on 16 January 2007 and closed on 23 January 2007. The issue price was Rs. 550 per share.

There was much joy when the IPO was oversubscribed by nearly four times, at a time when IPOs were not faring too well in India. This was a significant achievement for an apparel business. All the long days and nights spent on aeroplanes travelling across continents, to brief bankers and investors had borne fruit.

The Group now had the funds to double its production capacities. It also established a design centre and corporate office in Gurugram. A new integrated IT system and the launch of a retail brand in India, were also envisaged.

However, there was no time to rest or celebrate. The Group now had to meet the new expectations of the investors and the shareholders.

A new era was dawning for Deepak and his dedicated team.

Demerger: To Accelerate Growth

HoPFL had two types of businesses. The first business involved manufacturing garments for its clients. The second business, christened SDM, involved sourcing, distribution and merchandising plus marketing activities. Deepak was planning to bring all the manufacturing activities under one umbrella and manage the SDM business as a separate entity.

Deepak had observed that both his sons were very bright. As part of succession planning he thought it wise to have two businesses managed as two separate verticals. So, House of Pearl Fashions Ltd. (HoPFL) was demerged, in 2014. The business was split in two streams. The manufacturing business was christened Pearl Global Industries Ltd. (PGIL). The outsourcing vertical of the business was launched as PDS Multinational Fashions Ltd.

Deepak continued as the Chairman of both the companies, driving and supporting the businesses. The PDS business was 85 to 90 percent out of the UK and Europe. The PGIL business was 90 percent in North America, comprising of the USA and Canada. The two verticals were in different markets and product categories. They did not compete with each other. As a result of this demerger, the business now operates through these two companies.

Pallak Seth, the elder son of Deepak, born on 13 August 1977, manages the PDS business. The younger son Pulkit, born on 5 February 1980, manages the PGIL business. Both the companies are listed on the stock exchanges.

To register the new companies, the Group had to seek various permissions from the Government and the stock exchanges. The restructuring involved various due diligences, which were ably managed. The institutional compliances ensured that the moneys were deployed for the declared purposes and the various accounting standards were followed meticulously. The Group ensures that all statutory compliances are met, which makes due diligences seamless. Sandeep Sabharwal, the Company Secretary, who managed the various protocols, says that he has been enriched by his work experience at the company. He has learnt to manage the Company Secretariat and take decisions independently.

A Global Company

Thus, the DS Group, (Deepak Seth Group, comprising of PDS and PGIL), is the first garment manufacturing company which has gone global. It has created marketing and manufacturing subsidiaries worldwide. This gives the Group tremendous competitive leverage. If Bangladesh grows, it has a manufacturing base there. If Indonesia does well, it has a factory there. Now, Vietnam is doing well. So, there is an operation there. If the Indian business gathers momentum, the Group has factories there. Whichever part of the world does well, they already have an operating base there.

Deepak improves the performance of his team by expecting more from everyone. He has managed several challenges in his business journey. Now, he wants to ensure that his senior managers have the sagacity to overcome obstacles on their own. Sandeep Sabharwal says, "The Group has performed well even in tough times, due to the strong leadership of the Chairman. He can spot challenges and opportunities even in adversities. He takes care of thousands of families and is a father figure for all of them. He ensures that the company grows for the benefit of his employees and workers. He has a soft corner for his team even though he appears to be tough. I underline that."

A director comments, "Deepak is very sincere and hardworking. Sometimes, he is not able to join a board meeting in Delhi due to his travel schedule. Then, he gets up early in the morning and joins the meeting at 8 am from New York by video link. He briefs us about the market and the future trends."

Dr. Rajiv Kumar says that during college, he did not think that Deepak had in him the commitment, which characterises his career. Being a professional economist, he understands how gruelling it is for anyone in India, to nurture a business to a global level. He says, “Not only has Deepak really worked very hard, he has also built a very good team. He deserves every bit of the praise, recognition and glory that he is getting. Now, he has emerged as one of the largest Indian garment exporters, working in many countries.”

Sandeep says “Our Chairman is a good professional. He creates wealth for the employees and the company. He has successfully built a business, commencing from a garage. He has created an Indian multinational company. He is a true visionary.”

Businesswise, Deepak continues to be a firebrand.

His wife, Payel, says:

"He thinks of the business round the clock. At night, he sleeps with the mobile phone next to his bed.

If he gets a call in the middle of the night, in any part of the world, he takes it."

21
The Lady of Dignity, Payel, who Keeps it Together

Payel is Deepak's silent pillar of support on whom he can lean anytime, anywhere. She looks after him round-the-clock, managing every detail to make him comfortable. She is a lady of few words.

Deepak has a hectic travel schedule. He could be in New York for two days, then in Bangladesh for three days, then four days in London, again five days in Hong Kong. His travel schedule is gruelling. Payel is his constant companion on these travels. She has learnt to survive on very little sleep, when she travels with Deepak.

Payel ensures that his medicines are always in his travel suitcase. She ensures that the medicines are also in all their homes in Delhi, London and Dubai. Thus, Deepak is never without his medicines. Payel is always quiet, unflappable, but inevitably very effective and efficient. It is a boon when Payel travels with him, for she takes care of all the administrative arrangements. This liberates Deepak for his work.

Payel accepts Deepak's arduous lifestyle and has adjusted to it. She accompanies him on most of his travels, so that they can spend some time together. Many businessmen work zealously till the age of 40 to 45. By then, the business is established and stable. So, they pull back a bit. However, Deepak does not know the age factor. Even at the age of 70, he works more than anyone else. He flies around the world visiting the various offices and factories, for about three weeks every month.

"No pain, no gain" is Deepak's operating principle, and Payel accepts it. To achieve something in life, one has to sacrifice some comfort zones. She realises that to succeed constantly, Deepak has to travel and work ceaselessly.

However turbulent a situation or however heated a discussion is, Payel is always supremely serene. Payel complements Deepak perfectly with her distinguished, tranquil smile. Always poised, Payel is a picture of calmness.

She is always attired in simple but very elegant Indian dresses, with a preference for cottons. The fancy brand names of London, New York or Milan are not for her. She is happy to be wearing simple Indian apparel and using Indian accessories. However, she does want Deepak to be well attired, as he interacts with buyers and vendors across the world. She will shop for the best linen shirts and trousers for him in Italy. She also insists he buys his suits from Armani.

Early Wedding Years

Born on 28 May 1958, Payel was just 18 years of age when she married Deepak on 22 January 1976. Harish Seth recalls the joyous celebrations at the wedding of Deepak and Payel. Deepak's brothers led the wedding procession and danced with gusto. The Punjabis love dancing the "Bhangra" dance. Payel's family was one of the traditionally rich and aristocrat families of Delhi, headed by Lala Ram Pershad. He had four sons, including Mr. Badri Pershad, Payel's father. The Group was known as the Chunnamal family. Payel's forefathers had been involved in a project to establish north India's first textile mill.

The "Chunnamal Haveli" is now a heritage building in Delhi's Chandni Chowk. The drawing room is 50-feet long, 25-feet wide and 30-feet high. A marble slab in Urdu states that the house was built in 1848. This was 99 years before India became independent. The family bought the first car in Delhi. The first telephone instrument in the city was installed at their home. The family also owned Delhi's first theatre, Rama Theatre, where the first Indian talkie was shown. The theatre now houses a museum. Payel's cousins yet live in the grand home. Tourists also visit it to admire its grandeur and architecture.

The Seth family used to interact with some relatives of Payel. So, Harish and his brothers thought, that Deepak and Payel would make compatible life-partners. The marriage was finalised through Lala Beni Pershad, Payel's uncle.

After the marriage, Payel recalls an incident in 1979 at Kollam beach in Kerala state. Deepak and Payel were rowing in a small boat in the sea. As it edged closer to the shore, they had to disembark. Unfortunately, the small boat started wobbling. It was about to capsize. Payel did not know swimming and was petrified of the water. Deepak pulled her out, carried her on his shoulders and swam out of the sea to the shore.

A friend of Deepak who met them in Bombay, on their way back from their honeymoon, describes Payel as "incredibly pretty, as beautiful as a doll, with a gorgeous smile and twinkling eyes; she was absolutely devoted to Deepak and loved him absolutely."

Payel had lost her own father, Mr. Badri Pershad, as a child. He had passed away at a young age during a heart surgery in

London. While Payel was assured of a comfortable lifestyle in her family home, she always missed the care and love of her father. The vacuum remained, for nobody in the world can replace a father. Her pious mother, Mrs. Rajni Pershad, nurtured Payel and her brother Sanjay with tenderness.

The first few years after the marriage were trying on Payel, due to the exacting work hours that Deepak had to keep. The garment export industry is a tough business, where the entrepreneur has to literally slog with his front-line workers, in the initial years. The exporter has to execute the order by the due date and ship it on schedule. If there is a delay, the order is cancelled or the payment is withheld, resulting in losses. Deepak would be leaving the house at 6 am and would return home the next morning around 1 am or 2 am, for a few hours of sleep. Then, he would dash out again. Deepak worked every Sunday too.

Krishen Seth recalls, "Payel would wake me up, all seven days of the week around 1 am to tell me, 'Dipu (Deepak) has not come home yet. Please call the office and find out where he is.'" There were no mobile phones in the late 1970s. So, Payel and Krishen would stand at the window in their family house, waiting for Deepak to return home.

Payel blended beautifully into the Seth family, with Deepak's parents, grandparents and his elder brothers and sisters-in-law. During those early years of concentrated efforts, Deepak would be travelling almost a fortnight every month. Later, Deepak and Payel moved to an independent villa in Vasant Vihar. Deepak's parents visited his house regularly, to meet Payel and their grandsons, Pallak and Pulkit, especially when Deepak was travelling.

Payel had realised that Deepak loved having people around him. His mother too was very fond of people and enjoyed having relatives visit her. Deepak has followed his mother's footsteps. Every two or three days, he would organise a dinner for the entire family. Sometimes Deepak attends two weddings or parties in an evening. Payel transformed herself into a gracious hostess.

The Dedicated Wife

Shy and reticent, Payel prefers to remain in the shadows, though she is Deepak's solid partner for the last five decades. She is happy to let Deepak shine in any party or situation. "Perhaps I have had a calming influence on him, for earlier, he was a firebrand," she says.

However, businesswise, Deepak continues to be a firebrand. Payel adds, "He thinks of the business round the clock. At night, he sleeps with the mobile phone next to his bed. If he gets a call in the middle of the night in any part of the world, he takes it."

Rakesh Kapoor, the former Global Chief Executive of Reckitt Benckiser plc., UK FTSE-listed multinational consumer goods company, is Deepak's neighbour in London. He considers Deepak as a "super special person". He also feels that every successful business person has a steady, rock-solid foundation at home. According to him, Payel is the strong foundation in Deepak's life. He adds, "Deepak has taken many risks in his career. He has also worked very hard. He could do this due to Payel's strong support."

It is not easy to achieve a harmonious balance between family and work in life. Rakesh adds, "I personally do not think you can achieve a true balance in life. It's impossible. You have to give up something in life to get something else. And I think you can only give up something provided you know, there is some cover or support that you have. Deepak is incredibly successful in his work and in his relationships. He owes a lot to the solid support of Payel and his family at home."

Payel can keep cool under all circumstances. However, she also knows how to put her foot down when required. In 2007, when Deepak and she were on the way back from London, the customs officials on Delhi delayed them. It was Payel, who admonished them, "The wrist watch Deepak is wearing is within the permitted limits. And it was bought many years ago. Not now. And you should remember that he started his career on a scooter, visiting dealers the entire day, in sweltering heat. It takes a lot of time and effort to climb up, step by step. You should know this and respect it." The officials were speechless and stepped aside.

Gracious Hostess

Payel is a splendid and gracious hostess. Deepak entertains guests almost four days a week at home or at restaurants. Payel works with Deepak to decide the menu depending on the type of guests coming home. The menu varies depending on whether the guests are Europeans, Americans, Indians, vegetarians or non-vegetarians. Before the party, Payel will spend time in the kitchen to ensure that everything is ready as per the plan. The "paneer" (cottage cheese) in the "butter paneer" has to be succulent enough, the chicken has to be tender enough and the "parathas" or "dosas" have to be crisp and warm when they arrive on the dining tables.

At the parties, Payel ensures that all the guests are comfortable and at home. She will always have a few soft-spoken, kind words for every guest. Sometimes, Deepak gets busy looking after the drinks of the guests. Then, Payel spends a few minutes with every lady guest, asks about her welfare and her children and ensures that she is being served.

Payel never forgets anything. She remembers the names of all the persons she meets, their children and even their birthdays. Whenever she meets any person, she will ask about the children by name and what they are doing. Payel is immensely popular with all her nephews and nieces.

Payel always carries herself graciously. With Deepak's hectic travel schedule, it is Payel who remembers the birthdays of every nephew and niece and the marriage anniversaries of all the family members.

A Devoted Mother

After Pallak and Pulkit were born, Payel devoted herself completely to their upbringing and studies. Their school homework was always completed under her guidance. She personally monitored their progress. She loved her cute, well-behaved sons and focussed on nurturing their values.

Pallak says that his personality is a mix of his parents. He learnt business modelling from his father. However, many of his other personality traits came from his mother. Payel is always calm and unflappable. She is an achiever and can never stand still. She is always exploring new ventures.

Pallak reflects that his ability to take risks and initiate new businesses, came to him from his parents. He had watched Deepak innovate in the garments business. He had also watched Payel build and manage Little Pearls, the educational venture. He admires his mother for her energy and drive. She kept pushing the boundaries to the next level but always in a very pleasant way, with a smile on her face. His parents taught him to always ask, what more can I do?

Deepak and Payel were dedicated to their ventures and businesses. Nevertheless, they always ensured that they had ample family time together. Pallak recalls, "They have always been there for us. I have my own children now. I see how difficult it is to balance work and family. My parents are amazing role models." It required dextrous balancing by Deepak and Payel, to keep growing the business and yet ensure regular family time. Birthdays, wedding anniversaries and New Year eve parties are always celebrated together.

Pallak summarises the lesson he learnt from his parents about relationships very pithily, "Your business is like a rubber ball. If it falls to the floor, it can bounce back. However, your health and your relationships are like glass balls. If these balls fall to the ground, they shatter. Then, the pieces stay there on the ground. So, it is important to hold your health and relationships close to your heart."

Payel is very modest about her efforts to raise her sons and to keep all the family members together. She says, "It is a very Indian characteristic. We invest in our children. Then, the next generation does it for their children. You do it selflessly, without any expectations."

Payel is also keen that the next generation should continue to strive to achieve and excel. She says, "Even the kids here in the Little Pearls School have seen it all, done it all. The children here are pre-schoolers. They are so smart. They are hooked on to Internet and Facebook. It is good for their knowledge, but the social media should not become obsessions."

She adds, "It is a bit scary. What is new in life for them? What is there to look forward to, for the next generation?"

Harish feels that Deepak has managed the family relationships very sensibly. He says, "Deepak never steps on anybody's toes in business or in the family. He did that creditably in our large family. Now, he does it in his own family too. If he needs to counsel his sons, he will do so. It stems from his experience and maturity, from knowing the right thing to do."

Payel plays a very centric role in keeping the entire family together, enjoying a warm and affectionate rapport with the two daughters-in-law and the grandchildren.

Managing an Elegant Home

With a taste for style and an eye for detail, Payel also manages a gorgeous home. The furniture and furnishings are stylish. Every cushion is in its place, every painting or photo is always rightly placed on the walls or the mantelpiece. No speck of dust can ever make its way to any piece of furniture or a statue.

Their home is warm and friendly. Payel and Deepak have sourced furniture and paintings from all over the world, but everything blends in their homes. The paintings are by their favourite artists like Manjit Bawa, F. N. Souza, K. G. Subramaniam, Ram Kumar, M. F. Husain and S. H. Raza. They make the walls come alive with colour and vibrancy.

Deepak's classmate at college, Dr. Rajiv Kumar also appreciates their aesthetic sense. "Their home is a very beautiful place," he says.

Eventually, a home is made up of warmth and friendships. Payel's homes radiate hospitality and affection. On a Sunday morning, Payel moves from room to room in the house, making the rounds, with a few maids following her. She ensures that the cutlery is polished immaculately, the linen is well stored and the lawn grass has been manicured perfectly. It is never easy to run a good, efficient home. Payel does it effortlessly.

Evolving into an Entrepreneur

Payel is a devoted wife and dedicated homemaker. She is also an entrepreneur and businesswoman. She and Deepak were pioneers in starting Hopps, perhaps India's first departmental store, in South Extension, New Delhi's posh locality. Hopps was a multi-product branded store, selling jewellery, men and women's apparel, household linen, premium pens, etc. Delhi's elite was lured by a store, which could be in Oxford Street in London. Payel, Deepak and their partner Vinod Gujral managed the store.

Pulkit has tremendous respect for his mother. "She is a wonderful human being who has supported my father in every way, by always being by his side. She has unconditional love for everyone in the family and is always ready to do anything for everyone. On the business side, she has done well with a jewellery business in the past and now with the school, Little Pearls. She is also active in philanthropy through "Arpan". She is a very good-hearted person. Being with her grandchildren in Delhi and London and with the children in the school, gives her a lot of joy. She has always provided love, affection and anything asked for, in just a heartbeat. She has done everything to keep the family strong, through my Dad's long journey of setting up businesses around the world."

Chand also admires Payel's evolution into an entrepreneur with Deepak's support and motivation. "Payel ran a successful jewellery business for many years. Then, another store called

Hopps was launched in South extension. Then, she pioneered the educational ventures like Little Pearls and Peekaboo, which are fantastic institutions."

He adds, "Now, Payel is a mature lady. She was just 18 when she got married, shy and quiet. She has transformed herself into an entrepreneur." Chand credits Deepak for creating many entrepreneurs around him. "He has inspired his wife Payel also to become an entrepreneur," he says joyously.

From being a homemaker, Payel has evolved into a comprehensive businesswoman. Her forays in the multi-product department store and the jewellery business helped her to polish her skills in managing people, customers and inventories. She has also sharpened her commercial skills.

However, Payel was not happy only doing business. Her heart was in education and in contributing to society. Now, Little Pearls serves the needs of the community in Delhi. In the Arpan Project, children from low-income families and slums receive free education and meals at the school.

Payel sums her passion for her work by saying, "For me, work is important to keep the brain ticking."

Close friends say, Deepak would not have been the Deepak that he is, without Payel. Simultaneously, Payel would not have been the Payel she is, without Deepak. They complement and support each other. The shy bride of 18 years has matured into a successful entrepreneur.

22
Pallak: Northwestern to Norwest

Pallak was very popular with his classmates at Northwestern University in Chicago. He was good looking, smart and enjoyed meeting his friends. He was a high-energy student and loved extra-curricular activities. His dark navy-blue colour convertible BMW 328i car, a gift from his mother, added to his charisma. Not many youngsters owned this model at college. He had recently organised an “India Week” at his University. About 50 top businessmen from the USA and India had participated in the symposium, to promote India as an investment destination.

Pallak graduated with honours from Northwestern University with a BA in Economics and in International Business. After graduation, he accepted a job at a strategy and innovation management consulting firm based in Chicago, managed by professors from the Kellogg School of Management and the University of Chicago.

During the summer holidays of 1995, he flew to Delhi to spend some time with his parents. He loved his sprawling home in Delhi where he could swim and relax. He was scheduled to commence work in October in the Chicago firm. Now, he was looking forward to meeting his cousins and friends in Delhi.

Pallak relished chatting with his parents. During one of these discussions, Deepak suggested to him that he should consider returning to India and joining the business. “The business is growing, you will enjoy building it,” Deepak told him. Deepak also briefed him about an opportunity to grow the business in Hong Kong.

Deepak already had a company in Hong Kong servicing Lerros and other buyers. Hong Kong was a huge apparel hub, covering China, Vietnam, Indonesia, etc., in Southeast Asia. Deepak felt that the next generation should have an overview of the global market, before getting busy with the nuts and bolts of the business. Hence, Deepak briefed Pallak about the Hong Kong business.

Pallak ruminated for some days. He loved living in the USA. He had many friends in the country. He had been offered a fabulous job. However, he also realised that working in the family business, offered him opportunities for rapid professional and financial growth. Finally, he agreed to go to Hong Kong to foster the business. A new chapter was commencing.

Learning the Ropes in Hong Kong

One of the largest customers of the Group in Hong Kong was ABM Retail. The customer was being serviced from India. Deepak was keen to strengthen the relationship with this large customer by opening an office in Hong Kong. So, in October 1998, Pallak boarded a Cathay Pacific flight to Hong Kong.

Pallak rented a small 1,000 square foot office in Hong Kong. He had an accountant named Sudhir Kumar who managed the finance function. He recruited a merchandiser known to Deepak named Beyond, a Chinese girl. So, the small team of three, with a big dream, started managing the business. A new company Norwest was launched in 1999. The name Norwest was chosen by another accountant Rajiv Makhija, because Pallak had studied at Northwestern University in Chicago.

Pallak met ABM Retail and told them, "We have established this office here, to offer you a range of product categories and to serve you 24 by 7." The customer was delighted. Deepak was well networked in the garment industry. He and Pallak informed all their clients about their new office. So, these clients started visiting Pallak to source garments from the Far East and China.

Deepak flew to Hong Kong every two or four weeks to support and guide the young 21-year-old Pallak. For Pallak, it was the best way to start his career. He says, "I developed my EQ (emotional quotient) and CQ (commercial quotient), by observing my father closely as a child while growing up. His continuous support at the commencement of my business journey was precious."

In the first year, Norwest achieved a turnover of USD 10 million and earned a profit of USD one million. It was a thrilling moment to savour. To generate a profit of USD one million, in the very first year of your work life, in your first assignment, is indeed a milestone. Pallak recalls, "When you are 21 years of age, just out of university, earning a million dollars, it gives you tremendous reassurance. If the start in your career is right, you can build on the confidence. If you have a setback in the beginning, then you lose some hope or slow down."

He adds that the team was able to deliver in the very first year, due to the support of his father. "He convinced me to move from Chicago to Hong Kong. Then, he helped me to start a new venture. Finally, he gave me full support from day one."

Pallak had no practical business experience. He recollects that whilst his father guided him, he refrained from micro-managing the business. Many business leaders cannot let go, even when they appoint bright managers to manage their businesses. Deepak gave his elder son a free hand, but was always there whenever he needed support. Pallak talked to his father as often as he desired, sometimes, many times a day. He adds, "I learnt the business from him. He gave me mature counsel and was in Hong Kong as often as I wanted."

The business in Hong Kong kept growing. Pallak was young, enthusiastic and ambitious. He had tasted success and was hungry for more. He focussed on building a robust team in the merchandising and finance functions. He also refined his understanding of the business and his execution skills.

Having spent three years in Hong Kong, working on the supply side of the business, Pallak was seeking additional challenges. Deepak already had a company, Poeticgem in the UK, managing large customers and imports. Pallak moved to the UK to get a grip on the demand side of their business.

Building the Business in UK

Deepak had partners in many countries in the world, where they managed the businesses. A key lesson that Pallak had learnt by observing his father, was the importance of having outstanding business associates. They had to be entrepreneurs in their own right, who could expand the business.

Pallak studied his father's business model meticulously. He saw how his father incentivised the partners by giving them a share of the business. Pallak was also inspired by the business model of Li & Fung Limited, the large Hong Kong-based organisation which was growing rapidly. Li & Fung grew by fostering companies. He introspected how the Group could grow, by affiliating with entrepreneurs and providing them the freedom to grow.

He was keen to take the business to the next level by building on the entrepreneurial model that Deepak had innovated. Deepak had entrepreneurial business partnerships in Germany, USA, UK, Australia, Canada, etc. Now, Pallak launched a drive to bring some more vibrant entrepreneurs on board. The business had to grow constantly. "Growth" was the sacred "mantra". He added more verticals to the business, widening the customer and the product base.

Entrepreneurial Model

The entrepreneurial model had started in 1979, with Arun Gujral moving to Germany. After that, Deepak had teamed with entrepreneurial partners in 11 countries. Gradually, the operating principles and practices of the entrepreneurial model had been refined by Deepak. He always selected partners whom he knew personally or had a relationship with.

After the demerger of the parent company in 2014, a new business entity, PDS had been carved out. Deepak was the Chairman of PDS. Operationally, it was led by Pallak, as the Vice-Chairman. PDS was listed on the Stock exchanges in India after the demerger. PDS has gradually evolved into a global fashion-led supply chain business. By early 2010, the Group had about 20 subsidiaries.

When Pallak entered the business, he saw the value in the entrepreneurial model. He multiplied it aggressively, with some variations. Pallak went into overdrive to find entrepreneurial parties in the industry. He searched for the best possible partners, even if he did not know them. He scanned the market for professionals and offered them opportunities for becoming businessmen partners.

Pallak sought capable partners. He studied his customers, their staff and even competitors, ferreting for good talent. He would meet potential high-energy professionals and tell them, "You should join us. We will set up a business together and share the profits." He targeted successful professionals with solid industry experience, who were managing independent companies. He deployed head hunters to furrow out high performers.

Pallak then elevated the entrepreneurial model by introducing checks and balances. So, the entrepreneurial partners, blossomed into 50 business associations in various countries, with diverse products and value propositions.

Pallak also started building strategic partnerships with other apparel companies, in innovative product ranges. His goal was to partner with new businesses and managements to grow rapidly.

Typically, PDS would hold around 70-85 percent share in the new company. The entrepreneurs who joined would get between 15 and 30 percent share, depending on the size or scale of their network. Pallak's unique proposition was that the new recruit would be a "co-entrepreneur". He would earn more through shared profits at the Group, than the typical salary cum bonus route in the corporate sector. Though the entrepreneur CEOs had a share of the profits, they did not have to invest in the business. The Group invested 100 percent in the businesses.

Pallak says, "Basically, I built on my father's formula to expand the business through partnerships. I also studied how Li and Fung scaled up their enterprise by acquiring many companies. I decided to create a nursery of entrepreneurs."

The financial stake in a venture, is the motivating factor for many CEOs to partner with PDS. Many of the CEOs had worked with established companies for about 10 to 15 years. They had stable careers. PDS matched their salaries and offered them a financial stake, without having to invest a cent. The financial equity lured many dynamic professionals, to become entrepreneurial CEOs. It was a Hub-and-Spoke model of managing the business, with PDS being the central hub of funding and management services.

The Modalities

The relationship between the Group and the partner-entrepreneur is lucidly scripted in a Legal Deed and a Memorandum of Understanding (MOU). The MOU covers all ownership, shareholding, operational and separation aspects. It details several clauses to ensure seamless operations. These embrace percentage shareholdings, formation of a board, responsibility for delivering the annual plans, funding, etc. After getting 15 to 20 percent equity in the company, the partner-entrepreneur CEO, becomes a co-owner of the business. He is expected to devote his undivided time and expertise to the business. The Legal Deed underscores that the business has to be managed within the legal, commercial, transparency and ethical values of the parent organisation.

The CEO is responsible for managing the daily operations of the company. He is also responsible for the banking arrangements and installing a Management Information System (MIS). These roles and responsibilities are delineated in the Agreement.

If a new relationship does not deliver results in about three to four years despite the best of efforts and intentions, then the business is reviewed. About 70 percent of the partnerships deliver in the long run. The results in the first 24 to 36 months, show whether a partnership is delivering or not. Typically, the first year is a loss. The second year has a smaller loss. Normally, the third year yields a small profit. Generally, the fourth year is profitable and it pays back the investments made hitherto.

In case there is a parting, then it is in line with the well-defined Memorandum of Understanding (MOU), in which the separation package is covered.

In determining the separation packages, Pallak says that he is inspired again by his father. As a child, he had observed how Deepak worked with his business partners. He recollects Deepak's ability to compromise to make things work. Deepak was always very fair in his dealings. He would conciliate where possible, but could also be firm if necessary.

The Platform Model

PDS had started investing in companies with design capabilities to bring them under its umbrella. PDS is thus akin to a venture capital company for apparel businesses. Gradually, it outgrew the Hub-and-Spoke model. PDS has evolved into a holding company, christened internally as "The Platform".

Three Criteria for Onboarding

PDS invested in new businesses based on three specific criteria. The first criterion was that the party should bring a new customer base; for instance, customers from new markets like Australia and Canada. PDS and Rajive Ranjan teamed to establish Techno Design. The company focussed strategically on the German market. It generates a turnover of over USD 100 million annually.

Second, the party should be in a geographical location where PDS did not have a presence. For example, PDS identified entrepreneurial talent in Turkey, Sri Lanka, etc., where it did not have operations. PDS found the best talent, brought it on board and established new businesses. It teamed with Ms. Esra Ercan, CEO of Spring Near East and Mr. Safak Kipik, Director of Operations (Turkey, London and Hong Kong), to harvest new markets. Spring Near East has an annual turnover of around USD 90 million. After Ms. Esra Ercan passed away in February 2020, Mr. Safak took over the leadership of the business.

The third criterion for bonding, was that the party should have a distinct product category specialisation. So, PDS identified parties which had expertise in knitwear, footwear or home items. Gradually, PDS built a network of companies in apparel and consumer goods. Thomas Muller specialised in denim. He teamed with the PDS Group to set up Zamira Fashions in Hong Kong, to supply denim products. The business has an annual potential of USD 50-100 million.

Pallak also scanned for drive and a positive attitude among potential partners. Above all, he rifled for ethical values and integrity. He told his new partners, “My philosophy is simple. I am providing you, with the same opportunity, which my father gave me. With the support of the Group, you can create a company bigger and more successful than PDS.”

Mosaic of Partners

Pallak gradually built a constellation of companies run by business partners. None of these new companies were acquired. All of them were new creations. The partners were "sweat" equity entrepreneurs. The new companies were created without any bank loans. They had zero long-term debt. The firm relied on internal accruals to invest in the business. The profits were retained and reinvested in the new businesses. Keeping the company debt free, has almost been a religion within the Group.

PDS had woven a mosaic of business partners, who had a unique customer base or presence in a new geographical location or a distinct product expertise. Thus, the Group evolved into a global multinational.

Managing this novel organisation required a new culture. Pallak knew he would have to ensure freedom and flexibility for the new CEOs. They were stars in their own companies before joining the platform.

There were three types of business partners, who led the subsidiaries. First, there were successful professionals from large corporations, who joined to establish their own businesses with PDS's support. Second, there were entrepreneurs who needed finance and management resources, to expand their businesses. Finally, there were home-grown talented employees, who had the potential to lead independent businesses.

The lure for these entrepreneurs to join the platform, is the independence to achieve. They enjoy it. They have the opportunity to expand their businesses with the Platform's infrastructure and financial strength. They relish the best of two worlds. First, they have a business to manage as independent entrepreneurs. Second, they are a part of a global business which provides them support and the opportunity to grow. Finally, they have an opportunity to share the profits. And, get rich.

Platform and Financial Support

The role of the CEO is to ensure revenues and profits by providing customers with innovative designs, excellent quality and impeccable execution. PDS acts as a venture capitalist in the fashion supply chain. Each CEO has his own team and is accountable for the profits of his unit.

The Platform plays a central function, providing financial, IT, legal, HR and administrative services to all the companies. Each business is independently managed; however, it has to be in alignment with the firm's ethics and ethos.

The platform is managed from the Bengaluru office in India and the Hong Kong office for the financial and banking functions. Functions like IT, Audit, HR and Legal are managed from India.

The Annual Planning exercise is rigorous and commences four months before the new accounting year. In the first stage of Annual Planning, the sales, sourcing and margins are reviewed. Next, the budgets of the subsidiaries are studied and finalised. Finally, the aggregate corporate budget is concluded, embracing all the businesses and the corporate offices.

The finance team undertakes an annual review of the profit and loss statements, of all the businesses. It monitors the performance of all the units through an SAP-enabled MIS. The finance team has installed risk management frameworks and undertakes continuous reviews.

The senior management team has periodic meetings, when the performances of the businesses are reviewed. The meetings also cover key parameters like receivables, payables, cash flows, working capital management, etc. There are also regular meetings to review risk management, internal audit, IT, SAP, social and ethical compliances.

PDS's vendor base is ethically audited to ensure high standards, offering a sustainable product portfolio and multiple sourcing options. "We always do the right thing. That's a big USP. The large retailers put their trust and confidence in PDS because they believe in us. We do not put the customer's brands, our brand or our reputation at risk. So, the customers trust us," comments Omprakash.

Entrepreneurial Spirit

When Pallak joined the business, he was just 21 years old. Most of the people he was recruiting were in their 30s. Now when he is in his 40s, most of the senior managers are in the late 40s or early 50s. So, the average age of the team has increased from 30 to 40 years. Nevertheless, it is a team which is very young at heart, considering their unabated, aggressive growth plans.

The business had expanded across countries. It had established sourcing operations in India, China and Bangladesh. Pallak also started operations in Canada and a logistics business in the UK, in the early 2000s. There were additional ventures like direct marketing operations in Chile, a license apparel division in the UK and an entry into the home and furnishings category. Furthermore, there was the launch of a branded retail operation in the Middle East through a joint venture with a British firm, FG4, to design clothes for Arab children. PDS also pioneered direct marketing operations in Bangladesh, Australia and India.

Pallak had established operations in Turkey, Germany, Sri Lanka, Spain and Bengaluru in India. In 2014, the business also commenced operations in Cambodia, Belgium and Pakistan. Techno Design in Germany and Yellow Octopus were launched in the UK. Fabric sourcing commenced from Shanghai. Manufacturing operations started in Bangladesh in 2016, followed by an entry into the technology business in 2017. The pace of expansion and growth has been relentless. There is never a silent moment at PDS. Every day is a hectic day.

A Million Garments, Daily

PDS now employs over 150 designers, who create 10,000 styles every year for around 200 customers, in 22 countries. It has four factories in three countries, with a production capability of 36 million pieces per annum. It works with 400 compliant vendors, in 10 countries.

The DS Group (including PDS and PGIL) ships over a million pieces of garments daily to customers worldwide.

PDS is now positioned as a design-led sourcing and manufacturing powerhouse. Sainsbury's, Next, Asda's George and Tesco top its customer list. The Group has grown without a single acquisition. It is a “Plug & Play” design-led sourcing platform.

The company's unique business model has made it one of the world's largest suppliers of fashion apparel. "We are a large company, working with many independent business units. So, we can be very agile and entrepreneurial," explains Pallak.

Management reports, SAP reports and accounting statements, do tell a businessman how the enterprise is faring. However, there is no substitute for boots on the ground and visits to the retail stores. The sights and sounds of the markets, tell their own story. It requires an astute mind and a discerning eye, to walk around in a store and understand the preferences of the shoppers.

Deepak and Pallak travel about 12-15 days every month, to various countries to hold personal meetings with the local teams. Pallak also has monthly review calls with all the 45 CEOs to comprehend the pulse of each business. Every quarter, there is a review meeting where most of the CEOs are present. He also speaks to the CEOs on the phone as often as required. He is also available to them for consultation at any time.

Operating Philosophy and Values

Pallak has evolved his own management axioms in managing the large team. First, he completely trusts the people who work with him. He also tells them, that he trusts them. Then, he also makes them feel that they are fully trusted. Trust, has to be felt.

Second, there is a framework of checks and balances to ensure compliances and governance. Third, having established trust and an operating framework, Pallak gives the teams the autonomy to deliver.

An organisation needs motivated and hungry people to grow. They need to operate independently to deliver. "Micromanagement is a waste of time. I spend my time and effort on the businesses that are under-performing," says Pallak. He believes in choosing his partners with great discretion. Then, if they do the right things for the business, there is no need to be looking over their shoulders all the time. Double guessing the decisions of the senior managers, is the easiest and the best way to destroy morale and a business.

The subsidiaries operate independently with different names. The partnering firms are managed through financial disciplines, budgetary controls and governance.

Values and beliefs, are the soul of a company. An organisation is defined by how it behaves with its employees, customers, vendors and the regulatory institutions. It is important that the organisation should be value driven, with strong corporate governance and ethics for long-term survival.

Pallak is acutely aware of the importance of ethical values in an organisation and having an upright reputation in the market. The key values of the Group are integrity, trust, customer centricity and transparency with each other. These principles bond all the stakeholders and the companies in the Group. Deepak and Pallak have frequent meetings with all the stakeholders and partners, to define and embed the core values.

Free Hand to Deliver

Trust is the bedrock on which long-term relationships are built in the Group. It is also important to give people autonomy to operate and deliver. Finally, there is a framework to ensure that the free hand to deliver, is guided by a code of conduct.

Deepak gave his son a free hand to manage the business and invest in any venture he desired. However, he always recommended a more gradual and phased approach for growth. Pallak agrees in retrospect that Deepak's cautionary approach, helped him to build a strong and stable foundation for the business.

Pallak elaborates, "A lot of parents do not let go. Dad did not interfere. Occasionally, he used to put his foot down on some issue. In hindsight, looking back, my Dad's decisions were right. I think it is very important to get his opinion on the decisions we take."

Deepak also helped Pallak to evaluate and finalise the terms with new parties, in the early stages. He was just out of his teens when he was scanning and finalising future partners. Typically, the parties he was hiring had worked for 10 to 15 years in the business. Pallak was a decade or so younger than them. Yet, he was persuading them to leave their established careers, join a new venture and begin from a scratch. So, Deepak's presence and involvement brought experience to the discussions.

The rock-solid support from Deepak, added tonnes to Pallak's self-confidence and his drive for aggressive growth. He recollects that he had Deepak's support, at the back of his mind from day one. He says, "My Dad had built a sound financial base for us. I had nothing to lose, if I failed a little in the beginning. I had the courage to take risks and initiatives in business, since I knew that I had a fall-back. It gave me the confidence to keep pushing and moving forward. So, Dad's support and confidence were very critical. Without his support it would have been difficult for me to do business. Without his guidance, it could be paralysing at times."

Pallak considers his father a pioneer in the fashion industry. Deepak was the first to install an assembly line for garment manufacturing in the factories. He was also a pioneer in establishing offices across the world to improve customer service. Deepak started from zero and through sheer tenacity, honesty and financial discipline, built one of the world's most successful fashion companies.

Pallak also observes that Deepak trusts people and gives them the support to build businesses. However, if the results are not in line with plans, Deepak can become extremely hands on to solve the problem. Pallak explains, "He gives confidence to all his business associates, that he is there for them in times of need. What impresses me most about my father, is that he evolves with the times. He has never been considered old school. His knowledge and advice are always relevant. He is the best mentor to have in business."

23
The Harvard Experience

The Owner/President Management Program (OPM) offered by Harvard Business School (HBS) is a prestigious course. HBS's top management programs like the OPM are considered life-changing experiences. It became a turning point in Pallak's evolution as an entrepreneur and as a businessman.

Over a cup of coffee, Pallak would often tell new recruits, "PDS is a building, standing strong without an architectural plan." The OPM at HBS provided the architectural plan for PDS to him. It changed his thinking in a fundamental way. Analysing the case studies about the best companies in the world, provided business frameworks to him. They generated ideas on how to manage the business opportunities and challenges, as the organisation grew. The case studies now act as guides when he is managing complexity. They tell him, how other successful companies and businessmen manage growth.

HBS structured Pallak's thinking. The program gave him the confidence that many of his past decisions based on his instincts, had been perfect for the business. The new benchmarks gleaned from the case studies and the class interactions, enabled him to validate his business approach. The new frameworks were giving him a global perspective, on business challenges.

At Harvard, students learn from the programs they enrol in; but they also learn abundantly from their classmates. The programs at HBS allure students from across the world. So, a class of 50 participants, could have students from 20 to 40 countries. The discussions in the class and the after-class interactions with the fellow participants, bring a global perspective to the students. Pallak met some vibrant businessmen and entrepreneurs from around the world. The group assignments and the discussions over lunches and dinners, cement friendships for life. Students from Harvard bond very cohesively even after the programs, through well-managed alumni associations across the world.

Harvard relies on the case study method in its programs. The class is divided into smaller learning groups of about six to eight participants each. The learning group memberships continue throughout the period of the program. However, the fraternity of the groups continues even after the course. Many of the learning group members become business associates. They support each other's learning, evolution and progress for years after the program.

New Horizons

The OPM Program inspired Pallak to set up new companies. He also established a business in the water technology space, with potential for growth.

The idea to deploy PDS as a growth platform came to Pallak from his interactions with Professor Lynda Applegate of Harvard Business School. He realised that the PDS framework could enable, guide and mentor the constituent companies. The "levers of influence" framework, could provide the tools and appliances to manage a large number of dispersed businesses.

The Danaher Corporation case study inspired Pallak to develop business systems, to standardise operations and foster operational excellence in the units. The Zappos case study imparted lessons, on how the operating culture of a company can distinguish it from others. A culture which encourages excellence and creativity, can be of significant strategic advantage in a competitive industry. The Google case study helped Pallak to redefine the role of a manager and a leader in a business. The General Electric Company case study, gave him concepts on sharing the best practices of the PDS across different business units.

Pallak reflected on the frameworks that he had learnt at HBS. He realised that an entrepreneurial team is managed through beliefs, boundaries, diagnostic and interactive tools. The PDS belief system advocates that people and their values should be respected. Next, the boundaries define the reputation and financial risks that are non-negotiable. Then, the diagnostic functional tools like budgets, performance indices, balance sheets and cash flows help to manage the business. The interactive tools are the reviews, through which all the businesses share their best practices and ideas.

Harvard's PDS Case Study

After completing the OPM, Pallak requested Professor Boris Groysberg to join the advisory board of the company. At the anniversary celebrations in Bangkok, Professor Groysberg conducted a four-day workshop for the team of 140 managers.

Harvard Business School has written a case study on PDS, covering its unique platform of companies and how ingeniously they are managed. (PDS: Ring-Fencing the Ranch by Professors Dennis Campbell, Tarun Khanna and Director Kerry Herman, N9-721-361, August 11, 2020). The various guidelines or levers of influence deployed to manage the companies in the Group, are expounded in the case study.

Deepak and Pallak were delighted. A Harvard case study on their business, deployed to teach business models to Harvard MBAs, is indeed a feather in the cap for the Group. The young man Deepak, who serviced his first order for 6,000 shirts from the garage of his house, now featured in a Harvard Business School case study along with his son.

"The company relies on strenuous effort, not just on pure hope.

For, hope is not a strategy.

The youngsters who lead the company, do not mind some operational chaos, as the Group grows.

Chaos leads to creativity.

And, Profits come from disciplined execution."

- Pallak Seth

24
Building Professional Partnerships

Pallak sat in his office, with a blank sheet of paper on his table and a pen in his hand. He was confronted with a problem and was determined to resolve it. The Group was focussed on the UK and Europe. Now, he was keen to penetrate the USA markets. The number of companies on the Platform were increasing rapidly. However, many of them were focussing on the same customers. This created confusion. Pallak did not want five teams from the Group visiting the same customer, with similar samples.

The subsidiaries had strong domain experience, led by fiercely independent entrepreneurs. They were always chasing new businesses in new countries. Each business operated as an independent silo. Pallak wanted to forge them into a team, which shared knowledge and wisdom.

He wondered how to prevent the companies on the platform, from competing for the same customers. It often led to cannibalisation. He hoped to arrive at a Group consensus, without being over-granular.

Boundaries and Risks

Pallak also made calls to his business heads to get their views. He and his core team finally agreed on two internal guidelines. The first was christened the Boundary system. Whenever multiple Group companies competed for the same customer, Pallak and the Board would decide who would service the order. The best team would be selected on the basis of the products, design content, geography, logistics and the relationship with the customer. This would ensure that the Group companies, do not compete with each other for the same customers. The guideline would also help to protect prices and margins.

The second guideline ensured that the companies on the PDS platform become collaborators. If a company introduced another associate to a customer, both would share the profits in some ratio. The company which executes the order, gets a larger profit share. The company which introduces the customer, also gets some share.

Managing Risks

The management of risks is very crucial in the garments industry. Risks range from credit worthiness to fulfilment of all the compliances. Compliance encompasses legal, ethical and social provisions. All of them impact the reputation of an organisation.

The Group is acutely aware of the various risks concerning the business. The risk exposure is always high, when a business operates in numerous countries. The Group has to constantly monitor all the units for ethics and compliances.

The Group has internal processes to ensure that the businesses operate within the prescribed ethical parameters. There is zero tolerance for anything that impacts the welfare of the workers or the reputation of the company.

To ensure accounting hygiene, PDS operates with two compliance teams. The first team undertakes the scheduled audits of all the operating units. The second team focusses on surprise audits. Both the teams report to the board. The compliance team has 45 managers who review around 400 operations, in various countries.

Collaborative Model and Executive Board

Pallak was keen to forge all the stand-alone subsidiaries into a plus billion-dollar business, with a core vision and strategic plan. In October 2017, he organised a Leadership Meeting in Dubai, to chalk out a Group strategy and a plan for the future. He thought it wise to let all the partners debate and agree the operating principles of the company, to ensure unified compliance.

Pallak was keen to encourage sharing of information about best practices, markets and central services like IT and HR. There were also potential synergies in bulk buying of raw materials like fabrics. For instance, 10 factories buying 10,000 metres of fabric each, could get a discount of one or two percent. However, one entity buying 1,00,000 metres of fabric, could negotiate a higher discount from the textile mill.

Pallak discerned the need for alignment across all the businesses and for upgrading capabilities rapidly. Social and ethical compliances were also of serious concern to customers. Deepak and Pallak appreciated that though the business was led globally, it would have to be managed locally in each country. Their vision was simple: to be the preferred business partner of the top retailers and also be the preferred employer of professionals.

After the meeting in Dubai, Pallak formed an executive board, comprising of eight business heads, the Group Chief Financial Officer (CFO) and the Group Chief Operating Officer (COO). The board would focus on two objectives. First, build a common corporate culture. Second, ensure that all subsidiaries operate within the core values and protocols of the business.

The role of the executive board was to define the future strategy of the Group. It would also concretise governance policies, which were non-negotiable, which all the subsidiaries would follow.

The executive board constituted two councils to ensure adherence to PDS values and operating practices. The Ethical Compliance Council reviews policy issues, which impact the reputation of the company. The Business Conduct and Dispute Resolution Council manages issues involving subsidiaries, employees and vendors.

Three Verticals

The business now operates three verticals. The first vertical is the core business of design-led sourcing. This continues to grow organically. Every year, the Group partners with new companies, by identifying the right leaders with competent and motivated teams.

The second vertical nurtures units which need support. It onboards smaller companies (USD 10 to 30 million in revenues), which need sustenance as standalone businesses. These units benefit immensely by joining the Platform, since they get access to finance and management systems. The sourcing business is growing by 10 to 15 percent per year. It contributes to the prosperity of the newly boarded companies.

The third vertical is the establishment of a venture capital fund to invest in technology-driven fashion companies. PDS invests in ventures in fashion, retail and supply chain ventures, which target customers of the future. The idea is a unique blend of capital, domain expertise and global talent.

There are four stages in the venture funding process. The first stage is the "Idea Stage", also known as the pre-revenue stage. Then, the venture enters into the "Seed Stage", earning a revenue of around USD one million per year. In the "Early Stage", the venture is expected to have a turnover of USD one million to USD five million every year. Finally, the venture reaches "Growth Stage", when its revenue is more than USD five million annually.

The global retail and supply chain businesses are being disrupted by new technologies and start-ups. Businesses can survive only by keeping lean and nimble. Learning continuously, has become an essential ingredient of success. Hence, PDS has established a USD 15 million venture capital fund, to bring deep domain expertise to young entrepreneurs with exceptional educational backgrounds. Many bright youngsters, have brilliant ideas in sustainability and digitisation. However, they cannot grow their ventures, due to inadequate funds. The firm partners with such potential entrepreneurs and provides them with financial and management inputs.

The criteria deployed to select the ventures to fund, are clearly defined. They are selected on an anvil of three parameters. They should involve technological innovation or value chain novelty. They should be environmentally sustainable. Finally, they should meet the corporate standards on social ethics. Most of the companies on the platform are design-led supply chain companies, catering to markets in the USA, Europe, UK, Latin America, etc.

Levers of Influence

PDS has created a set of internal guidelines to facilitate operations. These are called the "Levers of Influence Framework". They are basically a set of protocols, with which all the subsidiaries operate. Each subsidiary works within the operating principles and values of the Group.

The subsidiaries have annual budgets and key performance indices (KPIs). These are monitored monthly. In the toughest of economic times, PDS has grown, due to its robust operational guidelines.

Pallak concentrates on areas of potential risk like customer management, credit, currency fluctuations, compliances, cost-effectiveness and complaints. He terms these priorities, the "Six Cs".

PDS has lucid parameters, to manage these risks in the subsidiaries. It ensures that it has a large basket of 200 customers, comprising of global brands, high street retailers and hypermarkets. The top 20 customers contribute 70 percent of the total revenues. No single customer contributes more than 15 percent of the turnover.

To manage the credit risk, PDS secures credit terms from customers and maintains adequate insurance covers. It also monitors receivables and overdue debtors regularly. To manage currency risks, the business buys and sells in the same currency; otherwise, immediate forex cover is taken. To ensure compliances, the Group adheres to an internal code of conduct. The firm projects turnover purely on compliant capacities. It also undertakes annual factory audits.

PDS covers cost risks by adopting the best global practices for cost-effectiveness. It micromanages costs and undertakes continuous reviews through 15 financial controllers. All these professionals are Certified Public Accountants or Cost Accountants.

The organisation has evolved from informal consultations to executive board meetings, from informal channels of communication to formal information systems. Town hall meetings, WhatsApp groups and news bulletins, ensure that all the constituent companies are abreast of developments.

Factories: Sri Lanka and Bangladesh

PDS's entire supplies were sourced from captive factories based in Southeast Asia. None of these factories were owned by the Group.

Many large new customers like GAP, Levi's and H&M were keen to work with suppliers, who had their own factories. Retailers in Europe and the USA, preferred to work with vendors who provided value-added services like designing, branding and financing. They wanted seamless execution of orders. Customers were also gearing for technological disruptions from mobile and online shopping to drone deliveries. Middlemen were gradually being squeezed out. The garment industry was going through a silent change.

Therefore, PDS set up manufacturing facilities in Bangladesh and Sri Lanka. It commenced manufacture of its own garments in 2016. The factories in Bangladesh were established at a cost of USD 50 million. They produce garments for the subsidiaries on the Platform and other customers.

PDS had established four state-of-the-art production units in Bangladesh, India and Sri Lanka. They manufacture babywear, children's wear, school wear, shirts, ladies' apparel, and casual and formal bottoms. The manufacturing units helped to add new product categories. They also demonstrated the Group's commitment to invest for future growth. The initiative helped the company to onboard new US customers, who were keen to work directly with manufacturing businesses. Large US retailers were delighted to work with PDS, which had its own factories. The customers could get a wider range of products and assured delivery.

PDS aimed at 20 percent turnover from its manufacturing operations and 80 percent from design-led souring operations. Its factories have about 6,000 machines, generating an annual turnover of USD 200 million.

Even though the Group has its own factories, the top ten factories which produced garments for it in the 1990s, continue to work with it. PDS's operating philosophy comprises of a sound sourcing strategy, professional conduct and fairness in all dealings. This has ensured that the buyers and the supplier factories, which worked with the Group 40 years ago, continue to do so even now. Businesses eventually depend on healthy relationships; the Group has nurtured its customer and vendor relationships over the last 45 years.

Salim Khan is a renowned Indian film script writer. He says that a good human being is a person whose assistants and friends, have been with him for a long time. Similarly, a good business is characterised by customers and suppliers, who have been with it for a long time.

Establishing production facilities also necessitated investments in IT, logistics, technical manpower, etc. This has enabled deployment of new technologies and digital tools, to manage the business efficiently.

Focus on Sustainability

The fashion and retail sectors are undergoing a major metamorphosis globally. The triggers are radical changes in consumer behaviour and shopping habits, supply chain innovations and augmented focus on social accountability and sustainability. Environmental and social goals have now become as important as financial goals. Deepak and Pallak realised, that businesses have to discern the way the wind is blowing and become effective agents of change. Otherwise, they will be blown away by the new winds.

There is significant focus on sustainability in the garments industry. Companies are making efforts to produce recyclable clothes, reduce packaging materials and prevent clothes from getting wasted in landfills.

Handbook: Bible of Values

The Handbook on PDS Core Values and Behaviour provides guidelines on how employees in the Group, should conduct themselves and their business. The 16-page Handbook, describes the basic operating values of the business. These are trust, integrity and ethics, people first, entrepreneurial spirit, transparency, collaboration and teamwork, social responsibility and customer centricity. Each employee is required to read the Handbook and sign acceptance. The core value is summed in one line on page 13 as, "In matters of style, swim with the current; in matters of values, stand like a rock!"

PDS's Metamorphosis

The business evolved into a "Hub-and-Spoke" model wherein PDS onboarded entrepreneurs based on their product specialisation, geographic advantage and customer bases.

Next, the Group transformed itself into a "Platform of Capabilities" enabling teams, ensuring best practices and standardisation through the levers of influence. The Group had also established its own production facilities. Now, the business has evolved into a "Collaborative Model", fostering inter-business cooperation, deploying the best teams and mentoring of stakeholders.

Building Culture, People

The business has blossomed due to a strong performance-oriented culture. Training and development of managers and staff on an unremitting basis, has strengthened the foundation of the business. Like large multinational companies, the firm has crafted a business induction programme, called the "PDS Business System" for new employees. It familiarises the new entrants with policies, procedures and operating guidelines. The induction also covers the importance of customer centricity, compliances, people management, internal controls, etc.

There is also a "Leadership Academy" which enhances leadership skills, amongst managers with growth potential. The Academy offers programmes to develop functional and leadership skills. These forums are also deployed to articulate and implant the core values of the firm.

To empower employees, PDS has partnered with Navex Global to provide a whistleblowing service. Any employee can make an anonymous complaint on any issue. An independent team from the company conducts a fair and confidential investigation. The report is tabled to the executive board.

The entrepreneurial model of business, a best practice of the DS Group, has now become a part of its ethos. Senior managers are incentivised and rewarded on the basis of their achievements. This drives them to surpass their goals.

Future Challenges

The future of the apparel industry is challenging, due to the volatile market. E-commerce has heralded major disruptions in the industry. Nevertheless, PDS aims to grow in double digits. The growth is being driven by the entrepreneurial hunger and spirit of the Group. Despite the changing retailing scenario, the business is confident of doubling its turnover in the next few years. The Group is also focussed on getting a strong bottom line. “Profits come from discipline,” affirms Pallak.

The company is virtually debt free and invests its own profits in new ventures, backing ambitious entrepreneurs. During the last two decades, the Group has acquired only three companies. Yet, it has grown organically to more than USD 1.2 billion in revenues. It has 45 businesses, with 76 subsidiaries. It has offices or operations in over 22 countries, four factories and about 7,000 employees. PDS has spread its wings to countries ranging from Brazil and Chile through the USA, UK, Europe to Myanmar and Cambodia. Nine of the subsidiaries in the portfolio, contribute 78 percent of the turnover. Due to the unique strengths of its business model, PDS has become a large global fashion company. The DS Group (including PDS and PGIL), has now become a leading global apparel business.

Lessons Learnt

Pallak has curated the key lessons that he has learnt in the business over the years, as follows:

Values

1) The culture of a business organisation, is the secret sauce of its success. It is a vital strategic asset, though invisible. It is not easy to replicate the culture of a company. Culture, has to evolve.

2) Values are the foundation of a sound business. We must hire and promote people based on their adherence to corporate values and ethics.

3) In life, some people help you; they come as blessings. Others may let you down or not measure up to expectations. They come with lessons. You have to learn from the lessons and not be disillusioned.

4) Good is never good enough. Always keep raising the performance bar. However, never set unrealistic goals.

5) An encouraging and team-driven culture, is a major competitive edge.

6) Always respect people and treat them, the way you would like to be treated yourself.

Leadership

1) Strong leadership is required during challenging times. Fanatic levels of focus, discipline and passion are necessary to achieve goals.

2) A fish smells from the head. How the leader of the company behaves, impacts the attitude and behaviour of the entire team. So, the leader has to be highly conscious of his conduct and style.

3) A leader needs to have a strong Emotional Quotient (EQ) and a robust Commercial Quotient (CQ).

4) Do not ignore problems. They do not vanish. Take them head on and resolve them. Always catch the bull by the horns.

5) Never fall into a comfort zone. Always keep the eye on the ball.

6) If you share what you earn with your team members, then they will multiply it manifold for you.

7) Do not ever, burn bridges with anyone in personal and business relationships. You never know, when you may have to walk back in life.

8) Always be fair with all your business partners. They should never get the feeling, that you are supporting one over another.

9) What goes around, always comes around. So, always be reasonable with people.

10) It takes years to build trust. However, one single instance can destroy it.

11) Never procrastinate, finish all the tasks on the same day.

Management

1) Hire people for their uncompromising integrity and potential. A person can acquire and strengthen the requisite skills over time.

2) There is no substitute for simple hard work. Pure brilliance is not a substitute for diligence. However, brilliance plus application can deliver astounding results.

3) Avoid debts. It puts pressure on the business and on the entrepreneur.

4) Never compromise on financial disciplines. It is better to earn less, but sleep peacefully every night.

5) Never look at what other people are receiving in your company. They are getting what they have earned and deserved.

6) The first loss, is the best loss. So, if a business is not delivering results, it is best to exit.

Recipes for Success

Over the years, Pallak has gradually evolved his own recipe for success in business.

Values are vital: He says, "The secret of success is having exceptional people who are motivated to build the company. All our associates know we are a value-driven organisation. We hire and promote people on the basis of our core values, as affirmed in the Value Handbook. The entrepreneurs know they have a free hand to deliver. However, they have to be aligned with our values."

Think long: He insists on looking at the long-term picture and does not take decisions based on short-term considerations.

Light candles: Pallak innovated in an industry, where companies are generally family managed. He has kept the business debt free. The business is light in assets and has a scalable model. He has buttressed many entrepreneurs, who have evolved into successful co-owners. Thus, he has lit many candles, which radiate wealth and opportunities.

Recruit young: He believes in recruiting young people in their 20s and 30s. He finds them smarter, ambitious and hungry for growth. Pallak believes in recruiting people smarter than himself. "Young people have an innate need to succeed," he feels. The business employs professionals from over 22 countries.

Ignore mistakes: Pallak has created a culture where employees are permitted to make mistakes. It is not a culture of fear. He smiles and says, "I tell my people, 'What does not kill you, will only make you stronger.'"

Encouragement: He has also built a culture where team members do not criticise opponents or competitors. They are encouraged to outperform them. Finally, the team is practical. Everything in business is not always fair; so, the best option is to be resilient and deliver.

Win-Win Formula

The operating philosophy and dynamism of the Group has brought some of the best customers to its fold. Global brands like Matalan, Primark, Next, Sainsbury's, New Yorker, Asda/George, Arcadia, Tesco, Takko, TKO-Evolution Apparel, Inc., Superdry, Jack Wills, La Halle, Kroger/Fred Myer, Inditex Group, Giant Tiger, C&A and Pep&Co are some of the businesses that work with the Group.

The team has created a partnership mindset, wherein team members focus on making the cake bigger. They do not fret about who gets how much. They treat the customers as partners in growth and develop strategic relationships with them. The organisational culture is to reduce all issues to digits, so that they can be calibrated. Whatever can be measured, can always be managed.

Pallak is now engaged in projects to unify the Group companies through joint financials. He is also exploring motivating the senior management across companies, through an employee stock ownership plan (ESOP). The goal is to reward collaborative efforts across multiple subsidiaries.

He adds, "The youthful company relies on strenuous effort and midnight hours, not just on pure hope. For, hope is not a strategy. The youngsters who lead the company, do not mind some operational chaos as the Group grows. They believe chaos leads to creativity."

In following Deepak's example of fostering entrepreneurs, Pallak has created a win-win model of business. Young entrepreneurs who had the spirit but not the capital, found a home in the firm.

The DS Group (including PDS and PGIL) is now scurrying towards a turnover of USD 2 billion. Its customers are delighted with world class service levels. Everyone is a winner.

"My Dad is a man of many parts. He has always treated us as children, but also as his friends.

In business, he has always given us a lot of autonomy from the very beginning. He treats us as equal partners.

He works with the highest ethical standards. He has never backed out of any commitment made to any staff member, who has performed.

He has built the business on the principles of entrepreneurship, motivation and mentoring people.

He coaches the staff, to perform to the best of their abilities."

- Pulkit Seth

25
Pulkit's Entry

Living and studying in New York was a fabulous experience for Pulkit. Coming from a caring family in India, he had to live on his own in the city that never sleeps. The experience taught him to be independent and self-reliant. He enjoyed his studies and performed well academically, at the New York University, Stern School of Business. He made some good friends at the university. Many of them are close to him even now.

Deepak would travel to New York often when Pulkit was studying and would guide him. He was very keen that Pulkit should do well at studies. Whilst a business career awaited Pulkit, Deepak knew that a sound academic grounding was always a huge asset in life.

Pulkit looked forward to Deepak's visit to the USA every month. Pulkit would always accompany him to meet the customers, even as a student. He recollects, "It was useful for me to see how my Dad interacted with people of different backgrounds and cultures. He was always able to convince them and win their trust. It was a great education for me."

Pulkit joined the USA business in October 2002 after graduating. He worked with the German and UK operations also. He studied the garments market, familiarising himself with various aspects of customer management. Pulkit visited all the customers with Deepak, to understand their operations and needs.

Having familiarised himself with the markets, Pulkit moved to India to understand the manufacturing and sourcing operations. Subsequently, Pulkit moved to Hong Kong to work there. This office, coordinated the sourcing of garments for their own Lerros brand, from Bangladesh and Indonesia.

Pulkit's induction into the business was very quick. He had complete responsibility from the first day. His challenge was to grow the Hong Kong operation rapidly. He concentrated on sourcing garments for key German clients and for their USA business.

Dealing with a business in entirety, exposed Pulkit to all aspects of the business from sales and customer servicing to sourcing and production. He already had a strong grounding in the finance and commercial functions, as he had majored in them at the University. Pulkit was therefore able to interact easily with the experienced commercial and accounting heads.

The exposure in the Hong Kong business, laid a robust foundation for Pulkit's leadership and career. He was managing sourcing, marketing and merchandising. In 2004, he moved to India, which was a major production hub of the company.

Building New Factories

Pulkit focussed on strengthening the manufacturing footprint for the business across the world. The factory in Indonesia had started in 2002. Another factory started operations in Bangladesh in 2004. The Vietnam factory was acquired in 2017.

There were many hurdles to cross when the factories were being built. Pulkit recalls, "We always tried to learn from our mistakes and move forward speedily. My Dad travelled with me to various countries and locations. We worked tirelessly in laying the business foundation in these countries. We recruited the best talent to work in our factories."

The Group has now become the most diversified apparel manufacturing business in India. It has manufacturing facilities in India and Southeast Asia. A dispersed production strategy gave a strong competitive edge to the company. During the nightmarish Covid-19 pandemic, having multiple factories across countries enabled the Group to continue production and supplies to all its customers.

Now, PGIL can produce more than 80 million garments annually. It also has partnerships with loyal third-party suppliers. The company has established 18 production plants in India, Bangladesh, Indonesia and Vietnam. It has a strong in-house team of 75 plus designers, based in thc USA, the UK, Hong Kong and Spain.

Pulkit had also become friendly with a pretty young girl named Shifalli, a classmate at school. Their friendship blossomed into love, even though Pulkit was based in New York and she lived in Delhi. Pulkit says, "It was easy to manage the long-distance relationship. My mother had told me to get married to the first girl I fell in love with. Mummy also made it very easy for my brother and me, by welcoming our wives with an open heart. Luckily, we are in a happy marriage and blessed with two great children."

Deepak's Plans for Continuity

Pulkit is quick to acknowledge his father's contributions towards his development and also that of the business. "My Dad is a man of many parts, playing numerous roles. On the personal side, as a Dad, he has always treated us as his children, but also as his friends. In the business, he has always given us a lot of autonomy from the very beginning. He treats us as equal partners. He is a wonderful father who has always given all that he can, to his family and friends. He works with the highest ethical standards. He has never backed out of any commitment made to any staff member, who has performed. He has built the business on the principles of entrepreneurship, motivation and mentoring people. He coaches and encourages the staff, to perform to the best of their abilities."

Simultaneously, Pulkit finds his Dad to be a very adventurous person, considering the global business he has built. He adds, "His drive to grow and expand the business is incessant. His experience gives him the ability to gauge issues correctly. He always generates new and creative ideas."

Pulkit's advice to youngsters is to ensure a very solid education, certainly a master's degree, after the undergraduate education. The world is ever changing and getting very competitive. So, a solid education and the ability to focus are important. The next ingredient for success, according to Pulkit, is sustained work despite setbacks.

Deepak gave responsibility to both his sons, very early in their business careers. He groomed them by giving them a free hand, with minimal guidance. With their strong financial family background and upbringing, the sons could have taken it easy. However, their view was that our father has built a global business; now, how do we grow it and take it forward?

Pallak and Pulkit have driven the business to a totally new level. They had a simple formula. From the beginning, they recruited the best people in the market and incentivised them with equity or profit sharing. Then, they gave them the freedom to bloom on their own.

Over the years, they have built an array of companies which are basically managed by entrepreneur-managers. They ensure governance and provide financial help. The brothers, Pallak and Pulkit, complement each other to grow the business.

Mr. Ahuja of Shahi Exports comments, "Both of Deepak's sons are well established. They have clear roles. Their business is well organised."

Awards and Accolades

The Group has received several awards from reputed foreign retailers and exports institutions like Apparel Exporters & Manufacturers Association (AEMA), Apparel Export Promotion Council of India (AEPC), Export Promotion Council, etc.

Macy's, USA, has appreciated the company with a Five Star Exports Recognition. JCPenney presented a memento to the Group in 2005, appreciating its extraordinary contributions. In 2006, the Group was honoured with a Purchasing Partnership Award by JCPenney.

Loblaw, the largest Canadian food retailer, has awarded the Group a KPI Score of 100 percent, for on-time shipments.

The Group has received an award from AEPC, for Highest Exports in Woven Garments for five years. Pulkit was the winner of Highest Exports by a Young Entrepreneur Award, 2008, 2009, 2010 and 2012.

In year 2014-15, the Haryana Government presented PGIL with a State Export Award for outstanding performance in exports. In 2015-16, it achieved the first rank for the Highest Global Exports, in the Rs. 100 crores to Rs. 500 crores category.

PHOTOGRAPHS

17. Sitting Mr. Ram Nath Seth and Mrs. Chand Rani Seth (Grandparents of Deepak Seth). Standing Mr. Madan Lal Seth and Mrs. Mina Seth (Parents of Deepak Seth).

18. Mr. Madan Lal Seth and Mrs. Mina Seth, parents of Deepak Seth.

19. Mr. Madan Lal Seth, father of Deepak Seth.

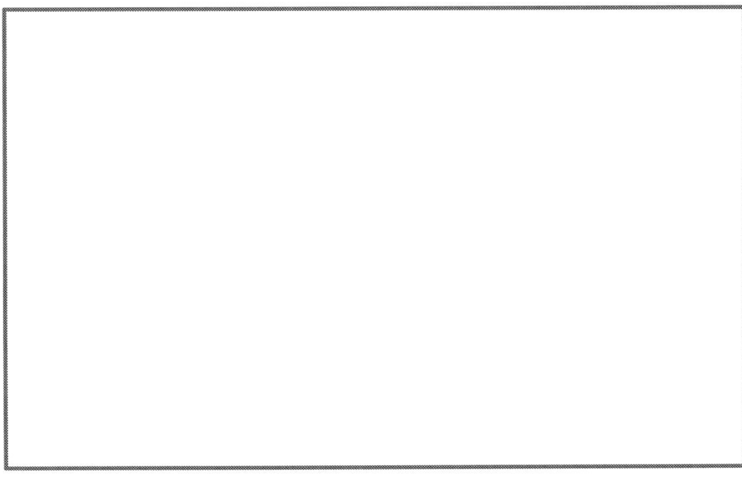

20. Mr. Madan Lal Seth meeting Shri Lal Bahadur Shastri, former Prime Minister of India.

21. Deepak Seth with his brothers in 2017. Standing, Deepak, Krishen. Sitting, Chand, Mahesh, Harish.

22. Young Deepak Seth, in college, 1970.

23. Wedding reception of Deepak and Krishen. Left to right, Deepak, Payel, Mrs. Charat Ram, Mrs. Rita Seth, Mr. Krishen Seth and Mrs. Suneeta Seth.

24. Wedding of Deepak, his parents, brothers Chand, Harish, Krishen and Mahesh, and their wives Suneeta, Madhu, Rekha, Rita. Also, young Amit and Varun.

25. Payel at her wedding, 1976. Mrs. Suneeta Seth (wife of Mr. Chand Seth) is on the left. Mrs. Beni Pershad, (Payel's aunt), is in the centre.

26. Payel and Deepak Seth.

27. Payel as a child, with her parents, Mr. Badri Pershad and Mrs. Rajni Pershad.

28. Deepak and Payel Seth.

29. Deepak and Payel, with parents and sons, Pallak and Pulkit.

30. Deepak with brother of Payel, Sanjay Pershad and family. From Left to Right: Sanjay, Anshuj, Deepak, Anu, Payel, Ayush, Ashray.

31. Deepak and Payel Seth with sons, Pallak and Pulkit.

32. Deepak Seth with his sons, Pallak and Pulkit.

33. Deepak and Payel Seth with Pallak and Faiza.

34. Deepak and Payel Seth with Pallak and family. The children (left to right) Alif, Aria and Ayat.

35. Deepak Seth with his elder son, Pallak.

36. Deepak and Payel, with Ritu and Rakesh Kapoor.

37. Deepak and Payel Seth with Shifalli and Pulkit.

38. Deepak and Payel Seth with Pulkit and Family. Standing in front are Dheer (grandson) and Sahana (granddaughter).

39. Deepak and Payel Seth with Pulkit and family.

40. Deepak Seth with Sahana, granddaughter.

41. Deepak Seth, as Chairman of the Government Hostel Management Committee in 1972, handing over a cheque to Dr. T. K. Tope, the Vice- Chancellor of Bombay University, for the Staff Welfare Fund.

42. Deepak, Payel and Pallak Seth with Arun Gujral and family. From Left to Right: Arun, Pallak, Payel, Neha, Kiran, Deepak.

43. Deepak and Payel Seth with Ashok Sanghi and Kamini Sanghi.

44. Deepak and Payel Seth with Ashutosh Bhupatkar and Madhulika Bhupatkar.

45. Deepak Seth with Narendra Aneja and Rajendra Aneja.

46. Deepak at a reunion of classmates of Jamnalal Bajaj Institute of Management Studies.

47. Deepak greeting Mr. Chandra Shekhar Singh, former Prime Minister of India.

48. Deepak Seth with Prime Minister of India, Mr. Narendra Modi (seated seventh from left), representing Garments Industry in India. Deepak is seated third from right.

26
IT and Digital Revolution

Gaurav Puri joined the DS Group in 1997, as the IT manager in one of the factories in Gurgaon. He was impressed that a company manufacturing garments, had its own ERP systems based on the Unix and Oracle platforms. Within a few weeks, he realised that dedication would open the doors of progress to him in the Group. Gradually, he rose to occupy a senior position in the corporate office. He joined the in-house team, working on developing an elaborate ERP plan.

In early 2007, Deepak and Pulkit realised that they needed a single IT solution which would integrate the different business processes, on a common platform. After a rigorous study of various ERP products, System Application Product (SAP) was selected as the best suited for the Group's business model.

Gaurav and a core team of 20 professionals started implementing the new system. Within two years, SAP had been implemented in the UK, Bangladesh and the USA businesses.

Gaurav then had the challenge of implementing SAP in all the factories. The technical team completed the roll-out in the Gurugram factories, before moving to Indonesia. A small team of six IT professionals implemented the new system in the factories in Indonesia, Chennai and Bengaluru in India, then in Hong Kong and Vietnam.

As a result, the entire manufacturing operations of all the PGIL factories are on a single SAP platform. The moment there is an enquiry from a customer, it is recorded in the system. The SAP application commences with the costing of an order. Then, the continuous progress and execution of the order is monitored in the system, till the payment is received from the customer.

After an order is costed, it goes automatically to Pulkit for his approval. Then, the system generates a detailed budget. The purchase orders, the production processes and finally the invoicing, are all embraced by the system.

The introduction of SAP covering the entire business process from enquiry to cash realisation, ushered efficiencies and speed in execution. Remote IT wires and programmes had intertwined an array of operations, factories, branches, vendors, suppliers and customers. The integrated operation weeded out delays and inefficiencies.

Benefits of SAP

The management of an order was laborious prior to the introduction of SAP. The order was costed on an Excel sheet. The Purchase Order (PO) was sent to a supplier through an e-mail. The supplier would download the PO. He would issue an invoice and inform the delivery date to the customer. All the communications were through e-mails or telephone calls.

The entire operation depended on a person who communicated via e-mails. If the person was on leave, the chain of activities would be stalled. The IT team therefore decided to introduce the SAP-ERP system.

With the introduction of SAP-ERP, the entire business process is automated. Every enquiry from a customer is recorded in the system. The software costs the order. After the costing is finalised and accepted, it is loaded in the system, generating a

Bill of Materials (BOM), for executing the order. Then, a PO is automatically generated. The supplier gets the PO. PGIL receives a notification when the PO is accepted by the supplier. At shipment time, various documents like the invoice and bill of lading are loaded in the system. These are verified by the shipping team.

When the goods reach the company's factory gate, the store manager generates the Goods Receipt Note (GRN) in the system. It records the delivery of goods received from the supplier and serves as a proof of receipt.

In the manual system, if the company received 195 rolls of fabric instead of 200 rolls, it would be intimated through an email. Now, the store manager just enters the actual quantity received in the system. It gets communicated to all concerned. The reconciliation with the PO is automatic. The difference is highlighted and communicated to the supplier.

The supplier acknowledges the short supply and invoices accordingly. The Accounts team cross-checks the invoice, with the entries in the system and then releases the payment.

SAP helps the business to track the physical movement of goods and maintains accurate financial accounts. Manual recording of goods, was always prone to some human errors.

The Barcode

The Group has a new initiative, barcoding in the Gurugram factory, to ensure tighter control on the production. A barcode is attached to every garment. Any ordinary worker can affix the barcode. Then, his colleagues in the factory scan the garment, at each stage of the production process.

Each garment is tracked digitally, as it moves through the various production processes. So, a freshly stitched shirt may go for washing, finishing, pressing, packing and despatch. The progress of the shirt would be monitored at every stage. Its precise location can be ascertained at any time. Thus, the system has digital information on every garment, by specific customer order, in the factory.

Barcoding has many advantages. The progress of every garment, is clearly recorded at each stage. Earlier, the garments were tracked manually, by making entries in an array of registers. Barcoding has made it possible to track every garment, by purchase order, colour and size throughout the production process. It contributes to speed, accuracy and timeliness of information.

Barcoding is particularly useful to ensure that customer orders are executed in entirety, as the despatch date nears. Orders are complex to execute. An order for 1,00,000 shirts may be split into five colours like white, cream, blue, green and pink. Furthermore, each of the five colour shirts is categorised by sizes like small, medium, large, extra-large or even double extra-large; so, five more variants. Thus, an order for 1,00,000 shirts, really means 25 sub-orders with varying requirements of colours of fabrics, buttons, threads, etc. The buyer prescribes specific quantities for each of the 25 variants.

Ensuring that each variant is completed on time, is an intricate process. The IT system will show at what stage each variant is in the plant, at any time. As the despatch date draws closer, production managers get sleepless nights, worrying if all the variants by colour and size are ready. If some shirts of a specific colour are not ready, the barcoding system helps to identify their location in the factory. Then, their production can be accelerated.

Chip Technology, RFID

The Group is also experimenting with an electronic chip technology, the RFID (Radio Frequency Identification). A chip is tagged to every garment. The progress of each garment can then be monitored through various phases in the factory. The chip is removed from the garment before it leaves the factory and can be recycled.

The RFID chip has an advantage over the barcode. The barcode has to be stitched into the garment, but the RFID has just to be affixed, which is easier. During the heavy wash in the laundry, the barcode needs to be covered. The RFID chip can withstand heavy washes too.

Line Planning to Optimise Production

The Group has also introduced a tool to ensure that all the production capabilities in the factories, are being optimally used. The Line Planning tool allocates production across factories, depending on the pending orders and the available capacities.

For instance, the company receives orders for execution over the next six months. The planning team allocates the orders over various factories, depending on the product variants they specialise in and their current work-in-progress. The planning team prepares a schedule, indicating which factories will produce the garments and the dates of completion. The scheduling of production lines, is generated in the SAP and is available to all the managers.

The tool helps management to assess the aggregate capacities in all the factories and their utilisation. The free capacity in every factory is highlighted. Starting with the Gurugram factories, the application is being extended to the factories in Chennai, Bengaluru, Bangladesh and Vietnam.

Line Planning has become a core tool for the management. It ensures that all factories are utilised in an optimum manner. A planning manager has to press a button on his laptop. He immediately knows the free capacity available, by factory, anywhere in the business.

Automation of Material Requirements

The production process of garments is more intricate than of many other products, even automobiles. In manufacturing a car, the various materials and components that go into it are detailed in the Bill of Materials (BOM). They do not vary for the same model. The colour of the car and the upholstery fabric can vary. However, in the garment industry, every shirt, trouser or blouse is a new product. Every garment has varying requirements of materials like fabrics, buttons and zippers, in an assortment of designs, sizes, colours, etc.

Producing a simple shirt or a jacket is a multi-layered process. Producing a skirt or a trouser may involve four or five types of fabrics. Furthermore, it can involve 20 to 30 types of trims and other items, including the zips, buttons, threads, etc. So, producing a simple skirt can involve procuring 25 to 35 items.

Executing an order for trousers means procuring the fabrics, linings, buttons, zippers, labels, etc., aggregating to 25 to 30 materials. Stitching an outwear garment like a jacket would require 40 to 45 types of materials.

Even a simple, humble, mundane button is a complex inventory item. The planner has to determine how many buttons are required for every jacket. Then, he studies the sizes of these buttons. A jacket can have many buttons of varying sizes, i.e. 12 L, or 15 L, or 18 L, etc. Then, the planner reviews the colours of these buttons and the characteristics. A red colour jacket for ladies, may have black or white colour buttons. Then, the planner determines the aggregate requirements of the buttons of various sizes, colours and designs to execute the order.

The manufacturer has to map the various materials, with the garments to be produced. For instance, if the jacket has a zipper, then the type and size of the zipper has to be determined.

Thus, every material (SKU or stock keeping unit), required to produce the jacket has to be planned. The exact requirement of each material has to be calculated. This can be a laborious process.

In the standard SAP process, assessing the requirements of these materials could take about two to three days. The Group has created an automated process in SAP, which compresses this time to just two and half hours. The Group has created a single screen, which identifies the various items and the quantities required. On the basis of this exercise, all the materials and components can be requisitioned from the vendors.

Order Closure Process

When an order for a particular style is completed, the Group prepares an "Order Closure Process Report", which is unique to the organisation. There could be some items of inventories, which may be left over after executing the order. These items have to be accounted for.

The Group ensures a high degree of accountability amongst its professionals. Every order is evaluated independently for its contribution to the bottom-line. The company has a "Net Contribution Analysis" statement. It shows the variances between the budgeted prices and the quantities of materials, with the actual prices and materials consumed.

The statement also shows how much the company has earned per garment produced. All the expenses incurred to produce the garment are included, so that the contribution shown is accurate.

Business Intelligence Reports

In a digital era, top managers are perpetually hungry for more information. However, they are also desperately short of time.

Managers will increasingly appreciate that, less is more. So, the IT team decided to create a platform where all the critical information about the various units, is presented graphically to the top management in a succinct style.

The team listed 40 KPIs (Key Performance Indicators), which are relevant for the business. The KPIs are parameters like sales, gross and net contribution, manufacturing and finance expenses, etc. All the businesses in India and abroad are assessed on these indices.

Deepak can now select multiple KPIs and compare the performance of the various businesses, with a few clicks on his laptop.

The team has developed a platform which presents the information through viewer friendly graphs and pictures. Deepak now does not have to wade through a sea of digits, to understand how any unit is performing.

PGIL is endeavouring to establish a single global platform, to enable the management to review any parameter across units. For instance, a planner may wish to ascertain the manufacturing cost of a skirt in India, Vietnam, Indonesia or Bangladesh. A tap on a laptop, will tell the planner the cost in these locations.

A small team of six IT professionals, sits on the third floor of the office in New Delhi. It coordinates the IT activities and platforms in all countries. The team operates in shifts to cater to businesses in different time zones.

Gaurav extolls the appreciation and support from Deepak and Pulkit to accelerate the various digital initiatives. They ensure that the senior management across countries, support the transformation of the operations, into a digitally managed global business.

27
Story of Lilly & Sid: B2C and Digitisation Venture

Christmas was approaching. However, Emma and Imran, a young couple in London, were flustered. They had trudged the length of Oxford Street thrice, visiting various stores to buy new clothes for their children. However, they could not spot anything that Lilly and Sid, their children would love for Christmas. So, they decided to manufacture some creative clothes on their own. They decided to launch their own children's line of clothing. As the ancient adage proclaims, "Necessity is the mother of invention". A new business and brand, were taking birth.

Emma worked as the design head of a large retailer in the UK. She knew the technicalities of garment production. Imran, her husband and co-founder was an IT professional. This was the perfect combination to introduce a new brand of online clothing for children. They launched their brand in the UK, named it after their children as "Lilly & Sid". Within a decade, the revenues grew to a million pounds.

After a few years, their growth started plateauing with the limited infrastructure and resources. This is when they started scanning for a partnership.

Entering the B2C Segment

About 1,807 kilometres away from London, NorLanka was a PDS company started in 2010, to manage the business in Sri Lanka. It is a supply chain solutions provider to over 25 brands and high-end global retail chains. The value-added solutions provided to customers ranged from design to market research. NorLanka is one of the largest exporters of baby and kids wear, with an annual turnover of over USD 100 million. It ships over 20 million garments every year.

NorLanka has its own factory with about 350 machines and 800 employees, in Thambalagamuwa in Trincomalee district. It also has 30 other factories across Sri Lanka affiliated to it, each having about 300 machines. These factories provide direct employment to over 16,000 workers in the rural areas.

PDS has invested in 1,200 machines in these factories. It shares its knowledge of the craft and its best practices with these factories, thereby augmenting their efficiencies and output. It also guides these factories on improving their safety, hygiene and productivity.

NorLanka augments its own manufacturing capabilities and of its 30 business partners, through continuous research. It believes in the entrepreneurial spirit and drive of the partners.

Joining the Platform

"Lilly & Sid" approached PDS in the late 2019 to join its platform. They had heard of its reputation of providing a springboard to entrepreneurs, for growing their businesses. The Group had always been a business to business player (B2B). However, it was evaluating the business to consumer (B2C) space also.

Pallak turned towards the Group's largest sourcing arm for kids and baby wear, NorLanka. It had done B2B business since its inception. It was one of the largest global exporters in baby and kids wear. The CEO of NorLanka was excited to work with an additional quality brand on the B2C platform. The B2C business would be a new initiative in terms of forward integration. It was new territory for the business.

A Chartered Accountant by profession, Periwal had joined the business 2014. He is the CEO of the Sri Lankan business. He hails from the colourful Indian town, Jaipur in Rajasthan state. After a due diligence, PDS decided to acquire a majority stake in "Lilly & Sid".

"Lilly & Sid" derived multiple synergies when they teamed with PDS. They had access to more designers and quality control processes. As the Group buys many raw materials in bulk for its partners, it gets lower prices. The partners can also access the Platform's technological prowess and data analytics, leading to sharper business decisions. Faster feedback through data analysis also contributes to improved product mixes and inventory management.

"Lilly & Sid" have added new products in the mother and women's categories. These have met with an enthusiastic consumer response. The plan is to launch the brand in Asia and other markets.

NorLanka has expanded its product and customer portfolio. No product contributes more than 30 percent of the total portfolio. Similarly, no customer contributes more than 15 percent to the revenues. NorLanka has worked diligently to ensure that it does not have any concentrated dependencies in the market. It is now expanding its footprint in the USA, Germany, Middle East, China and Australia.

B2C (Business to Consumer): Impact on Margins

The advent of online sales is also leading to a restructuring of margins, between the retailers and the manufactures of apparel. Traditionally, retailers have enjoyed the bulk of the margins. Retailer margins are high, as they incur expenses like store rentals, show room maintenance, displays and floor staff salaries. With online sales augmenting, many such traditional costs of the retailer will disappear. The split of margins between retailers and manufacturers may also get reviewed.

Digitisation Initiative

Cabaraal in Colombo wanted to buy a new mobile phone. He does not have to visit five or six shops to learn about the various models of mobile phones and their prices. He just visits an online portal on his laptop, to assess all the options and prices. Cabaraal saves his time and effort. He also avoids parking hassles. Digital technology now enables Cabaraal to compare models, features and prices of various brands of mobile phones on a single platform.

Online sales of apparel augmented during Covid-19, as brick and mortar shops were shut. The online fashion retailer, Asos in the UK, improved profits by 329 percent in the year ending August 2020. Online sales of casual clothing spiralled during the lockdowns, giving a rollicking boost to the revenues and profits of the online sellers.

There was massive stress among many large retailers who were pure brick and mortar operations. They could not take advantage of online sales during the Covid-19 lockdowns. They had not assimilated the changes in consumer behaviour in their business models. Their revenues dropped sharply. Some businesses rolled down their shutters.

Online businesses are gaining ground, as the option offers many advantages to the consumers. Online companies like Amazon had been growing astronomically worldwide, even before Covid-19. The pandemic triggered a major boom in their revenues.

The concept of a digital platform to enable business, was on PDS's radar for some time. The online boom in sales during Covid-19 accelerated the digitisation drive.

Dizbi Pvt. Ltd. was established as the technology arm and as an independent company on the platform. The initiative is also a forward business integration initiative in IT. The goal is to develop software, digitisation and IT systems, which contribute to the business.

Periwal says, "The name of the company, Dizbi, just came from my head. It is small and catchy. I like it. It is easy to remember. We now have this amazing domain, Dizbi.com. It is a profit centre. All the 20-software staff and developers work full-time in the company. It is an independent company which serves the Group companies as well as external clients."

Dizbi monitors IT solutions, information and research which can benefit the Group. The goal is to make PDS a digital and efficient organisation and also sell its services to external clients.

Deepak laid the foundation of the Group, on an entrepreneurial model of profit sharing.

He chose entrepreneurial business heads, who managed the businesses independently, with profit sharing.

28
A Company of Entrepreneurs

It is a universally acknowledged business fact, that business leaders contribute their best and surmount unscalable hurdles, when their remuneration is linked to their contribution. Gold and glory are great motivators, since time immemorial.

Business is people. Then, for a business to continue blossoming, the people heading the businesses should flourish too. Deepak realised this axiom as early as 1979, just a few years into the garments business. Despite the availability of a mountain of electronic business tools like e-mails, video calls and ERPs, Deepak realised that business is done by people. Eventually, there is no substitute for a businessman, sitting across a customer in London or New York, closing an order. So, Deepak knew he needed partners who ran the business, as owners. He realised that his business philosophy would have to be, "Care and Share", to grow the business rapidly.

Deepak recognised that he could not be present everywhere. He knew he had to empower his CEOs to deliver. Thus, he evolved the unique entrepreneurial model, wherein each CEO managed his own business. The leader could thus prove whether he was ready for more challenging assignments in the Group.

Deepak thus laid the foundation of the Group, on an entrepreneurial model of profit sharing. He chose entrepreneurial business heads, who managed the businesses independently, under his leadership, with profit sharing. His goal was to provide his business partners, with the motivation to excel and earn.

Pankaj Bhasin, the CEO of the woven division, applauds Deepak's vision of the entrepreneurial model, "It has given opportunities to many entrepreneurial leaders to run the businesses as their own. They work on the philosophy of earning, to earn," he says. The philosophy basically means that any CEO can earn as much as he desires, through his incentive programme. He has to keep adding to the wealth of the enterprise, through higher revenues and profits.

"This entrepreneurial culture acts as a huge motivating factor for the people to outperform. They feel that they are the owners of the business," comments Krishna Kanodia, who now works as the CFO, Poeticgem, London.

The entrepreneurial system is an integral part of the culture of the DS Group, (including PDS and PGIL). People do not want to deliver only 100 percent, but 120 percent plus. The leaders see themselves as innovators and creators of wealth, not just pen pushers. The more profit a leader earns for the company, the higher is his share.

Trust: The Glue

The partners are delighted to have a share of the profits of the company without having to invest any money in it. It is also a massive motivation. From being an employee, the entrepreneurial manager is transformed into a profit-sharing partner. Deepak's sons, Pallak and Pulkit have also aggressively adopted the entrepreneurial model for growing their businesses.

Trust is the glue which binds an employee to his leader. Sharing of profits with an employee builds trust. He is assured that he will be aptly and amply rewarded for his endeavours.

Deepak trusts his people, gives them clear directions, shares the profits and maintains good relationships with them. This is the essence of the company's operating philosophy. In this entrepreneurial model, the CEOs become partners. They drive the businesses as if they own them. The CEOs respect Deepak, are loyal to him and deliver their best. This is a key reason why many managers have worked in the Group for decades.

In pioneering the entrepreneurial model, Deepak has also evolved into a businessman, who builds organisations around people. He finds the right people. Then, he lets them build their companies around them, the way they deem fit, so that they can deliver results. Deepak does not build organisations around charts. He builds organisations around leaders.

Nursery of Entrepreneurs

Deepak has transformed the Group into a nursery, for creating budding entrepreneurs. Sanjay Sarkar, says, "We have become a company of entrepreneurs." He has worked with the company from 1997 onwards, after leaving British Oxygen. He learnt two important lessons after joining. First, take ownership of the entire process and achieve the goal. Second, take decisions. The management will overlook a wrong decision. However, inaction is inexcusable. Leaders should not vacillate. They must take decisions and keep the needle moving.

Whilst the business heads have a free hand in managing the business, they work with business plans and budgets, agreed before the year commences. There is continuous guidance available on tap from Deepak, round-the-clock. Any CEO from anywhere in the world, can call him at any time, to seek his views on any subject. Deepak has thus become a consulting interventionist cardiologist. Whenever any business has a blockage of any type in any function, he clears it.

Arjun Puri works as a Director with Kmart Australia, a chain of retail stores, which does business with the Group. He says, "I cannot imagine Deepak sitting with a book in his lap in a corner. He is always on the go. No sooner he finishes one project, he is on the next. Every time I meet him, he comes up with some new ideas. That, is Deepak. He is a high energy person. He values entrepreneurship. He likes to hire a lot of entrepreneurs, for he is an entrepreneur at heart himself. He will recruit anybody who has entrepreneurial ability. Then he will give the potential candidates an opportunity to work for him. He tells them, 'Listen, I will give you a break to be a part of the business. Your entrepreneurship will decide how far you can go in this organisation.' He trusts people a lot. He gives them ample independence. He attracts entrepreneurs, so the business grows. I have seen the Group grow, because he has attracted the appropriate people to the organisation and created a productive traction".

The garment business is fiercely competitive and cost-effective. The Group has not merely survived, but has emerged amongst the top players.

Deepak is 24 by 7 into the business. Close friends say that even when he sleeps, he dreams about shirts and trousers. He keeps himself fully abreast of the developments in the garments industry in India and worldwide. He monitors all aspects of the business. If there are any changes in fashion, design trends, fabrics, production technologies or customer preferences, Deepak would know about it. This deep involvement, earns him the respect of all the entrepreneurial CEOs in the business.

Deepak travels across countries for about 15 to 20 days every month. He travels to markets, talks to customers and employees, to learn how the business is shaping on a constant basis. The "boots on the ground" habit exposes him to developments in the market and the industry on a constant basis. For him, visiting the customers and their retail outlets is akin to online learning.

Encyclopaedia of Knowledge

Gradually over the last five decades, Deepak has become an encyclopaedia of the particles and segments of his business. This micro involvement and knowledge are necessary, as every few months, the Group is either catering to a new customer or a new country.

Deepak takes many risks while investing in new countries. However, he assesses the risks carefully. He always keeps initiatives ready to stay ahead of the curve. When countries like China, Bangladesh, Nepal, Mauritius and Vietnam were developing as supply centres, he was quick to establish factories there.

Deepak had also lived through the quota system, when he was focussed on mastering its nuances. When the quota system was withdrawn, he adapted to a quota-free regime with agility. Later, Deepak realised that the next big challenge would be delivering on the slate of compliances and governances mandated by the customers. So, there have been significant changes, as the business has evolved over the last five decades. However, Deepak and the Group were quick to anticipate these changes and galvanise for them. Thus, besides having a business vision and charismatic personal qualities, it is crucial to remain ahead of trends in an ever-evolving market.

Dr. A. Sakthivel, Chairman of AEPC, says, "I know Deepak from 1990 when he was elected to the AEPC. From then onwards, he has been a good friend and a well-wisher. He is one of the finest gentlemen I have come across, friendly, lovable and helpful to others. Even though he has built a large corporation, he has no airs. He talks to everyone, is very simple in his behaviour and is also admired by the younger generation. He is a role model for companies and exporters in the industry. He started very small and has built an empire now. However, he is still the same person I met, 30 years ago. He is very hard working. Only people close to him can understand his ethic of hard work."

Anand Bhatia joined HoPFL in 1992 as a management trainee, after completing his MBA. He now manages a large factory in Gurugram. He says that Deepak Seth has an aura about him. "Whenever he talks, everyone listens to him. He is an inspiration. After 48 years of work, he is still on his toes 24 hours a day. He expects the same dedication and application from his team. So, after all these decades of working with him, I too have developed the habit of being alert round the clock. Mr. Seth is very sharp."

All the managers know that you do not play cards with Deepak. He sees through every situation lucidly.

Managers who have worked with Deepak for decades opine that he respects honesty and integrity. They say if you have made a mistake and lost a million dollars in a deal, just go to him and own it. He will never talk about it, ever again. However, if you try to cloud or obfuscate the issue, there will be serious ramifications.

Deepak has his business on his fingertips. His teammates show him many charts and statements. However, he already has the figures in his mind. He calculates his monthly profit and loss statement mentally, in his car from the airport to the hotel or from his house to the office. Says Anand Bhatia, "We show him all the sheets in the office, but he already has all the key ratios in his mind."

At the 25th Silver Jubilee anniversary of the company, Deepak presented Anand Bhatia with a Long-Service Award. In his response, Anand said, "He is a fatherly figure for me. I have learnt a lot from him. I feel a part of the business. I learnt from Mr. Deepak Seth the art of management by working on the ground myself. I spend a lot of time on the production floors. I do see all the papers that come to my office. However, I know what is on them. I calculate the figures, as I walk and work on the production floors. This is an art I have learnt from Mr. Seth."

Deepak carries the business with him in his mind. At the monthly review meetings, attended by 12 to 14 senior managers, he knows exactly what questions to ask. If a slide with a hundred figures is shown to him, he will identify the few relevant figures and focus on them. He keeps abreast of all key developments in all the departments, be it production, merchandising or finance.

Many businessmen have a phobia of figures. However, data and spreadsheets do not daunt Deepak. If he gets a statement with 1,000 sets of figures in it, he will know which are the one or two pieces of data to review. He can separate the grain from the chaff. All these personal and professional qualities have earned Deepak the respect of his entrepreneurial partners. They too contribute to making the Group, a company of self-driven entrepreneurs.

"My basic values like honesty and hard work came directly from Papaji. He worked from 7 am to 9 pm or 10 pm, straight 12 to 13 hours daily. He worked on every Saturday and Sunday. He was always travelling for work on every weekend.

I also remember people coming during Diwali to our house to give gifts to Papaji. He would not even meet them.

He would tell the guard, 'I do not want to meet anyone. Do not let anyone with gifts enter the house.'

So, Papaji and his professionalism built the foundation of values in my life."

- Deepak Seth

29
Business Is People

"I cannot let you enter this building," a guard told Deepak at the factory gate in Naraina. "But I have a meeting at 2 pm and need to collect some papers from my office," Deepak told the security guard. "Today is Sunday. The factory is closed. Do you have any identity card?" the guard asked Deepak.

On a Sunday morning at 11 am in 1980, Deepak was completely flummoxed. Normally, he does not get flustered easily. He had to collect some papers and had driven alone to his factory office.

A rather baffled Deepak told the security guard, "Why do I need an identity card? I own this factory, that you are guarding." "That is what you say. Why should I believe you? I have never seen you before," replied the obdurate guard.

Deepak did his best to convince the security guard to let him enter his own office premises. However, the guard was adamant. He did not know Deepak. So, he would not let him enter. There were no mobile phones in 1980. The security guard would not even let Deepak use the landline in his watchman's cabin to make a call. So, Deepak visited an adjoining factory to use their phone, to call the Administration Manager to instruct the guard to open the factory gate for him.

In ten minutes, Deepak returned to his factory to a tearful, profusely apologetic security guard, "Sir, I have just joined a day ago. I did not know you. I have my instructions that I cannot let anyone enter the factory on a Sunday. Hence, I stopped you. Please forgive me."

Deepak was very upset at being barred from entering his own factory. However, he did not say a word to the guard. He merely picked up the papers from his office and left.

On Monday morning, Deepak summoned the security guard to his office. The guard was in a state of panic. He was literally trembling as he entered Deepak's office. Deepak asked him to sit on a chair. "How can I sit in front of you," asked the jittery guard. "Please do," insisted Deepak. The HR manager was also seated in the room. Then, Deepak told the security guard, "I have called you to commend you for your work yesterday. You were absolutely right in preventing me from entering the factory, since you did not know me. So, I am giving you a cash award and also recommending that you should be promoted as security chief for this unit. Thank you, for your commitment."

The security guard was in tears as he left Deepak's office. He had thought that he would be fired. He told the HR Manager, "Aisa sahib aaj tak zindagi me nahi dekha" (I have never seen such a boss in my life).

Transforming Lives

Mamthaj hails from a town called Mandya, with a population of about 1,31,000, in Karnataka state in India. She shifted to Bengaluru in search of a good job. She joined PGIL in 2016 and has been working as a supervisor in the factory since then. Before joining the company, she had worked for 15 years in another garment factory. She has earned a promotion. Her job enables her to lead a balanced personal and professional life. She says that belief in oneself is important, but hard work too, is critical to grow in life. Her goal in life is to continue to work hard and provide a good education to her children. She considers her manager as her role model. He inspires her and she looks up to him.

Far away, Vietnam was developing rapidly into a modern country, after the trauma of the great war from 1 November 1955 to 30 April 1975. Thirty years after the war ended, Nguyen Thi Tuyet started her career as a seamstress in 2005 in Hanoi in PGIL Vietnam. In five years, she was promoted as a "Jumber" (high-skilled seamstress in Vietnam). In 2014, she was promoted as a Line Supervisor. Her production line continues to be one of the most productive, in the factory. Her team members are stable and highly industrious. She married in 2009 and has two children. Her parents-in-law support her, by taking care of her children. She has grown in her job and is also able to balance her family and work.

Happy Employees: Assets

An organisation is the sum total of its leadership, its vision and the people that work in it. Strategy, technology, systems and brands are all vital. However, without good quality and dedicated employees, the best of strategies cannot deliver. Employees who are happy with their work places and who love going to the office every morning, are the real assets of any organisation. Happy employees automatically enhance efficiencies and productivities. The Group provides medical facilities in the factory premises. It also sponsors employee football matches.

The DS Group (Deepak Seth Group, including PDS and PGIL), has endeavoured to make the Human Resources (HR) function an integral and vibrant part of the business. HR is not a mere support function. Wages constitute about 30 percent of the cost of a garment. Therefore, HR plays a vital role in improving productivity and ensuring profitability. Says

Ashutosh Sharma, who heads the HR function, "From the very first day, I realised that my role would be much more than that of conventional HR Manager. It would be a business role." After the interview with Deepak for the job, he realised that he would have to focus on the real business issues.

Learning from Father

The business has a very granular Employees Handbook. It briefs the employees about the company, its values, mission and codes of conduct. It also details the expectations of employee behaviour in the offices and on the factory floors. Under this Code of Conduct, no abuse of any mental or physical nature is accepted in the company. The well-defined "Code of Conduct" is implemented right from the factory floors to the Board room.

Managers are invigorated by the policy of the company to train and develop staff, so that they can be promoted. Promotion from within the Group boosts the morale of the staff. High rewards to star performers also motivate the young and ambitious staff.

Women constitute the major part of the labour force in the garments industry. Row after row of women working on sewing machines, is a common sight in any garment factory in the world. Whilst men undertake the cutting and sampling tasks, women handle the stitching and embroidery work. It is very important in factories to ensure that employees observe protocols and keep their distances to avoid any instance of eve teasing or harassment. These proactive steps to preserve the dignity of all the employees, have added to the reputation of the Group as a happy place to work.

Deepak imbibed the values and principles to manage the business from his own father, Mr. M. L. Seth. He says, "Papaji was a great professional. Lala Charat Ram was his boss. Lalaji had a formidable reputation as a tough taskmaster. My best education came from talking to Papaji. It was a fantastic education. I was inspired. My basic values like honesty and hard work came directly from Papaji. He worked from 7 am to 9 pm or 10 pm, a straight 12 to 13-hour day. He worked on every Saturday and Sunday. He was always travelling for work on every weekend. I also remember people coming during Diwali to our house to give gifts to Papaji. He would not even meet them. He would tell the guard, 'I do not want to meet anyone. Do not let anyone with gifts enter the house.' So, Papaji and his professionalism built the foundation of values in my life."

Laws of Lands

The Group ensures that it complies with all the laws of the land, in all the countries it operates in. It ensures timely payment of all statutory dues like the provident fund, Employees' State Insurance and gratuity.

As the garments industry is very labour intensive, the labour unions are usually very strong. It is common for the labourers to complain or protest, if they are treated unfairly. The DS Group employing about 30,000 people, endeavours to ensure that all employees are always treated humanely. Thus, over the years, the company has built a reputation as an organisation which cares for its workers, women and the underprivileged. As a result of these proactive steps, there has never been a strike by the workers.

The garments industry is a tough, cost-effective business. An exporter can lower the prices, to secure an order and keep the top-line growing. However, without margins and a strong bottom-line, the top line is meaningless. So, just giving discounts is not the panacea to managing the business in the garments industry. The ingredients of success in the business are loyal customers and vendors, thrifty purchasing and financial prudence. Humane HR practices, are a critical component of the recipe for success.

Fruit Salad and Rigorous Work

It takes a lot of HR work behind the scenes, to make an organisation humane and dynamic. A fruit salad is a delightful dish to view and eat. However, it takes several hours to prepare the dish. Each fruit has to be cleaned, peeled and cut. Then the seeds have to be extracted. Next, each piece of the fruit has to be placed alluringly in a fascinating format. Then, the collection has to be garnished and embellished with dried fruits, cherries, cream or ice-cream. Finally, the collection has to be plated.

So, managing a company with a vibrant HR function involves detailed work in processes and systems. The organisation structure has to be clear and known to all the managers. Intentions and plans have to be reduced to policy manuals so that roles and responsibilities are clear.

The Group agrees Key Result Areas (KRAs) with the senior leadership team. The incentives of all the managers are linked to their KRAs. This ensures a performance-oriented culture.

Early in his career, Deepak had realised the importance of frugality in the cost-effective and highly competitive garments industry. He always frowned on overtime payments, unless they were strictly necessary to execute an order on schedule.

In 1979, he had observed the high cost of manufacture in one of the production units in Naraina, Delhi. After analysis, he tracked it down to the inordinate overtime being paid to the workers. So, he paid a few brisk visits to the factory in the nights to check on the work. He discovered that some of the supervisors and their workers were sleeping in the nights and claiming overtime. When the workers realised that Deepak was making surprise visits to the factories in the nights, the overtime costs evaporated.

Now, Deepak and his managers do not need to visit the factories in the nights to check on overtime costs. The costing of the garments is computerised to the last cent. The teams which operate within budgets, earn higher incentives.

Careers, Not Jobs

There is a significant advantage in recruiting people early in their careers, in the garment industry. People who work on the production floor, refine their skills over decades. There are not many schools or colleges which teach garment manufacturing, washing, pressing or packing. A skills development programme in the company ensures that young aspirants are recruited, trained and motivated to stay with the business. The Group motto is, "We do not merely offer jobs; we offer careers."

Learning and Development Culture

Organisations prosper when its employees grow. Motivated, ever-learning, energetic employees are keen on advancing their careers. They make companies prosperous. In pursuing their own goals, they add to the wealth of the business too. The

Group has developed a culture of cheering learning and development among its employees, at all levels in the business.

The Group has many initiatives to encourage learning and development among its staff. The goal is to enhance management skills and workforce productivity.

30
Training for Leadership and Growth

It is an unwritten axiom that people like to progress in their lives. Every person wants tomorrow to be better than today or yesterday. The DS Group provides regular training to all employees to enhance their skills. PGIL has established skill development centres in Chennai and Bengaluru, for the staff. Training is imparted in the classroom and also on the job, where the supervisors guide the staff.

iLEAD (Leadership Development Programme)

The Group's iLEAD programme is designed to develop the leadership skills of managers. It covers coaching in four sections, "Learn, Engage, Accelerate and Disrupt".

The programme crafts individual development plans for potential leaders and provides them with professional counselling. It consists of four modules that groom a manager to lead himself, his team and a business. The duration of the programme is 11 months. There are regular reviews to assess the effectiveness of the programme.

Managers at the middle level are trained in influencing others and building effective teams. They also receive regular coaching and mentoring.

SEED for Supervisors

There is also a "Skill Enhancement and Employee Development" (SEED) programme for supervisors in operational roles. The six-month programme is designed to enhance the capabilities and productivities of supervisors. The programme fosters leadership skills, to groom supervisors for promotions to managerial positions. The 15 modules are designed to improve an employee's understanding of himself and develop self-confidence. It fosters a "buddy system". Team members and colleagues motivate and guide each other for effective performance. The career progression programme trains supervisors in the company to evolve into managers. After completion of the programme and a thorough assessment, about 10 percent of the supervisors, are promoted to managerial positions.

Global HR Management System

To bond all employees across countries, PGIL has launched "Pearl ONE", a human resource management system (HRMS). It has partnered with a company that provides digitised HR solutions. With this digitised platform, employees can connect to the HR department with any queries.

PGIL also has a campus hiring and on-boarding programme, called "Aarambh" (Start) to select bright candidates and build their leadership skills.

Workers Engagement Platform

PGIL has also launched a "WE: Workers Engagement Platform". This is an android-based mobile solution. The application enables real-time communication and engagement with all the employees. The versatile mobile platform engages workers constructively and enables instant communication.

The in-house developed platform, provides information, which a worker may need daily. It provides quick access to training manuals, government schemes, ethics helpline, emergency contacts, etc.

Roshan Lal works in the laundry section of the factory in Gurugram. The platform tells him the training programme he has to attend during the day. The platform also tells him all the government schemes he can avail of. For instance, he can access his Aadhar Identification card, Ayushman Bharat Yojana (free healthcare scheme of the Government of India), Employees State Insurance status, Provident Fund balance, etc. A single click gives the worker access to all his personal data.

The managers or supervisors can send information and announcements to their workers, through the mobile platform. Videos promoting learning and skills enhancement are also disseminated. The application is multilingual and can also be deployed to conduct worker surveys.

Human Resource Information Platform

The Group is also working to bring the entire human resource operation under a single technological umbrella. This will integrate the Human Resources function with the business operations and provide information on all HR matters.

"My Voice", Global Ethics Helpline

The Group is now a global operation operating in 22 countries. The employees in these countries need a confidential forum, to express their grievances or any issues that bother them. Through the "My Voice" facility, any employee at any level, in any unit, can report any unethical event, without revealing his identity. The company has launched "My Voice" to ensure transparency and confidentiality in dealings with all employees.

This is a third-party toll-free ethics helpline for the workforce. It is managed by "Intouch", which operates 24 by 7, all 365 days in the year. Any employee can use it to report any unethical practice, violation of code of conduct, redressal of grievance, breach of law, etc. Employees can raise issues without disclosing their identities. This is a multilingual platform, connecting all the units worldwide.

The complaints are forwarded to the Chief Ethics Officer. The Chief Ethics Officer assigns these issues to nominated persons for review. There is no interference in the work of the Chief Ethics Officer. This process ensures transparency. Thus, the company partners with its employees and vendors who want to support it, against any violation of the code of business.

"Simpliance": Online Compliance Tool

Compliances in the garment industry have increased manifold. The Group's policy is to ensure that all compliances are adhered to. It has launched "Simpliance", an online compliance tool. Its dashboard sends monthly alerts on recurring compliances to all the business units. The units can upload documents pertaining to registrations, licenses, inspection reports and certificates on this site. "Simpliance" also sends compliance scores to the units.

P.A.C.E - Empowering Women

There is also a special initiative to empower women employees. The "Personal Advancement and Career Enhancement" (P.A.C.E.) programme encourages women to improve their performance at work. The sessions discuss nutrition, health, family planning, HIV awareness, etc. The programme has led to an increase in morale, reduction in absenteeism and improved the quality of life of the women employees.

Training Rural Youth

The business participates in a programme to create a regular supply of skilled workers to manage the operations. The "Deen Dayal Upadhyaya Grameen Kaushalya Yojana" or DDU-GKY, is a Government of India rural youth employment scheme. PGIL has partnered with the Ministry of Rural Development (MoRD) and the Ministry of Textiles (MoT), to manage skill development programmes for village youth. The Group has established a mechanism to oversee the training of youngsters in the villages.

After completion of the three-month training period, the participants are offered employment in PGIL factories. The programme contributes to a steady supply of skilled workers for the company.

The 5S Initiative

PGIL has piloted the 5S Japanese management philosophy in the Gurugram factory. This method uses five Japanese words to manage a manufacturing workplace. These five words are: Sort, Set in order, Shine, Standardise and Sustain. The application of this system helps a company to reduce waste, minimise costs and improve employee commitment.

Insurance Benefits

Employees are the key strength of a business. PGIL insures all its employees in India through a range of policies to ensure their protection. The employees have life, medical and accident insurances. The policies also cover the employee's parents and immediate families.

"Great Place to Work" Survey

The company participated in an employee survey organised by the "Great Place to Work" Institute. Employees provided feedback about the culture of their work places. Such studies help management to refine policies to build trust with staff.

Wellness Initiatives

The Group also fosters mental peace and tranquillity at work. The PGIL Vietnam business conducted a workshop on

"Positive Living and Harmonising Relationships" at its factory. It provided tools and exercises to the staff to keep calm during work. The meeting covered basics like a positive way to start a new day, the art of observation and transforming complaints into opportunities.

Fostering Self-Development

The business provides a great learning ground. Managers and staff have the opportunity to understand the entire value chain in PGIL. Then, they are free to contribute, through new ideas and suggestions. In many large organisations with established systems, managers follow set protocols and precedents. In the company, the systems are defined, but there is ample opportunity for the enterprising manager to innovate. "The sky is the limit in terms of rewards and recognition, if you are a committed person," says Captain Vinod Vaish.

A HR executive comments, "There is tremendous learning to evolve as an HR leader. However, more important, the Group helps you to evolve into a business leader." The younger recruits are inspired, that their senior colleagues have worked in the business for 30 years and built careers.

The Group has evolved into a result-oriented organisation, due to its focus on delivery. Results matter. Whether it is a business, a manufacturing unit, a services department or a support services function, the ultimate result is crucial.

Deepak encourages his business heads to interact proactively with the local environment. He himself is not shy of networking with local government officials, when necessary. A PGIL factory manager recalls that some contractors were in collusion with the local strongmen. The latter were trying to control the local labour. This was impacting the factory operations. When Deepak learnt about it, he immediately briefed the HR Director to talk to the local police to resolve the issue.

Whilst being humane and caring, Deepak can be tough and demanding, should the situation arise. “One bad fish can spoil the pond,” he counsels all the departmental heads. Deepak tells them that it is their call to develop an employee who is not delivering. He insists on fair and just treatment of all employees. He has a heart of gold and cares deeply about his employees.

Captain Vinod Vaish who has worked with the Group since 2009, extols Deepak’s habit of taking rapid decisions. He says, “When I telephone Mr. Deepak Seth for some decision, I get it within two minutes. He does not delay any matter. He is often in the USA or Europe. The time difference is irrelevant. It may be day or night. You can text him. You can WhatsApp him. You get a decision immediately.”

People Commitment

The deep-rooted commitment to people, quality and success, mingles with the blood stream of the people who work in the Group. It becomes a part of their DNA. Even if some of them leave, they fondly reminisce their working days. Quite a few seek a re-entry. Deepak and his team never hold it against the returnees and welcome them back with open arms. Deepak’s stint at the HR department of ITC had taught him many lasting lessons. One key lesson was that every person in the company has to be viewed as a friend or a colleague and held close to the heart.

Over the last five decades, the DS Group has built a reputation for professional management, equitable treatment of staff and care for the employees. It is a preferred place of employment in the apparel industry, luring some of the best talent in the apparel industry.

Pulkit's Futuristic Leadership

Pulkit too has developed an eye for detail, like his father. His leadership style inspires his managers and staff. "You can storm Pulkit with 100 e-mails. You can be sure, he will reply to every e-mail. Again, you may load him with 150 bullet points on WhatsApp. He will separate the grain from the chaff and will reply to the relevant points. He can differentiate information from data," comments a senior PGIL manager.

The manager adds, "Pulkit sometimes takes a decision that seems untimely today. However, he knows that the decision is best when you look forward, five to ten years into the future. The investments in the PGIL factories are examples of planning for the future." This futuristic view, keeping growth as the guiding light, makes the business a dynamic place to work in.

An organisation is defined very substantially by the style of leadership of the top management. Deepak is a charismatic leader due to his passion, knowledge of the business and his quick decision-making. He is complimented in PGIL by Pulkit's process-driven style. Pulkit believes in a buy-in by all the stakeholders. He likes his team to generate options. Then, he chooses the best route forward. Deepak, Pallak and Pulkit are always approachable, whenever any manager has any issue to discuss.

The PGIL team bonds with Pulkit due to his youthfulness and his belief in collective decision-making. They do not have to dilute their views; they can talk to him heart-to-heart. He gives everybody an opportunity to speak. The HR team enjoys the consultative process. Pulkit is a highly method-oriented leader. He has his own views. Yet, during a meeting he goes around the table and asks each person, "What do you think is the best option for our business? The best way forward?"

Inspiring Managers: Diligence and Stamina

Deepak's own commitment and his diligence inspire his team members. He literally works in a virtual environment in multiple time zones. He returns from London and goes straight into a meeting in Delhi. After attending a review meeting, he takes a flight to Bangladesh to inaugurate a new factory. Later, he travels to Hong Kong to meet a customer. Then, Deepak heads back to India for a vendor meeting. He holds meetings at his home also over the weekends.

Deepak does not know the meaning of jet lags or time zones. If there is a meeting, he is there, irrespective of the time or the country. Younger members of his team are impressed with his energy and his balanced management of family, work and health. His wife Payel adds, "Deepak can travel 12 to 14 hours on a flight and then drive straight to a meeting. He does not need to go home to rest after a long flight. He refreshes on the flight itself. At the airport, he gets into a car and drives straight to the office."

Deepak is also admired for his immense stamina. Says one manager, "When we return from an overseas trip, on landing, we prefer to go home first. After resting for 30 to 45 minutes, we proceed to the office. Nobody drives straight from the airport to the office. However, Mr. Seth goes directly to the office. He may be returning at 9 am or 3 pm. The flights from the UK and USA to Delhi are of 10 to 20 hours duration. Deepak's house is between the airport and the office. Yet, he visits the office first."

Deepak Seth is now a legend in the garment export industry. Due to his vast experience, he is considered a fountain of knowledge. Captain Vinod Vaish adds, "You go to him with an issue. He has the acumen to identify the problem immediately, due to his sharp intellect and experience."

Captain Vinod Vaish observes that Pallak and Pulkit have inherited Deepak's discipline and work habits. He says, "The two sons are following in the footsteps of their father. In nine years, Pulkit has matured and has taken the business to a new level. He thinks 10 to 15 years from today. He told me to go to the interior states and buy 10 to 20 acres of land for a mega-factory. There is also a constant focus on ethical practices and the welfare of the employees. Whenever I sit with the Chairman or his two sons, I learn something new from their vast experiences."

"Pearlites": Alumni Network

There is a very strong, though informal, alumni network. Every day, the HR department receives at least two to five applications, from ex-Pearlites who want to re-join. HR has created the term "Pearlites". It is the name for anyone who works in the Group, irrespective of whether the person is yet employed or has left.

There is thus, a brand value in working with the Group.

31
Laxmi's Story and Developing the Hinterland

Laxmi is the daughter of a farm labourer in Jharkhand. She attended the village school and studied till the eighth standard. Her attendance in school was erratic due to the frequent violence in the Naxalite area (zones prone to intense violence due to armed and militant insurgencies). Her parents were reluctant to let her travel to school, petrified for her safety. However, Laxmi was keen to have a productive life. She did not want to squander her life toiling as a labourer, on a landowner's farm. Life is a gift from God, she thought. She did not want to waste it.

Laxmi's school teacher heard that a garments company was opening a factory in the state and was recruiting youngsters to work in it. However, the selected candidates would have to travel to Delhi and undergo training for some months. They would be paid a stipend during the period, which would cover all costs and ensure some savings.

For Laxmi, this was a godsend opportunity. However, she had never stepped outside her village in her life. She only knew her parent's dilapidated one-room house and the ramshackle village school. Her parents would not even think of their daughter going out alone to a big city like Delhi and living among strangers. Finally, they relented when they heard that the company, would be taking care of all the arrangements in Delhi. Moreover, there would be other girls from Jharkhand who would be participating in the programme. The clinching factor in making the parents agree was that after the training, all the girls would return to Jharkhand. They would work in a garment factory being established by PGIL.

So, Laxmi joined a group of youngsters from Jharkhand, to be trained at PGIL's Skill Centre in Gurugram. There, they would train her for three months, of which one month would be "On-the-Job Training" (OJT). After this stint, the interns would be placed in the factories with a salary.

Life Changing Experience

Laxmi and her teammates, will progressively upgrade themselves from an unskilled category of workers to semi-skilled workers. Finally, they will get trained to become fully skilled workers. Their remuneration will improve, as their skills enhance. Then, Laxmi will be able to send some money to her parents and siblings every month. When the factory commences production in Jharkhand, Laxmi and her teammates will be transferred to work there.

Thus, an entire stratum of society is lifted upwards in terms of skills, incomes and social mobility, due to the company's internship programme. It is a new beginning, for a new generation.

The interns get exposure to living in a large city like Delhi and get trained. They also garner a Certificate from the Ministry of Rural Development (MoRD). Laxmi and her friends from a tribal village, will earn a livelihood and also contribute to their families. PGIL manages similar programmes in Chennai and Bengaluru cities, with batches of 35 lady candidates each.

Cities like Mumbai, Delhi, Chennai and Kolkata lure workers from across various states in India to work in factories.

Typically, states and towns which are industrially developed, attract workers from states like Bihar, Uttar Pradesh, Jharkhand, Chhattisgarh and West Bengal. Industrial development has been relatively slower in some of these states.

These states are now focussed on improving their prosperity by encouraging investments in industry. Local labourers migrated to work in large cities, outside their own state. Now, they are finding it possible to secure employment in their own states.

If a local worker can earn Rs. 8,000 (USD 107) per month in a factory in Jharkhand, he will opt to stay in his own home state. Even if he earns Rs. 12,000 (USD 160) to Rs. 12,500 (USD 167) per month in a large city like Gurugram, he would prefer to stay in his hometown in Jharkhand. In Gurugram, he would have to spend Rs. 6,000 (USD 80) for a room and food on a shared basis. So, he would be left with just Rs. 6,000 (USD 80) to Rs. 6,500 (USD 87) per month. This is less than what he would earn at home, where his accommodation would be free. Moreover, at home he can spend time with his family, relatives and friends.

Return to the Countryside

In Indian states like Chhattisgarh, the local government is giving a fillip to industrialisation and construction projects. Local labourers increasingly prefer to work in their own home states. So, workers from the eastern states of India, may gradually be reluctant to work in large cities like Gurugram, Mumbai, Bengaluru or Chennai, due to the high costs of living.

The larger cities like Bengaluru in the South of India are also short of workers. PGIL had to recruit 110 workers from other states like Madhya Pradesh and Jharkhand and bring them to work in their Bengaluru factory. These workers are provided with dormitories. Their accommodation is in the proximity of the factory, to reduce commuting time. The company is running this pilot to study its impact on productivity, morale and absenteeism.

Employers in India will increasingly have to adopt the Middle East model of employment. The companies which bring the workers from other states, may have to provide a holistic life to the workers including accommodation and medical benefits.

In the future, labour-intensive industries like garment factories, will increasingly shift to smaller towns or the economically slow, but ambitious states. Minimum wages will continue to increase in major metro towns like Delhi, Chennai and Bengaluru due to higher costs of living and rentals. Fashion garments which have higher margins could be manufactured in factories based in the cities. However, the manufacturing of garments with low margins, may gradually shift to smaller, low-cost towns.

The foray into the regional hinterland to set up garment factories, will also contribute to economic development in these areas. Industrial activity in the semi-rural areas generates employment, incomes and lifestyle-changes. As the local people get more cash in their hands, they spend more on food, hygiene and education. They also spend more on communication devices like mobile phones and internet.

Thus, the strategy of PGIL, to expand beyond established hubs like Gurugram, Chennai and Bengaluru will generate development and progress in the interiors of the states.

Make in India, 2014

The establishment of various factories by PGIL, was in consonance with the call given by the Prime Minister of India, Mr. Narendra Modi, to "Make in India". The initiative was launched in 2014 to encourage companies to manufacture in India. The goal was to transform India into a global design and manufacturing hub. The Group's apparel manufactured in India and abroad, were already being sold in retail outlets across the world.

Indian Leadership, Garments

The strategy of expanding in the hinterland of India will pay dividends in the long run. Rising costs and weak infrastructure in some key garment manufacturing countries, will propel India as a lead country for manufacturing garments.

For instance, Bangladesh is handicapped by infrastructure issues like the weak availability of power and road networks. Sending a truck from Gazipur to Chittagong port, a distance of about 270 kilometres, could take six to ten hours due to road congestions. If there is a major roadblock, the truck could take even three days. In Vietnam, the minimum wages are rising. The labour in the country prefers to work in the high-paying electronics industry. So, establishing a footprint in the regional hinterlands, could provide a strong competitive edge to PGIL in the future.

A shift of industries to the developing states in India, could result in lower costs of production. Governments in these states are offering incentives, tax concessions, subsidies, etc., to lure corporations. Costs of living and labour are also lower than those in metropolitan towns. So, production of garments in low-cost states, may provide a very strong competitive advantage to India in the global markets.

32
Sharing and Caring for People

Roopesh Kumar was very apprehensive. He had just been diagnosed with cancer. He had married a few years ago and had a young daughter named Alka. Now, cancer can be a life-changing ailment. There are always deep concerns about how the family will manage the situation. Sitting at his desk in the Merchandising division in 2002, Roopesh wondered what the future had in store for him. His biggest concern was losing his job, due to prolonged absences during treatment. Then, he would be financially pressed for money to get treated and to look after his family.

Roopesh's treatment lasted an entire year. He took days off, for the chemotherapy treatment. However, no salary deductions were made for the days he was absent. He could not attend to his office duties regularly, due to the hospital visits. However, nobody said anything to him. Deepak had given a clear brief, "Roopesh has to be rendered all assistance. No deductions will be made for his leave days. He should receive full support." So, Roopesh was given adequate time and resources to get himself treated.

Next, Roopesh had to pay all his hospital bills. The insurance company would settle his claims only after getting all the bills. Roopesh needed the cash to settle his hospital bills. Again, Deepak instructed that an advance be paid to Roopesh. "Mr. Seth was like a deity who saved my family and me, at a very difficult time in my life," he says. Roopesh continues to work in the company.

The mother of another manager Ashok, went through a serious health problem. She was hospitalised. Ashok would rush to the hospital at odd times during working hours. Deepak told him to take any leave that he needed to care for his mother. Ashok just needed to send an SMS or a WhatsApp message to Deepak to inform him, that he was leaving for the hospital. He was not required to take any official leave, during the visits to the hospital to tend to his mother.

Ever sensitive to his team, Deepak learnt in 2002 that the new managers were being recruited at market salaries. However, some of the more senior employees who had joined earlier, felt that their salaries had not kept pace. Deepak immediately called a meeting of the senior managers from all the departments, including HR, banking, shipping, administration, etc. After listening to them, he refurbished their remuneration packages.

Vinod Nair, who works on the personal staff of Deepak, owns a two-wheeler. This was convenient during the weekdays to travel to his office in 2005. However, over the weekend, his wife and son desired to visit the malls to shop, see a movie or just have an ice-cream. His two-wheeler could not seat the entire family. He was reflecting on how to manage the situation. Finally, he made up his mind to buy a small Maruti car, so that his family could enjoy the weekends. He did not want to seek a loan from the banks. The monthly instalments and the interest would weigh on him. He decided to seek a loan from the company.

When Deepak heard about Nair's request, he advised him, "Why do you want to waste your money on buying a car? You need a car just for the weekends to take your family out. So, every Friday evening, you take one of the office cars with you to your home. You use it for the weekend and bring it back with you on Monday mornings. This way you will have access to a car over the weekends, without having to take a loan to buy it." Nair was delighted to have a company car for his personal use over the weekends.

During the chat with Nair, Deepak realised that his wife, Mrs. Nair was a qualified teacher. He offered her a job in the Group's Little Pearls schools.

Deepak spends a lot of time with new management recruits, ensuring that they are well-inducted and comfortable. During one of these interactions with new youngsters, he enquired why they had changed jobs. He learnt that many of them had left their previous employers, because they had not been paid their salaries for some months. He was shocked. Deepak ensures that salaries are always paid on time in the Group.

Captain Vinod Vaish asserts that there has not been a single instance, when the salaries of the employees were delayed.

Whilst Deepak can be humane in a deserving situation, he can be exacting too, if necessary. Alok a driver, would receive Deepak from Delhi airport, whenever he returned from abroad. On one such occasion in 1993, when Deepak returned at 3 am, Alok was not at the airport. Deepak could not even call him, for mobile phones came much later to the world. He walked up and down the terminal for about 45 minutes, searching for Alok. Finally, he hailed a taxi and went home.

In the morning, Deepak called Alok and asked him why he had not come to the airport. Alok replied, "Sir, I was at the airport. Somehow, I missed you."

Deepak was fuming. "How could you not see me?" he asked. Then Deepak got into his car with another driver and drove straight to Alok's home. He asked Alok's mother, "Auntie, where was Alok yesterday night?" Now, she did not know that

Alok had told Deepak that he was at the airport. So, she relied truthfully, "Sir, he was at home, sleeping the entire night."

Deepak's initiative to suddenly visit Alok's house and talk to his mother, sent a clear message to the other employees from the office staff to the managers, do not bluff. If you have made a mistake, tell the truth. Alok was let off with a reprimand. Sharma from the Accounts department opines, "Mr. Seth knows who is doing what, in the company."

Vineet Mathur had joined the business in India, with a time framework of about six months, after returning from Dubai, in 1993. He had done a stint with the DS Group in Dubai, as a Finance Manager. He was now looking for a role in finance in India. Deepak offered him the position of Senior Finance Manager. His mission was to restructure the accounting and finance departments. Vineet thought that he would complete the tasks within six months.

The proposed six-month plan, elongated into an 18-year long career. Over those years, Vineet grew and was promoted to Group Financial Controller.

Two factors contributed to Vineet working for 18 years, against the planned six months. First, Vineet realised that the Group was in a growth mode. He saw that Deepak was a very dynamic entrepreneur and had ambitious goals. Vineet also observed that Deepak was a bit discontented, as his vision was not getting delivered. Second, Deepak built organisations around people. When he realised that Vineet was keen to work abroad and planned to move to New Zealand, he transferred him to London. "That probably kept me going," explains Vineet.

Deepak is also known to be a very caring employer by his staff. A departmental head recalls that when his father-in-law passed away, Deepak was not in the country. However, on returning to India, Deepak went straight from the airport to the employee's house to meet his family and comfort them. Says the manager, "I have never seen an owner of a large business visit the house of an employee, just to offer his condolences."

Open Door Policy

Sundeep Chatrath walked determinedly into Deepak's office. He was not happy with the prices of a fabric that they were using. He thought that the company was paying a much higher price, than it should be. Deepak immediately told him to get fresh quotes. When he found the market prices lower than the prices that they were paying, he immediately changed the supplier.

Sundeep was impressed with Deepak's quick actions. He says, "Normally, owners of businesses do not go into rigorous detail, nor do they decide so fast. Managers know that Mr. Seth takes swift decisions and acts very fast. Whenever I visit the Chairman and tell him I have a small suggestion, he responds immediately by saying, 'Nothing is small. Tell me everything in detail.' He gives me his full attention and takes me very seriously. For me, this is a big learning."

Every employee from a newly employed worker to a full-time director, can walk into Deepak's room without an appointment. He can suggest how to improve a process or the business. He can even express his unhappiness on any issue. Deepak's doors are always open to any staff member, however junior he may be.

A quality which impresses Deepak's team, is that he does not have any ego.

Surender Dhillon adds, "Mr. Seth could be meeting a peon, a clerk or a director. He greets everyone with the same respect and affection. Personality is not defined just by qualification or affluence. How you meet people, how promptly you respond, how you celebrate events, how good a host you are, all define the personality of an individual. Success is admirable, but it is also necessary to be a good human being. Mr. Seth excels in all humane qualities." Managers find Deepak to be a very positive and approachable leader.

Deepak has a special bond with the factory workers. He himself learnt garment production on the factory floors. When he started thc business in 1976, he spent many days and nights on the floors with the tailors. He learnt how the fabrics are cut and stitched. He saw how the garments are washed, pressed, packed and despatched. In the nights, Deepak would go home for a quick dinner to his house in Vasant Vihar. Then, he would return to the factory at 1 am and stay there until 5 am, with the production workers. Those days being on the factory production floors, gave him granular knowledge of garment production, fabrics, buttons, threads, etc.

It was during those long nights in the factories, that Deepak developed respect for the floor workers. He saw their dedication and commitment first-hand, toiling in the nights to ensure that the shipment left on schedule. Hence, Deepak's doors are always open to any factory worker on the production floors.

33
Battling the Covid-19 Pandemic

The hurricane of Covid-19 in late 2019, brought the world to a complete halt. It was the biggest crisis that the world has faced since World War II. It disrupted lives comprehensively. Never was the world collectively bruised as horribly, as during Covid-19. Millions died due to the pandemic, unemployment reigned and fear stalked human beings. Isolation and loneliness lead to widespread depression.

PDS's three principles comprising of trust, people and partnerships, were all tested during the Covid-19 pandemic. Pallak says, "Our focus has always been sound risk management and financial prudence. This has contributed to our navigating the turbulent Brexit and the USA-China trade war. Then, Covid-19 brought the world to a grinding halt. We managed the Covid-19 turbulence also."

Pulkit and his senior managers, sat tense and anxious in their conference room, in Gurugram in early March 2020. Covid-19 was threatening to shut down the entire world. There were complete or partial lockdowns in Europe and the USA.

Covid-19 was a hard-hitting phase for all retailers. The best retail markets in the world had rolled down their shutters. All the top retailers of the world, who were the customers of the DS Group, had to shut their stores, due to the lockdowns. No cash was coming in, except through online sales. This was normally about 15 percent of the pre-Covid-19 sales. Most retailers cancelled all their pending orders in the last fortnight of March 2020. They stopped the exporters from shipping goods. This was the peak season of shipping for Indian exporters, as the bulk of the summer fashion merchandise is shipped in March.

Many retailers also stopped payments for the goods that had been delivered to them previously. Payments due in the month of March 2020 were also halted. The customers unilaterally increased the credit periods. Normally, retailers paid on delivery or between 30 and 60 days after shipping. These terms were elongated to 90 to 180 days due to Covid-19. This added to the woes of exporters, resulting in negative cash flows.

Thousands of containers were being packed at the factories. And, thousands of containers were at the ports, waiting to be loaded on ships. They all stood stranded.

"Blood Bath" on Streets

The stoppage of shipments had a cascading impact, as the goods being produced in the factories could not move out. The entire supply chain ground to a halt. Along with the supply chain, the cash flows also dried up. Many export companies and factories ran out of cash.

In the last week of March, the governments in India and Bangladesh also declared fierce nationwide lockdowns. They were struggling to stem the spread of Covid-19 infections.

This came as a shock to the manufacturers, who were already reeling under the blow of cancelled orders from their customers. Raw material supplies from China were also delayed. Manufacturing units were struggling. The DS Group was reviewing how to manage the cash flows due to the abrupt cancellations of shipments. Now, the Group had to deal with the second tremor of lockdowns within a week.

"It was a blood bath on the streets," summed up a leading garment exporter. The exporters could not do anything. Some retailers, who had inordinate debts, declared bankruptcies. Debts are fatal, in a downturn.

Deepak, Pallak and Pulkit, were determined to ensure the safety and continuance of all operations, despite all odds. Deepak's axiom had always been, "Every time the business goes through a problematic patch, learn to unlock new opportunities." This adage, became the "mantra" for the Group.

Thus, as the world went into a lockdown in 2020, many large retailers across the world cancelled orders or sought order pushbacks. The Group too had these issues. PDS losses aggregated to USD 70 million. However, due to its stringent financial disciplines, strong risk management policies and policy of insuring credit accounts, the business took only marginal credit hits.

The financial impact from the pushbacks and cancelled orders was also buffered due to the diversified customer base. PDS has around 200 customers, comprising of retailers, hypermarkets, etc. No customer contributes more than 15 percent of the business. Having a large basket of customers helped the company to buffer market shocks. The business also has a diversified country presence. The UK is its largest market, contributing around 40 percent of the business. Bangladesh is the largest sourcing country, contributing 45 percent of the supplies.

Salvaging the relationship with the Group's top customers was the vital priority. Pallak says that many retailers like Asda's

George, Tesco, Primark, Sainsbury's and Next acted responsibly despite the menacing times of Covid-19.

Covid-19 War Room

The DS Group (including PDS and PGIL), literally established a War Room to manage the Covid-19 fallouts in the various operating units. Deepak positioned himself in London. Pallak shifted to Hong Kong. Pulkit operated from India and Dubai. Deepak, Pallak and Pulkit were in touch with their senior management teams 24 by 7, assessing the situation and improvising solutions.

Covid-19 led to a sharp decline in sales of traditional brick and mortar outlets. Many retailers with loss of sales to online operators, were reducing manpower and costs. Large retail customers requested suppliers to supply basic products as required, without confirmed advance orders. For instance, an exporter may be producing millions of pieces of jeans. The customers wanted the manufacturer to store the jeans for them, without advance orders. When the stores run out of a particular size or colour of jeans, the retailer will place an order and expect prompt replenishment.

Deepak had given a clear brief to the management teams. First, keep operating expenses in line with revenues in the next few quarters. Second, ensure zero impact of the crisis on the net worth of the business in the balance sheet. All operating decisions would be taken, within these two parameters.

When the impact of Covid-19 hit the global markets, Deepak took some quick decisions. He realised that sourcing fabrics from China would be difficult, so he explored options in India,

Bangladesh, etc. He knew that many of his large customers in Europe and USA would slacken orders due to lockdowns, so he offered goods to his customers at attractive prices.

The Group factories also started manufacturing masks and PPE (Personal Protective Equipment) suits. Deepak also started planning for the next season. Many companies were flummoxed on how to handle the pandemic. Deepak started planning and executing for the next phase, post the pandemic.

Battling Covid-19

The Group focussed on dialogues with all the suppliers to defer supplies of raw materials for some time. It also opened channels of communication with customers to understand their financial health.

The Group's offices in many countries had to remain closed because of the lockdowns. The factories were quiet. The warehouses were isolated. There was an eerie silence in the business.

However, the staff was busy working from their homes. Their laptops, Wi-Fis and phones were always at work. The teams laboured relentlessly despite all the hardships. The offices and the factories were closed. Yet, the managers were able to keep the accounts and cash flows under control. There was constant communication between the managers, the staff and the workers. The workers had to be briefed and reassured. The sales teams were in close contact with the customers to ensure seamless communication.

The cancellation of orders and the consequences on cash flows had opened a huge can of worms. There were a host of operational issues to grapple with. The teams had to negotiate with the customers to reduce cancellations of orders and seek faster payments. All deliveries had to be re-scheduled, which was a logistical nightmare. There were new government protocols regarding re-starting factories. There were also new norms pertaining to staff health and safety, which had to be adhered to. Bank limits had to be recalibrated. Salaries had to be paid to the managers and staff.

Export companies were thus under intense pressure. Their cash flows had stopped completely. Customers were not paying. However, exporters had to pay their workers, staff and managers. They also had to pay their vendors due to their long-standing relationships. Owing to the lockdowns, banks were managing with limited staff. So, how does a business negotiate fresh credit limits? Every business was driven to bay. It was caught between the devil of cash shortage and the deep sea of adhering to commitments, in an unchartered environment.

All the Group units had to micromanage, keep a close watch on expenses and focus on being as lean as possible. Retailer payment cycles were long and getting insurance covers was tough.

In this "new normal" of uncertainty and cash scarcities, the Group regularly monitored the financial health and sales of its customers. Many large customers were facing bankruptcies and the Group was keen to avoid any financial hits.

The DS Group technology teams rose to the occasion. They generated avenues to continue the businesses across countries and frontiers, despite the lockdowns. Offices and factories were shut. Flights stood cancelled, so travel was impossible. Couriers were late. The Group had to make rapid and significant investments in video conferencing, 3D technologies, etc., to ensure that the business continued seamlessly. The staff, working from their homes, had to be trained to operate in this new virtual business environment.

Deepak continued to guide all the teams from his London War Room. He leveraged on his relationships in the industry to understand the market and provide insights to all the businesses. Covid-19 was an unprecedented crisis in the history of mankind. There were no readymade solutions in a manual or from a business school textbook. Everyone was at sea. Deepak's ability to ensure financial hygiene in the Group and to dialogue with major customers helped to light the way forward.

Deepak wore a mask and a face shield and marched through London, Dubai and Delhi, nurturing the business. "God is kind, everything is in control," he said. "The roots are here in India. So, it is always good to be back, even though many people are not wearing the mask," he said on returning to Delhi, after a long stint abroad.

The Group operates in 22 countries. So, the management of each country had to keep track of government advisories and notifications on a constant basis. There were daily announcements on protocols at work, staff management, social distancing, office working hours, etc.

Hobson's Choice: Credit

The top retailers normally have credit ratings from Moody's and insurance companies. So, it was easy to get credit insurance for the large retailers who are rated Triple A (AAA) in the industry. After Covid-19, it became very difficult to get insurance, even for the top retailers. Some of the large retailers like JCPenney and J. Crew went bankrupt. Within the span of a few months, the number of creditworthy retailers declined sharply.

Manufacturers were in an absolute gridlock. Retailers were ready to place orders; however, they wanted to pay 120 days after the delivery of the garments. The insurance companies were unwilling to insure these transactions due to uncertainties. The suppliers of the fabrics insisted on advance payments, since they were aware of the risks in the market.

It was a Hobson's Choice situation. Customers were going kaput or seeking credit; the suppliers of raw materials would supply only against advance payments. The banks were unwilling to advance loans without personal guarantees. The garment manufacturer was thus driven to bay. If a manufacturing firm executed an order, it risked a bad debt. If it declined an order, the firm yet had to pay for the fixed costs like salaries and rentals.

The DS Group was able to keep its head above the waters during the Covid-19 storms, due to its cautious policy of risk-management and credit insurance. Deepak insisted that the Group work only with creditworthy customers. Hence the Group was able to avoid exposure to many large retailers who had financial issues during Covid-19.

The Group did continue business with some retailers without credit insurance. These were large retailers, with whom there had been a long association. Deepak also relied on his "gut feel" to assess the buyers and their financial situation. There was always concern that the customer could file for bankruptcy. A retailer could go to court and say that they are bankrupt but need to survive. Then, they could stop all payments to their vendors and reorganise the business. However, the retailer still needed his vendors to become viable again. So, they paid the bills of their suppliers. If the retailer had classified the vendor as a "critical supplier", then the payment was principally assured. The vendor received preferential payment, if he was critical to the survival and success of the retailer in the long run.

Deepak focussed on strengthening relationships with the senior management of the large retailers. He tried to ensure that the DS Group was classified as a critical vendor by them.

Impact on Manufacturing

The manufacturing plants at PDS bore the brunt of the Covid-19 backlash. The factories had goods ready for shipment, but the orders were cancelled. The factories were carrying inventories of unused fabrics and trims, for orders on the machines. However, the machines had fallen silent. So, the factories with an installed annual capacity of 36 million pieces and projected annual sales of USD 200 million, were bleeding financially. Nevertheless, the business ensured payment of all statutory and worker dues.

Pallak opines, "A manufacturing business has massive liabilities. I had a lot of empathy for standalone manufacturing businesses, which were severely impacted."

Steadying the Ship

PDS being a people-first company, ensured that none of the 45 companies on the platform shut during the pandemic. Sound relationships with the bankers helped the company to pay all the vendors.

Some vendors did take hits ranging from USD 1,00,000 to USD 3,00,000, due to the culling of orders. The choking of supplies from China was a major concern, as Covid-19 continued its ravenous march. Pallak admits, "It has been a rollercoaster ride."

The focus of the Group was to keep a healthy balance sheet, maintain cash flows to pay employees and manage the suppliers, bankers and customers.

Though there was pain during Covid-19, Pallak's endeavour was to ensure humane and ethical management. He had refrained from relying on borrowings as the organisation grew. Thus, the company was financially robust when the Covid-19 crisis emerged. The company had grown by reinvesting its profits in establishing new businesses, without any significant debt. It is virtually a debt-free company.

Impact on Workers

The year 2020-21 was thus one of the most challenging years in recent decades in human and financial terms. However, governments could have minimised the impact of Covid-19 and the recessionary waves, by being proactive and micro-managing situations.

For instance, the Indian apparel sector went into downward spiral. The large global retailers cancelled current and future orders, as the retail outlets in their countries were shut. Indian apparel exporters had large inventories of finished products, raw materials, etc., which had to be written off. Garments are almost a "perishable" product, for they are manufactured against specific orders, dictated by prevailing fashion trends. Production in many of the apparel factories had stopped.

However, the businesses were required to pay full wages to the workers. Manpower costs constitute about 30 percent of the cost of a garment. Hence, the overheads burden is substantial on the manufacturers.

Many of the units were in danger of having to shut down completely. The apparel sector needed the active support of the government. For instance, the wages of the staff could have been paid from the Employees Insurance Funds. The factories had been contributing to this Fund. The government could have paid the salaries of the staff for about three months. Banks could have contributed by increasing the working capital limits of manufacturing units by 25 percent, without additional collaterals. Tax payments could have been deferred for some months, without any penalties.

These steps could have aided garment manufacturers to survive the crisis. They could have helped the factories to retain all their workers and provide them with food, accommodation, etc., during the grim patch.

With the lockdown in India, millions of workers, unsure whether they would have jobs later, walked back to their villages. When the lockdowns were lifted, many of the workers did not return immediately to the cities and to their jobs. This, crippled the manufacturing units.

Restructuring for Growth

Dr. Mahesh is optimistic about the future. He says, "You have to keep a positive outlook. Then, you can focus on what the customers want and endeavour to meet their needs."

Deepak restructured the business to ensure that it emerges stronger after Covid-19. The Group has reduced overheads to ensure that costs are in line with the income generated.

Many of the large retailers in the UK and Europe sense there could be an enormous consolidation in the apparel industry. They will work with select key vendors rather than a multitude. They will change the way they do business. Some large customers have approached PDS, to manage their sourcing operations or categories.

Large retailers need to prune their costs. They are reviewing whether they need big teams to manage their design and sourcing operations. They are studying whether they can sub-contract these tasks to professional companies, to reduce their overheads. They want to focus on their core strengths and competencies, which is retailing to consumers. With operations across 50 offices in 22 countries, PDS can provide global solutions to its clients. It can offer the right product, from the right factory, in the right country, at a competitive price.

In the future, large manufacturers too will want to onboard customers who have a strategy to grow together, rather than undertake transactional businesses. For instance, the DS Group (including PDS and PGIL), would like to work with large retailers who are looking to build long-term relationships.

Established manufacturers will prefer orders from customers who have acted ethically during Covid-19. They will not be too keen to partner with retailers who either cancelled orders or withheld payments. Manufacturers would opt to play safe and work with customers who conduct themselves ethically.

Many large manufacturers know that their customer base may shrink. Industry experts believe that the Covid-19 shakeout on the retail front, could see about 150 global retailers emerge strong. They have their teams and insurance covers, enabling them to get supplies.

Opportunities in Crisis

In every crisis, there are the seeds of growth. The DS Group is also discovering unexpected opportunities in the devastation wrought by Covid-19. The Group's responses to the Covid-19 catastrophe, could make a business school case study in crisis management.

PDS is planning to expand its platform after being approached by many medium-sized suppliers. These vendors have lost moneys and customers, but retain strong teams and complementary product categories. They are keen to partner with the PDS business.

PDS deployed its supply chain in China, employing 500 people, to produce personal protective equipment (PPE) like masks and gloves. This initiative kept its factories humming and also helped its customers, who sold these new products. Thus, the Group kept generating income and retained its people. Pallak has donated about half a million masks, to the Great Ormond Street Hospital Children's Charity in London. He has deployed the professional venture capital "PDS Growth Fund", to encourage sustainability initiatives. It will support start-up brands and disruptive business models to fuel future growth, especially those with a sustainability focus.

The Fund has already invested in Yellow Octopus. It has a reGAIN application, offering a multi-brand take-back programme. The goal is to revolutionise fashion recycling. Yellow Octopus operates in 21 countries in five continents. The Fund has also invested in Reflaunt Resell Service, a Singapore and London-based resale platform for luxury fashion brands. Pallak is establishing a structure and a team for the Venture Fund initiative, to evaluate opportunities.

The Group is also changing its course in other ways, due to the pandemic. Says Pallak, “Covid-19 has done what a CEO or a Chief Technology Officer could not do. We are moving very rapidly on the digitisation track. We want to diversify our sourcing base. We will supply fashion apparel. However, we will explore other categories also. Many of our customers have approached us to source cosmetics, masks and PPE gowns.”

Covid-19 has changed shopping habits across the world. Consumers have shopped online due to sheer necessity. They have enjoyed the experience of having products delivered to their homes, with a few clicks on their laptops. Most corporations across the world are evaluating “Business to Consumer” (B2C) distribution channels. This channel will grow exponentially in the future. PDS plans to invest in companies in the direct-to-consumer space, because online sales will augment.

PDS already has an arrangement with Lilly & Sid, an online premium B2C boutique brand, selling babywear. It provides PDS access to a direct-to-consumer channel brand, with a margin potential. The brand also leverages on the Group’s existing babywear sourcing base.

Pallak is confident about the future. He says, “We are going to come out of Covid-19, stronger and stable. It is an evolving target, but there will be incremental opportunities.” He overflows with optimism.

Hopes for Recoveries

The first quarter of 2020 was a financial setback for most exporters. PGIL galvanised in the second quarter and gathered momentum.

The process was gradual, due to the non-availability of labour. India's factories are manned by migratory labour from the countryside. An estimated 140 million migratory labourers had fled to their villages, when the national lockdown commenced from March 2020. They could not return to their jobs. So, reigniting production in Indian factories was problematic. The railways in India were shut. There were no trains to ferry the workers from their villages to the cities to work. Some workers returned by travelling on buses or arranging their own transport. Many factories struggled to reopen due to labour shortages. Moreover, the lockdown had not been lifted comprehensively. Various states and cities lifted the lockdowns in phases.

PGIL factories installed all the safety protocols for the workers. They were assured of a healthy and safe environment to work. The workforce was supportive and adapted to the new protocols. However, there were issues in getting all the workmen to the factories expeditiously, as regional and zonal lockdowns continued, depending on the severity of Covid-19. The managers were confident of achieving pre-Covid-19 levels of productivity.

PGIL revamped its operations and operated at 90 percent plus capacities, by the third quarter of 2020. The factories in Bangladesh and Sri Lanka also picked up steam.

However, retail demand continued to be 20 to 30 percent lower than the pre-Covid-19 era. The Group evolved a strategy to add new customers aggressively. It also executed a plan to get large orders from existing buyers, to utilise its capacities fully. Servicing existing and new customers, with tight watching of the financials, helped the business to fight Covid-19.

Long Term Impact of Covid-19

The trauma of Covid-19, has led to significant changes in human behaviour. Human beings will no longer consider themselves infallible. Nobody will ever take anything for granted, ever again. An invisible virus brought the entire planet to a complete halt. The virus was a great equaliser; it attacked with complete immunity. It attacked emperors and presidents; it attacked paupers. Human beings learnt to live in their homes, without going out for months. They also learnt to economise and live on savings. People learnt to work from their homes. Most people also learnt to buy what they needed, not what they fancied or what was great to own.

In the post-Covid-19 world, customers will be frugal and focus on savings for at least three to five years. So, the markets for consumer products could be rather cloudy for some years. During the lockdowns, many people from managing directors to janitors, have lost jobs. Many professionals have had their salaries slashed. A lot of people across the world, have lived on savings and borrowings. Covid-19 subjected families at all levels, to severe stress. Customers have downgraded to lower priced brands and have given up consumption of non-essential products. Poverty increased across the world, during Covid-19.

It will be some years, before middle-class customers splurge USD 2,500 on a branded handbag or USD 100 on a necktie.

New Retailer Strategies

The apparel markets and businesses have also changed irrevocably due to the Covid-19 lockdowns. Retailers have gone back to their drawing boards, to chart new strategies for a chastened consumer and market. Retailers are focussing on how to reduce their costs, since they expect some declines in sales over the next few years. This will create more dependence on vendors, for design and sourcing inputs. Many retailers will review their vendor mix, to have robust supply chain solution providers. Retailers are controlling inventories more tightly and insisting on faster deliveries.

Online Will Be King

During the lockdowns, consumers got habituated to shopping online for everything they needed, including their essentials like flour, rice and pastas. Online sales doubled and even tripled for some retailers. Online sales of all products, including apparel, increased. As brick and mortar retail outlets downed their shutters, online sales moved North. So, retailers will spruce their online portals.

Retailers are also reducing the number of outlets and building online distribution networks. They are also offering new options. A customer can book the order online and collect the merchandise from the nearest store. Retailers are also ensuring sanitisation, social distancing, masking, etc., to increase the safety in their stores.

Changing Customer Preferences

During the lockdowns, customers worked from their homes. So, dress codes got diluted. A suit or a tie was not considered necessary, even during a formal Zoom meeting. A shirt and jacket were acceptable. The sales of formal apparel took a beating during the lockdowns.

Sales of informal apparel like loungewear, athleisure and sleepwear boomed during the lockdowns. Knitted garments like the comfortable T-shirts also became more popular than formal office shirts. Retailers sold more shorts, athleisure pants and pyjamas than formal trousers.

In the post-Covid-19 era, formal wear is likely to make a comeback. However, customers having survived for months without suits and ties, will calibrate how much formal wear do they need in the future. If business can be done effectively in a T-shirt and shorts, then how much should a person spend on a formal Saville Row suit?

Harvesting the Power of 3D

The 3D software is a major business tool in the apparel industry. The technology allows the seller to show the complete details of any garment, like the fabric texture, the stitching and embellishments, even the way the fabric falls and drapes on the human body, etc., on a computer screen. The technology shows all these assorted features in stationary positions and also during movements. The seller can show how a garment will fit on different sizes of bodies, along with various colours and design combinations. So, buyers and sellers can do business of new collections, without even stitching a sample garment.

Thus, apparel collections are being finalised with the entire brand team working from home. The assortment creation for retailers has always been through meetings. The designers, merchandisers and buyers could touch and feel the samples. Now, 3D software makes it possible for buyers and sellers to envision a garment, without it being manufactured physically.

The 3D technology was in the market for the last few years. However, it gathered momentum and widespread acceptance during the Covid-19 era.

The technology is the best alternative to showing the actual garment to the seller. It saves time and is cost-effective, compared with the traditional mode of stitching samples and tabling them to the buyer. The seller does not have to expend time and money producing samples, for a successful sale. The technology is user-friendly; hence, adoption rates are high.

The virtual sampling also contributes to the sustainability drive. The customer is shown samples of the garments through digital images. No samples are stitched. This saves fabrics, time and the manpower to stitch samples. This is the way forward for new generation companies.

Moreover, business can be conducted virtually with the 3D technology. The buyer and the seller do not have to travel to meet. They can work from their homes or offices on their laptops.

New Technologies

It is possible that travel and face-to-face meetings may decline in the future, as compared with the pre-Covid-19 era. Customer preferences of garments, have changed during the pandemic period. Customers have become frugal and less fussy about their clothes and hairstyles. The pandemic has made fashion, less fashionable.

Some of these attitudes may continue even after Covid-19. In the apparel business, 3D tools were "nice to have". However, now they are mandatory, in the virtual business world. Similarly, the focus on presentations over video conferences will continue for some years. Till the last traces of Covid-19 are wiped out, there will be reluctance among people to travel freely. Hence, the computer screen will continue to be the emperor in businesses for a rather long time.

Deepak is the Chairman of PDS Group managed by his elder son Pallak and also of PGIL managed by his younger son Pulkit. He is constantly travelling to offices and factories in both operations.

Deepak can talk at any level. He can talk easily to a factory worker about the number of stitches per inch. He can also converse with the CEO of a global retailing company.

He is always talking with people and learning about the business.

34
Mr. Chairman's Role

The flight from Santiago in Chile to London, a distance of 11,690 kilometres, was of 14 hours and 35 minutes duration. However, British Airways would ensure a smooth flight with in-flight entertainment and good food. Deepak, Pallak and Omprakash had visited Chile to study the market. As they boarded the return flight, Omprakash wondered how he would manage the long flight. Perhaps, he could catch on some rest and sleep. Working with Deepak in any market in any country is hectic. Deepak moves swiftly from one task to another. There is no time to rest.

The moment they were ensconced in their seats, Deepak started reviewing the meetings which they had conducted, with prospective customers and partners. He discussed with Pallak and Omprakash how to manage the Latino customers. Every country has its own operating culture. Deepak was sensitising Pallak and Omprakash, to the way the Chileans did business.

For instance, when you do business with Indians, they get straight to the point. They dive into prices, quantities, terms, delivery dates, etc. They do not spend much time on preliminaries. However, when you do business in Latin America or in the Middle East, a lot of time is spent in establishing a personal rapport. "How are you? How is your family? How was your holiday?" These are commonly asked questions, before a business discussion commences. In some countries in the Middle East, where the businessmen have farms too, it is quite common to ask about the health of the cows and goats on the farm, before commencing the business discussion.

Throughout the flight, Deepak continued to discuss the Chilean visit with Pallak and Omprakash. He discussed various strategies on how to commence the business, how to build and maintain relationships with the partners and the employees. Next, Deepak started discussing the key drivers of the garment business in Latin America and how to harness them.

Clearly, Deepak was grooming Pallak. Omprakash, who had just joined the Group, was also getting inducted. Deepak slept a mere four hours on the long flight. The balance ten hours were spent in discussions on building the business.

Omprakash was flummoxed. Before boarding the flight, he was ruminating how he would spend the 14 hours on the long flight. After the flight, he realised that he had just been through a ten-hour master-class, on building a business and establishing best practices. He would always cherish the tutorial.

Multiple Roles

As the Chairman, Deepak plays multiple roles. Increasingly, he has evolved his role as that of a friend, philosopher and guide to his sons and the senior managers of the Group. "It is very enriching for us to travel with the Chairman or accompany him to any meeting. He knows when to listen to you and when to drive his point of view," says Omprakash.

Omprakash Makam, a Chartered Accountant by profession, had joined the Group in London in 2009, to manage the finances globally. After the initial four years, he had moved to Bengaluru to establish a corporate office for PDS.

He recalls his first meeting with Deepak to explore career opportunities. He was pleasantly surprised to observe that Deepak did not give the impression of interviewing him. "Mr. Seth had a pleasant way of talking. He discussed the finance function and how he saw me shaping up to add value to the business," he reminiscences. Deepak explains to new managers their roles in delivering results and forging a win-win relationship. Over the years, Deepak has refined the art of interviewing. He makes it an enjoyable chat. He believes in ferreting the potential in everyone and building on it.

Deepak is the Chairman of the PDS business managed by his elder son Pallak and also of PGIL managed by his younger son Pulkit. He is constantly travelling to offices and factories in both operations. So, he always has advance knowledge of the problems that customers and manufacturers are facing or are likely to encounter in the future. He is thus in a position to forewarn the CEOs, about the issues that their customers or vendors would be encountering.

Deepak as a person, can talk at any level. He can talk easily to a tailor in a factory about the number of stitches per inch. He can also converse with the CEO of Kohl's or Macy's about global retailing trends. He always talks with people and interacts with them. The person travelling with him on a flight, could be an employee or a competitor or from a buying office or just another traveller. He will take interest in the person and learn from him. If he thinks there is an opportunity to do business or any kind of work with the person, he will remember it and pursue it.

Strategic Focus

Over the years, Deepak has evolved his own management style. When he started in 1976, he would burrow into every miniscule detail. He would agonise to establish the best price for a button, a reel of thread or the project cost of a new factory. Now, as the Chairman of the Group, he has meetings with bankers, board members, employees and prospective partners. He seeks views on political and economic trends, market cycles, fashion, consumer behaviour, etc. Then, he ponders how all these variables will amalgamate, to impact the business and shares his perspectives with the senior managers. Deepak has developed the uncanny instinct, of looking at all aspects of an issue and making a balanced judgement.

The garments business is a people's business. It requires continuous interactions with people. Deepak has developed patient listening skills. He builds relationships with everyone he meets. He forges good associations with everyone at the table, whether a deal is signed or not. Then, he maintains those relationships.

Punctuality and Commitments

At 9 in the morning, Oxford Street from Tottenham Court to Marble Arch in London, is very crowded. It is one of Europe's busiest shopping street. It has over 300 branded retail outlets, luring about half a million shoppers daily. Every signal is a traffic jam. Shoppers from across the world are on the street, hunting for bargains in Marks & Spencer, Debenhams, etc. Omprakash was driving a car, with Deepak seated next to him. They were on their way to a meeting with NatWest Bank at Blackfriars. The snarls of traffic were delaying them.

Omprakash drove with utmost caution. He always did, whilst driving in London. He was new to the city and did not want to get booked for any traffic offence. Deepak realised that if Omprakash continued to drive, they would be late for the meeting. Deepak hates being late for a meeting or to keep anyone waiting. So, he asked Omprakash to stop the car and took over the driving himself. He drove adroitly and they were able to make it on time to the meeting. Omprakash recalls, "He did not think twice before taking the wheel to drive. Mr. Seth is known for always being on time." His punctuality and timeliness are emulated in the organisation.

The DS Group (including PDS and PGIL), ensures that commitments to customers, bankers, employees and business associates are always met. This has become a core strength. It gives the Group immense credibility in the market. If there is going to be any delay in meeting any commitment to anybody, Deepak is the first person to telephone and explain the situation.

Deepak believes that a good leader should practice what he preaches to his team. So, one of his habits is never to leave any decision or issue pending for the next day. He clears his table every evening before he leaves for his house. Every email received and every call made to him during the day, are answered before he closes shop even if it is late night.

Win-Win Business

Generally, businessmen like to be in a winning position in any negotiation. They like to hold the best cards. Deepak has a special interpretation of the win-win philosophy. In any business deal, he likes to see both the parties win. He likes to focus on maximising the gains from the business, so that both the parties prosper. Deepak does not focus on what percentage of the cake is his or that of the partner. His philosophy is, let's endeavour to make the cake bigger and enjoy it.

In starting a new venture, Deepak does the sums. If the project is feasible, he concentrates on identifying the best talent to manage the business.

Rakesh Kapoor observes, "Deepak is the type of businessman, who will have five percent share in 100 businesses, instead of 100 percent in five businesses. He has evolved a range of business models, depending on the partners he has and the operating conditions. He is always open to starting new businesses."

Rakesh Kapoor studies successful people to identify the qualities that make them unique. According to him, Deepak is a very special person because he knows how to generate trust, build and grow businesses, construct partnerships and empower women.

People who are successful, have some common characteristics. They are hardworking and driven. Ultra-successful people never stop learning. They are relentless in their pursuit of growth.

Deepak is perpetually thinking about how to improve the business and grow. He is not yet done. He is ready for many more rounds. Many people hang up their boots after they meet some goals in their lives. Deepak is nowhere close to that. He is relentless in his pursuits and ambitions.

Brilliant Executor

Deepak is a brilliant executor too, with his high energy and drive. A strategic vision, without execution prowess, is just a piece of paper. "Execution is everything" in business, more than in any other field. In an exacting industry like garments, delivery on quality, time and cost is vital. If the supplier falters on any one of these parameters, he can have an abortive customer relationship or a botched business. Says Rakesh Kapoor, "Deepak is an unbelievable executor. Probably, the best executor in the Group. If he was not brilliant in execution, he would not be where he is today."

As the Chairman of the Board, Deepak constantly guides the efforts of the CEOs and business heads. The retailing environment is getting more competitive. Some project is always in a turnaround phase. So, close consultation with the management team is always useful.

Surender Dhillon attributes Deepak's success as a leader, to his balanced mind and personality. He says, "This is the reason, I have been working for the company for the last three decades. Deepak started the business literally from a workshop, measuring 100 square feet. There were only five employees. He himself travelled on a Lambretta scooter. He used to carry samples on his scooter to meet customers in Delhi. Now, he has built a global business."

Deepak is a multi-tasker. He will be talking to a person in his office. Simultaneously, he will deal with incoming calls on the phones. He will respond to e-mails and WhatsApp messages. He will also give decisions to another colleague, who walks into the room. Deepak has mastered the art of managing three to five tasks concurrently, as the Chairman.

Deepak is a very consistent person. Many business leaders become mercurial as they grow. Deepak's consistency extends to his signature also. An accounting staff member observes, "There is no difference between Mr. Seth's signature today and what it was 10 years ago. I am bewildered by this. In my case, my signature changes every three to five years. That is not the case with Mr. Seth."

"He is a very charismatic man. He commands respect. People want to sit in the same room as him," comments a business head.

Garments Industry: New Challenges

Deepak and his team are also conscious of the significant changes taking place in the industry. These will impact the business over the next few decades.

1. *Online Business*

The growth in the sales of online businesses, is leading to momentous transformations in the industry. It is also impacting high-street retailers across the world. No retailer can ignore this phenomenon. The Group needs to ensure that its basket of customers, is active in e-commerce, for growth in the future.

2. *Sustainability*

The heightened awareness about sustainability and care for the planet, is a growing concern of all consumers. The youngsters of the world are deeply concerned about climate change, global warming, fast fashion, social impact of industry, etc., led by the indefatigable Greta Thunberg.

3. *Fast Fashion*

From the 2000s, fashion has become faster. Garments are launched to be replaced by new designs within months. Young shoppers prefer trendy apparel at higher frequencies. Fast fashion produces garments quickly in line with current trends. These garments are priced economically. Youngsters use these garments for short periods, till the trends last and then discard them. As these items are relatively inexpensive, they lend easily to impulse buying. The stores of Zara, Forever 21 and H&M are always crowded with young consumers, looking for high-fashion apparel and accessories at reasonable prices.

Fashion garment manufacturers like the DS Group (including PDS and PGIL), had to keep pace to meet the new needs of the market. This was exacting. Delivery times were curtailed, costs were under pressure and labour and environmental compliances had to be tightly monitored.

4. *Shorter Delivery Times*

The garment exports business has also become more complex due to the higher expectations of the buyers. Earlier, buyers provided five to six months' time for delivering the stocks after order placement. Now, they expect delivery within three months. For instance, in the 1970s and 1980s, an order placed in October was expected to be delivered by March or April in the following year. Now, retailers place an order in October and expect deliveries by January of the following year. Manufacturers have hundreds of employees on their payrolls, but their order visibility is just about three months.

Retailers insist on minimum time-gaps between ordering and delivery. Fashions change fast. They have to catch every opportunity by its forelock. Hence, buyers insist on speedy deliveries.

5. *Complexity and Advances*

The manufacturer is the last link in the garment chain. He deals with the suppliers of fabrics, buttons, labels, cartons, polybags, etc. The retailers do not have to deal with this multitude of vendors. They place an order and agree on a delivery date. The manufacturer has to manage the entire supply chain of the stitching, processing, printing, dyeing, embroidery, etc. Many of the vendors are located in Bangladesh, China or Korea. They insist on advance payment or Letters of Credit. These vendors insist on their terms, as there are few suppliers of many of these accessories.

6. *Changing Structure of Industry*

The structure of the garment exports industry has been changing over the last few decades. In the 1970s, a person could install 100 sewing machines, spend about USD 1,00,000 and become a garment exporter. Thus, circa 1975, there were an estimated 15,000 garment exporters in India. Due to competition and stringent governance requirements, many exporters rolled down their shutters. By the year 2000, there were only 1,500 garment exporters in India. This has now declined to about 500 viable exporters operating from India.

The decline in the number of exporters in India, has led to an increase in the number of garment exporters in other countries like Bangladesh, Kenya and Ethiopia.

There has been a rationalisation amongst the retailers also. Three decades ago, there were about 5,000 retailers who were being pursued by garment manufacturers. Due to consolidations and closures, there are just about 50 top retailers, who are creditworthy and can get credit approval from the insurance companies. There are fewer retailers, but they are larger and more powerful.

7. *Static Markets*

A challenge confronting the garments industry is that sales in some European countries, have been static or declining in the recent past. For instance, Germany's imports of apparel and textiles have remained stagnant around USD 70 billion, for the last many years. The population growth in countries like Germany, has also been sluggish.

Consumer priorities are also changing. The priority of most consumers was always to own a wonderful house, buy stylish cars and wear elegant clothes. Fashion and clothes were important. People wanted to be well-dressed with panache.

The advent of the digital era has changed some priorities of consumers. Homes and car are yet important. However, laptops, smart phones and digital tools have become the new status symbols. They have also become necessities. It is common for billionaires to be moving around in unbranded shorts and T-shirts. The brand of clothes a person wears, is becoming less important than the brand of his smart phone. So, consumer priorities are also shifting.

8. *Role of Retailers, Importers*

A major development in the industry is that large retailers and customers seek direct ties with the producers of the garments. Earlier, retailers were content to place an order with an importer and sign off. It was the importer's job to liaise with manufactures in various countries and deliver the garments to the buyer's warehouses. Now, large retailers have their own offices in the garment producing countries. These local offices scan the vendors, inspect the factories and ensure compliances. So, the importers are gradually being squeezed out.

9. *Value Services*

Increasingly, retailers will not just want garments; they will seek value-added services. They need designs, branding, inventory management, warehousing, etc. Companies like Hong Kong's Li & Fung render these incremental services. So, vendors too will have to modify their offerings. The DS Group has been a pioneer in offering design services to its customers.

10. *Fewer Retailers?*

Retailing of garments could become less glamorous. This will save costs. Many retailers are wondering whether they need large retailing formats, in expensive fashion streets to sell a pair of jeans or a blazer. They also ponder whether they need to pay astronomical fees to a movie star, to model a new dress. Eventually, all these expenses add to the price of a dress. Retailers who are unable to perceive these changing trends, could face immense pressures in the future.

The garments industry may have fewer brick and mortar retailers, with online sellers playing a larger role in the future. Existing garments suppliers will have to forge stronger relationships with the retailers. They will have to partner with their retailers. Some of the suppliers may also build their own brands and sell them through stores or online. So, the future of the garments industry, is pregnant with new possibilities and horizons.

2019 was a watershed year for large retailers. In September 2019, "Forever 21" filed for bankruptcy. There were 16 major bankruptcies in a single year. The garments market was entering unchartered waters. Covid-19 added to the turbulence.

11. Challenge of Costs and Inflation

About three decades ago, garments were manufactured in UK, Italy, France, Turkey, etc. As costs spiralled in these high-wage countries, production shifted to China, Morocco, East Europe, India, Kenya, Bangladesh, etc. The constant mobility of the supply chain to take advantage of lower production costs across countries, has helped manufacturers to contain costs.

The price of a garment depends substantially on its quality and the retail outlet. The mass retailers work on the volume game. Their strategy is to sell high volumes at low prices. Branded retailers like Tommy Hilfiger will sell a T-shirt at ten times the mass market price, with higher quality materials. A premium brand retailer like Stefano Ricci could be selling a T-shirt for USD 250, as it would be made from organic, Egyptian or Pima cotton. So, the FOB price of a T-shirt could range from USD one to USD 30. The USD one T-shirt could be retailing at USD three in a mass-retail outlet. The USD 30 T-shirt could be selling at USD 300, in a premium retail outlet like Louis Vuitton.

Garment manufacturers are confronted with the challenge of inflation in production costs. The prices of readymade garments cannot be increased sharply due to competition and the budget constraints of consumers. However, labour costs which are significant in manufacturing garments, are rising steadily in the developing countries. The prices of land for factories, power costs, etc., are also increasing. So, garment manufacturers will have to ensure significant production efficiencies, to survive.

The costing of garments is undertaken in US dollars, across the world. The inflation in many developing countries, like China, India and Bangladesh, was around five to seven percent annually, during the last few decades. These countries have also seen devaluation of their local currencies. For instance, the US dollar fetched eight Indian Rupees in 1984. By 2020, it fetched 73 Indian Rupees. The inflation in labour costs and raw materials in India, was neutralised, to some extent, by the devaluation of the local currency.

Retailers constantly seek lower prices. If a retailer was paying USD five for a shirt a decade ago, now he wants to buy it for USD four. He is also able to secure this price, since he can source from multiple suppliers, in different countries.

The key to surviving and ensuring profits, is to improve productivities and reduce costs. "In this highly competitive market, manufacturers can be profitable only by being very efficient, productive and ensuring perfect execution. It is a very tough business," opines Deepak.

12. Fashion Vs. Core Garments

Garment manufacturers have to strike the right balance in producing fashion items and core or basic items like T-shirts, shorts, etc. The margins are higher in fashion products, but they also need more skilled labour, which in turn costs more.

People: Backbone of Business

Every morning Deepak overflows with energy and is raring to go. Pallab recounts, "I have travelled with him from London to Hong Kong or Hanoi. We land at midnight. We plan to have breakfast at 7 am next day. We are all much younger than him. We could be late by about five or ten minutes. Deepak is always there before any of us." His energy and enthusiasm for building the infrastructure and business, keep him going.

To prepare himself for every gruelling day when he is in Delhi, Deepak takes a brisk walk on his lawns or spends time on the treadmill. He swims in the pool for 15 minutes or spends time in the sauna, depending on the weather. He undertakes stretch exercises daily to strengthen his back. To ensure that he has time for his morning routine, Deepak has a swimming pool, gymnasium and sauna at his house.

Success in the garments business requires immense flexibilities and quick decision-making. The speed to market has become critical, so every decision has to be literally instantaneous.

The manufacturer frequently has only 60 to 75 days from order to delivery. Then, the entrepreneurial model of the Group galvanises to execute. The senior managers are trained to take decisions quickly. "We avoid bureaucracy, too many meetings and discussions. We have to solve problems within minutes and at times, even seconds. When glitches emerge, we resolve them immediately. We cannot have a committee meeting. If we hold long meetings, the machines and the workers will remain idle. We cannot afford to waste any time. So, we take decisions immediately," says Deepak.

In the consolidation of the industry, partly triggered by Covid-19, it is possible that operating relationships between the large retailers and the large manufacturers will mature. There are fewer retailers and manufacturers now. It could be a more balanced relationship.

To avoid surprises in the business, Deepak has endeavoured to train the senior management team and install robust systems. He says, "We have competent teams running the business. We have professional managers and operating practices. We have policies, manuals and plans for various contingencies. So, we are able to manage situations. Nevertheless, I am aware that the buck stops with me, as the Chairman. It could be a major banking issue, a labour situation, a thorny government matter or a problematic customer resolution. They hit my table. Then, I have to resolve the issue."

Deepak maintains a full day work schedule, for all the 365 days in a year. He divides his time equally between the businesses managed by his sons. Although he leaves the day-to-day management to the sons, he is involved in all strategic decisions and management of key relationships. Garments is a highly personalised business. Deepak maintains close contacts with all the major buyers.

The success of the Group, according to Deepak is due to the endeavours and passion of his team members. He also respects the goodwill of the thousands of families, that make a living from the DS Group. He asserts, "The success of the Group belongs to the people who work here, the professionals who lead it and their blessings." He adds, "Our people are the backbone of the business."

A Businessman for All Seasons

During the last five decades, Deepak and his team have managed a fashion business in about 22 countries. The key countries like India, USA and UK have been through significant political changes and economic cycles.

India has had 12 Prime Ministers during this period including Mrs. Indira Gandhi, Morarji Desai, Chaudhary Charan Singh, Vishwanath Pratap Singh, Chandra Shekhar, Narasimha Rao, Rajiv Gandhi, Atal Bihari Vajpayee, Deve Gowda, Inder Kumar Gujral, Dr. Manmohan Singh and Narendra Modi.

One of the largest customers of the Group, the USA has had nine Presidents, including Gerald Ford, Jimmy Carter, Ronald Reagan, George H.W. Bush, Bill Clinton, George W. Bush, Barack Obama, Donald Trump and Joe Biden.

Another large customer of the Group, the UK went through nine leadership changes, including Harold Wilson, Edward Heath, James Callaghan, Margaret Thatcher, John Major, Tony Blair, Gordon Brown, David Cameron, Theresa May and Boris Johnson.

Thus, the DS Group worked through around 30 leadership changes at the President or Prime Minister level, in three of its major theatres of operations. Each leader brought economic and fiscal changes and policies to support an agenda. The Group observed, learnt and adapted, to manage the business through all these five decades of political, economic and fashion fluctuations. And, the Group stuck to the knitting, which is manufacturing great clothes for its customers.

PHOTOGRAPHS

49. Achievers Award, St. Columba's School Alumni (2002).

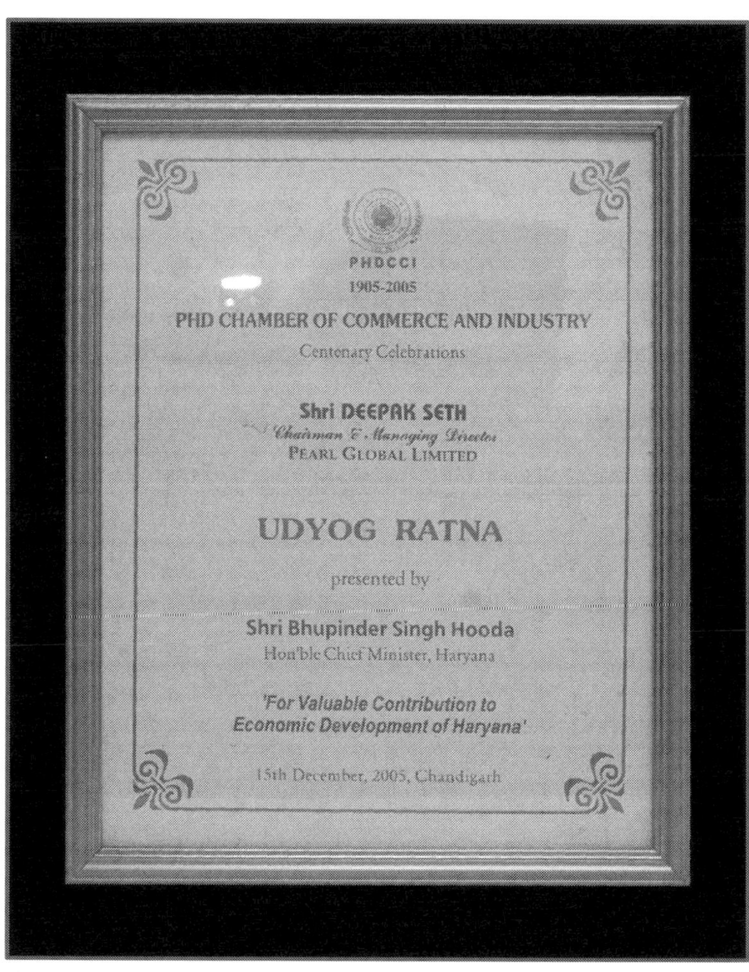

50. Udyog Ratna, for Valuable Contribution to Economic Development of Haryana, PHD Chamber of Commerce and Industry (2005).

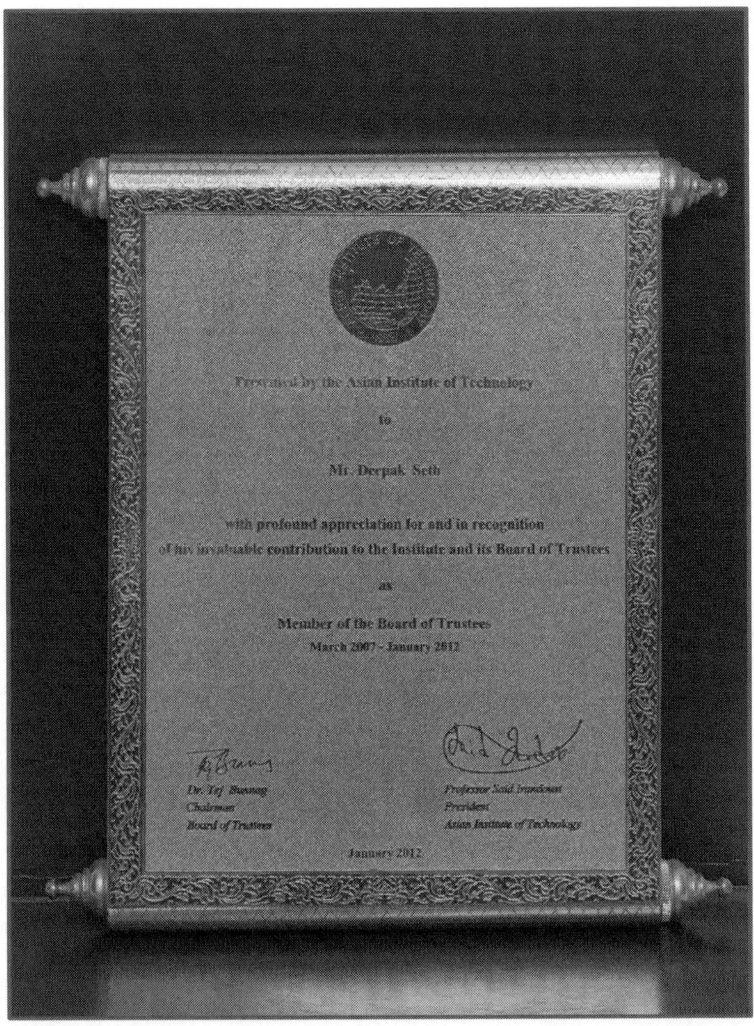

51. Member of the Board of Trustees (March 2007 to January 2012), Asian Institute of Technology.

52. Appreciation of Valuable Support and Encouragement, Pearl Academy of Fashion (2012).

53. 30 Years of Service to Apparel Industry, Apparel Exporters and Manufacturers Association (2012).

54. Guest Speaker, D. E. Society's, The Institute of Management Development and Research (2017).

55. Member – Managing Committee (2021), Garments Exporters and Manufacturers Association.

"Deepak is a very knowledgeable person due to his experience in the industry. He always contributes sound ideas. He always speaks sense, irrespective of whom he is speaking to."

- Dr. A. Sakthivel, the Chairman of AEPC

"Deepak is very well informed about business trends abroad. He is always positive and forward thinking. It is very helpful when he comes for our Association meetings. He has businesses across the world; he travels a lot. His views and impressions are useful."

- Mr. Harish Ahuja, Chairman of Shahi Exports

35
Playing a Role in the Industry

Deepak is a pioneer in the garments industry with five decades of experience in it. Now, he is perceived as a veteran. He is one of the key spokesmen for the apparel export industry in all meetings with the Government of India. He is also a vivacious member of the Apparel Export Promotion Council (AEPC). This is the official body of apparel exporters in India. It assists Indian exporters, importers and international buyers who want to import apparel from India. It operates under the aegis of the Ministry of Textiles, Government of India.

Deepak has always played an active role in various industry associations. He held the office of the Vice Chairman of the AEPC of the Eastern region for two years. He is also active in the Apparel Exporters and Manufacturers Association (AEMA).

Deepak works through various industry associations, to improve India's competitive advantages in areas like fabric quality and processing technologies. China has acquired significant strengths in these areas. Deepak has constantly pushed for India to excel. He is also widely travelled. His views are always sought on how to improve the ease of doing business in India.

Deepak is a permanent invitee to the AEPC meetings. This is a rare honour bestowed on professionals, who are experts in the business. He is respected for his knowledge and exposure to the global markets.

Meeting the Prime Minister

The Indian Prime Minister, Mr. Narendra Modi, was meeting a cross section of Indian industrialists and businessmen to seek their ideas on spurring growth. The meeting was organised by the NITI Aayog in Delhi in January 2020. Deepak was also invited to present his views to the Prime Minister. Deepak spoke about the travails of the industry and the support required from the government.

The government had made commitments on certain subsidies. These had been withdrawn suddenly. For instance, the MEIS (Merchandise Exports from India Scheme) for exporters, was withdrawn. In this scheme, the exporters received incentives, aggregating to around four percent.

The exporters were sharply impacted since the incentive was incorporated in their costing. They were upset. Four percent is the net margin on many consignments. Its withdrawal rendered many orders unviable. The margins of the exporters were already squeezed, due to the competitive pressures from Bangladesh, China, Indonesia, Vietnam and Cambodia.

So, Deepak told the Prime Minister that the garments export industry was surviving on a ventilator. He requested that the government should honour all its commitments to the exporters. Withdrawing assured incentives out of the blue, without any notice can hurt companies.

Second, Deepak told the Prime Minister that government policies should be valid for at least five years. Policies should not change every six to 12 months. If there is a five or ten-year policy, then businessmen can make some assumptions and plan accordingly. Manufacturing needs a long-term horizon.

Third, Deepak sought an improvement in the ease of doing business in the country. Deepak and the businessmen also sought more simplicity in the administration of various tax legislations. The Goods and Services Tax (GST) was an excellent initiative. However, there were around 250 notifications which made its execution very cumbersome.

The government is now introducing Faceless Assessment Scheme. It would be possible to file tax returns online. This is guided by a 70-page document, outlining the process. Deepak underscored to the Prime Minister that the procedures needed simplification.

Fourth, Deepak advised that the government should hire the best talent in the market. He said that the government should recruit high-quality professionals from business and industry and agree lucid key performance indices (KPIs) with them. They should be provided with attractive incentive programmes and the freedom to deliver. Then, things would get done.

Deepak felt commercial assignments cannot always be handled by bureaucrats from the Indian Administrative Service (IAS) or the Indian Revenue Service (IRS). Professional managers from the private sector, can contribute towards simpler procedures and faster execution.

The government has taken a number of steps to streamline procedures and reduce the possibilities of corruption in the country. Measures such as demonetisation, GST and bankruptcy code are all laudable initiatives. They will improve the investment climate in India. A major advantage of doing business abroad, is that most government processes and regulations are managed online.

Respect in Industry

"Deepak is a very knowledgeable person due to his experience in the industry. So, he always contributes sound ideas," remarks Dr. Sakthivel, the Chairman of AEPC.

The Chief Minister of the Indian state of Madhya Pradesh, Mr. Kamal Nath, organised a meeting of industrialists in March 2020. He wanted to brief investors about the opportunities in the state. "Deepak explained to the Chief Minister the expectations of an investor. He always speaks sense, irrespective of whom he is speaking to," adds Dr. A. Sakthivel.

There is tremendous scope for the garments export business in the future. India's share in the global garments manufacturing and exports business is yet limited. China exports about USD 150 billion worth of apparel per annum. Bangladesh exports are USD 34 billion. Indian exports are just USD 17 billion per annum.

India has strategic competitive advantages over Bangladesh. It has key raw materials like fabrics to manufacture garments. Bangladesh has to import the raw materials from China and India. India has a home-grown pool of managers and technicians. In Bangladesh, most management positions are occupied by Indians or Sri Lankans. India also has a vast reservoir of designers, merchandisers, etc., with formal education in their disciplines.

The market is huge and untapped. The key players in the garment export industry in India are socially well connected. They do not compete with each other, as in some other industries. Many of them are friends. There is enough business for everyone. So, relationships are very harmonious and not competitive.

Mr. Ahuja of Shahi Exports says that Deepak Seth is very well informed of business trends abroad. He adds, “Deepak is always positive and forward thinking. It is very helpful when he comes to our Association meetings. He has businesses across the world. He travels a lot. His views and impressions are useful.”

At the 100th anniversary celebration of PHD Chamber of Commerce and Industry (PHDCCI) in 2016, Deepak and the Group received an “Udyog Ratna Award” for their valuable contributions to the economic development of Haryana. The Institute of Technology presented an award to Deepak in 2012, in appreciation and recognition of his contributions as a Trustee.

A memento was presented to Deepak by the Apparel Exporters & Manufacturers Association (AEMA) in 2012, for completing 30 years of service to the apparel industry and for his valuable guidance.

The various Export Councils, frequently invite Deepak to participate in their panel discussions, on various issues confronting the garment export industry. Deepak willingly shares his experiences and perspectives, to give a momentum to the industry.

"Deepak is available to all of us at the drop of a hat.

He has never let down anyone from the family or even outside the family. You are proud of how he has evolved and grown. You hold him in awe and respect him. I often wonder how he could achieve this or that.

Deepak has the strength to handle stressful situations and emerge as a winner from them.

I can only say that God has been kind to us, to have him as our youngest brother."

- Harish Seth, Elder Brother

36
At Heart, A Family Man

The small boy aged six years, dressed in a formal suit, stood at the centre of the stage and spoke into the microphone, "I would like to congratulate my lovely grandfather and grandmother on their 50th wedding anniversary. They are a wonderful couple. They are also very loving and kind."

The audience of 250 guests at the Hotel W, Singapore Sentosa Cove, were impressed with the self-confidence of young Dheer, Pulkit's son.

After the declamation of the young child and a few more speeches, the band took over. Over an elegant dinner, the band played the best Bollywood, Punjabi and English songs for the guests. Then, the dance floor started rocking. About 200 guests were on the floor, dancing merrily till the wee hours of the morning.

Inspired by Mrs. Mina Seth, who loved bringing family members together, Deepak and Payel too love celebrating their joys with families and friends. So, their 50th wedding anniversary was celebrated with 250 of their family members, colleagues, associates and friends over four days from 20 to 23 February 2016 in Singapore. Each guest had been received at the airport and escorted to his or her room.

The three days of celebrations included a beach dinner, a sailing expedition and a festive dinner at the hotel. Participating in the celebrations were all the brothers of Deepak and their families, business associates and friends of

Deepak and Payel. Deepak had also invited his alumni friends and their spouses from St. Stephen's college in Delhi and Bajaj Institute (JBIMS) in Mumbai, to the celebrations. Every evening, Deepak was the first person on the dance floor. He was the last one to leave it, in the wee hours of the next morning.

In 2008, Deepak had celebrated his 60th birthday with equal gusto, with 250 family members, associates and friends in Istanbul, Turkey. Harish Ahuja, a leading garment exporter, remembers the wonderful time he had in Istanbul with his family and friends.

The Seth family bonds together to celebrate birthdays and anniversaries. The entire extended family numbering 51, went for a family cruise together in 2018. The youngest family member was Sonia, the seven-month-old daughter of Rishi, the elder son of Dr. Mahesh Seth, living in San Francisco. The oldest was Chand who was turning 75 years. The family spent some pleasurable days together on a cruise on "Vision of the Seas", a class ship by the Royal Caribbean International. This was an all-family event.

Brothers: Strong Pillars, Arms

Deepak was very clear from the beginning that the family is paramount. Even though he is the youngest of all the brothers, he enjoys tremendous respect from all of them. This is due to his family values. He is always there for the family and has a strong sense of fairness. Whilst Deepak and his brothers inherited their business acumen from their father, they imbibed the family bonding spirit from their mother.

At heart, Deepak remains a family man, close to his own family and his brothers and their families. Though he travels 15 to 20 days per month, he ensures that they have an extended family dinner, whenever he is in Delhi. All the brothers and their families attend these dinners.

Deepak comes from a family which bonds very tightly. He is highly respectful of the emotions and feelings of others. However, he is not afraid to call a spade, a spade. His eldest brother Chand says, "His frankness is an important quality. As my youngest brother, he has been a great source of strength. He always discusses with me whatever he is planning to do and how he will do it. He talks to everyone in his own family about his plans. Deepak's strength is that he listens. When you tell him there is a better way of doing something, he listens and acts on it."

The family is also united by WhatsApp groups, even though the members are spread out across continents. The five brothers have a "Seth Brothers" group. Then, the "Elder Seths" group has the five brothers and their wives as members. There is also a "Seth Famjam" in which every Seth, irrespective of age is a member. The youngsters in the family have a "Seth Youngsters" group.

Strong Relationships

"Chand and his wife Suneeta, being the eldest, have been sterling in keeping the family together. Deepak, being the youngest, has also maintained family relationships and given a lot of importance to them. He continues to do so, even to this date," feels Dr. Mahesh Seth, Deepak's elder brother.

He adds, "If I am not well, the first person my children call is Deepak. The bond has developed over many years. Deepak often travelled to New York for business. Whenever possible, he would insist that my entire family visits New York to spend time together. He also came to Michigan to spend time with us whenever possible. He attaches a lot of importance to the family." The Seth family is tightly knit. Deepak is incomplete without his family.

Harish comments that, "We are one big happy family. A lot of the credit for where we are today in terms of our family values and relationships, goes to Deepak. The younger generation of our sons, daughters, nephews and nieces follow the Indian tradition of tying "Rakhis". (An annual festival in India, wherein a sister ties a colourful thread on the wrist of her brother. The brother reciprocates with a gift and a pledge to protect his sister lifelong.) The younger girls also have their own family lunches. So, the fraternity prevails, not merely in our generation but also in the next. Deepak, in a certain way, has provided the support and platform for our closeness. I think he is instrumental in our being where we are today."

Respect and sensitivity towards the feelings of others, is the secret of the harmonious human relationships, that Deepak maintains. Many businessmen are successful, but are unable to maintain accord in their homes. Deepak has been able to build trust and loyalty in business and at home. He always stands by his word.

When the three brothers, Chand, Harish and Krishen decided to restructure their businesses, they asked Deepak to enable it. Deepak did it seamlessly. Deepak and his four brothers are pillars of strength to each other.

Deepak is savvy and understands how an issue can be addressed. Sometimes, he resolves an issue by saying little things to various persons, to build trust and bring everyone on the same page.

"Despite his hectic schedule and success," says Harish, "Deepak is available to all of us at the drop of a hat. He has never let down anyone from the family or even outside the family. I even enjoy him at work. When I have breakfast or lunch with him in his office, it is an experience. You are proud of how he has evolved and grown. You hold him in awe and view him with respect. I often wonder how he could achieve this or that. And then I think, we were probably wrong in letting him go on his own in 1987. It would have been better for all of us to have stayed together. Deepak had the leadership to generate growth. We lost out on that, I think. I am pretty sure of it. Deepak has the strength to handle stressful situations and emerge as a winner from them. I can only say that God has been kind to us, to have him as our youngest brother."

Harish adds, "Many people on seeing Deepak's leadership, conduct and maturity, do not believe that he is the youngest brother in the family. However, he is."

A unique feature of Deepak's personality is that however busy he is, he always has time for anyone who wants to meet him or talk to him personally or even on the phone. He has time for everybody. You can contact him anytime. He is there for you. Whenever any brother wants to talk to Deepak about any issue, his immediate reaction is, "Sure. When shall I come over?" He always makes time to talk to the family members.

An endearing trait of Deepak is that he is a very happy person. He is always cheerful. Friends who have known him for decades, say that they have never seen Deepak despondent. Sometimes, he is concerned. But he is never depressed. His philosophy is, however wretched the situation, "I will climb out of it. I will overcome."

Many successful people in the world are never content. Deepak has the ability to be happy, as he does not lose sight of the important issues. For him, family matters the most in his life.

Krishen recalls, "Even as a youngster, Deepak had a craze for excelling at everything he did. Whether it was studies, athletics or business, he wanted to be the best. Even now, he combines his passion with strong values. His first priority in life is his immediate and extended family, then business and everything else follows. He will go to any length to ensure that there is no disruption in the family relationships and that the bonds remain secure."

Thus, Deepak has become a consistently positive social person, ever-willing to help people, always ready to have a good time and very cheerful. He always has a joke up his sleeve and enjoys life.

Harish, his elder brother says, "The interesting thing is that today, the family looks up to him. He has always been a very fair adjudicator in any issue. He always listens to you. He gives you the confidence that nothing will go wrong. His message is, if anything happens, it will be managed. So, there is nothing to worry about. So, all of us, including the children in the family, adore him for what he has achieved. He provides comfort to all of us. He is magnanimous with the family."

Balancing Role: Own family

Deepak consciously strives to strike a sensible work-life balance. The way he has raised and groomed his two sons and the manner in which he integrates with their families is exemplary. He never misses the holidays with his own family and the extended family.

Deepak has also planned the succession in the business with prescience. He has personally inducted his sons, Pallak in London and Pulkit in New York, in the business. He has provided relevant exposures to them in almost every element of the business, in a range of overseas markets. In addition, he has ensured that they work with the same tenacity and focus which he has. The father and the two sons blend into a vibrant team. Sometimes, Pallak motors at 150 miles an hour to expand the business. Then, Deepak wisely slows him down.

The gratitude of the two sons is reflected in Pallak's words on his Dad, as, "He is the best father one could ever want. He has always been there for me and supported my decisions. He has always guided me, which has helped me to make the right decisions. He has a very strong character. His strength and energy are exemplary. He has instilled in me the values of sustained work, integrity, realism and flexibility to keep the team together. He is always fair in his dealings with everyone. He had great respect for his parents and always tried to keep his brothers and family together. I have never seen him fall out with anyone. He made sure, he never burnt any bridges. I was extremely fortunate to be born and brought up in such a supportive, loving and stable family environment. I have the most wonderful childhood memories and parents. My Dad is a great sounding board for me. He is my role model in personal and business life. Now that I have my own children, I aspire to be like him as a father."

In playing the role of a father, father-in-law and grandfather, Deepak has skilfully kept the family together. He is always open-minded and ready to have a family discussion on any issue and hear everyone's point of view. Deepak started a family business, but is very professional in managing it. He has well defined norms about who can spend how much and what can be charged to the company.

Makes You Believe in Yourself

Deepak's daughters-in-law also enjoy working with him. Pallak's wife, Faiza Seth, says, "An important thing I have learned from Papa is the emphasis on family commitments. He maintains relationships and keeps in touch with everybody. This is essential because we are human beings and we all need affection and family support. Papa always helps people. He does it so quietly."

Faiza worked with Pallak in the London business. She recalls that Deepak had advised her, "In business, first listen and only then talk." Deepak also created a climate of open communications within the start-up team. He was always counselling the young team, "Its fine if you make mistakes as long as you communicate with each other and learn from them."

Many youngsters in the age group of 25 to 35 years were used to a rather authoritative or dictatorial styles of management, based on hierarchy, in the 2000s. Deepak was ahead of the curve. He believed in open communications and was generous with the mistakes of youngsters. However, he sought honesty and transparency so that everyone could learn from errors. Deepak's operating style sharpened Faiza's people management skills.

Faiza finds it amazing that Deepak can talk easily to everyone. A person could be a sweeper or the CEO of a multinational company. Deepak can establish immediate rapport with both of them. He is versatile in communicating with people, irrespective of economic, social, religious, cultural backgrounds. This is a unique strength.

Deepak is also very accepting and supportive of people of various nationalities and religions. He manages a global business and is very open-minded. Faiza recollects the sensitivity and maturity with which Deepak finalised her marriage with his son. Pallak and Faiza were classmates at Northwestern University in the USA. They belonged to different religions and were just 21 years old. Deepak built bridges with everyone and ensured that the marriage was smooth and joyous.

Deepak trusts and believes the people, with whom he works. Faiza recollects that in London, Deepak provided them a platform to work, the initial capital, his network and his guidance. After that, he left them to run the business on their own. He gave them complete autonomy to run the business, not merely as a father but also as an entrepreneur.

Deepak's trust imparted confidence to the new team. The youngsters were inspired by Deepak's belief in their delivery skills. Faith in people, is a key ingredient in any success story.

According to Faiza, Deepak's strong faith in his sons, is the secret of their success. When a father believes in his children, is always there to guide them and is a springboard for ideas, he boosts the self-confidence of the offspring.

Faiza spent the first few years of her career working with the business in London. Investment banking fascinated her, so later she worked in equity markets with Lehman Brothers in

Hong Kong. She then completed her MBA from Stanford Business School in California, with an internship at Morgan Stanley. She started Casa Forma in 2007, an award-winning luxury architectural and interior design firm headquartered in London. She also started Soham, a charitable school for kids in Hyderabad, India. Faiza is also involved with business issues like sustainability.

Faiza says of Deepak, "Whenever I have a question or any issue, he is the person I go to. He is reliable, has good advice to offer and is always there for you. He is very supportive in exploring not merely professional goals, but also personal goals and hobbies. Between the two years at Stanford I had led a business trip to India and Pakistan. In Delhi, Papa helped me organise a meeting with upcoming fashion designers."

Faiza says, "My ability in starting businesses, is due to the confidence built by Papa's belief in us and his guidance. He believes that we can do it. That gives me the confidence that I can."

Daughters, Not Daughters-In-Law

Shifalli, Pulkit's wife also admires Deepak and says, "Sometimes people are just born to lead. It is something they do with ease, confidence and most important with empathy. This is how I would describe Papa. His sense of fairness towards all the people he works with, astonishes me."

Shifalli remembers an incident in 2001, which endeared the Seth family to her, "I was visiting London as Pulkit's fiancée and staying with them in their St. Johns Wood apartment. The extended family had come over to spend the weekend with us. One day, I slept till 11.30 in the morning. Mummy (Payel) and the others were preparing breakfast. One may have felt, that as the future daughter-in-law, I should have woken early and helped in preparing the breakfast. All Deepak said was, 'If Pulkit was sleeping, would we ever wake him up?' That statement truly touched my heart. From that day till today, nothing has changed. I have always been treated as a daughter in the family."

Sylvester Stallone to Nephews and Nieces

Deepak's zeal and zest for life impresses the younger generation also, in the extended Seth family.

Deepak's nephews applaud him as a fighter who achieves whatever he wants. They were always in awe of his muscles. The youngsters have been trying to beat him in arm wrestling since forever. However, he has always emerged victorious. Even now. He is seen as the Sylvester Stallone of the family by his nephews.

Deepak is a father figure and a great friend to all his nephews and nieces. Many of them remember him for spoiling them as kids, with his humorous and mischievous personality. Deepak visited the extended family at the Gangaram Marg villa, on all anniversaries, birthdays and festivals. He kept in close touch with all the nephews and nieces in the family.

The children recollect that the annual Diwali celebrations in their home, were always very spectacular. There were endless boxes of crackers that Deepak brought for the children. Even now, festivals are very special, since the entire family bonds. Deepak loves to keep up with everyone.

Varun, the elder son of Chand says, "Deepak Uncle has been my role model. He knows how to balance his life between work and family. He attaches a lot of value to time and is always very punctual."

Deepak had bought a new Toyota MR2 sports car circa 1983. It was a two-seat, mid-engine, rear-wheel-drive sports car, manufactured in Japan. It was a rarity. He immediately called Varun and let him take it for a spin by himself. Varun relished the experience. Deepak's love for cars fascinated his nephews during their teenage years. He always called Varun to his Vasant Vihar residence, whenever he was test driving a new car.

So, not surprisingly, Deepak is considered a truly amazing person by the children of his brothers. He is admired for having a heart of gold, always loving and giving. He is esteemed for being a wonderful son, husband, father, grandfather, uncle and friend.

Deepak is also appreciated for his quality of getting along well with people of all ages. The brothers' children observe that Deepak respects every person he meets, no matter who they are or what is their status. They admire him because he always remembers the entire family, no matter how busy he is. "Deepu Chacha's" (Deepak Uncle's) zest for life is infectious and the children constantly learn from him.

Deepak gives frank and sound advice to his own sons and his nephews and nieces. He treats all the children in the extended family with equal love and affection.

Varun summarises Deepak's achievements as, "His vision and entrepreneurship combined with hard work and continuous travel, are examples for us to emulate. He ventured into the educational field early on and has created India's best fashion institute, the Pearl Academy of Fashion. The accomplishments of his Group are endless. It has now evolved into a worldwide conglomerate, whilst working with the best global retailers and brands. I am so blessed to have a wonderful "Chacha" (Uncle) like him. I am super proud of him."

All the nephews and nieces love Deepak and Payel, for helping anyone who needs assistance. Deepak and Payel firmly believe in giving back to society. They manage various charitable organisations such as the "Mina Seth Clinic". The "Arpan" initiative provides free education to children living in the slums. Their ability to connect with people across socioeconomic backgrounds, professions, religions and ages endears them to everyone they meet.

Student of the Grandchildren

Nowhere is Deepak's ability to relate to others, more evident than in his relationships with his grandchildren. He is an astounding grandfather. He loves the children passionately. He hugs and kisses them. He jokes with them. He is the type of grandfather who sits on the floor, gets to their eye level and relates to them. Pallak's son Alif and his daughters Ayat and Aria simply adore their grandfather.

The warm heartedness of Deepak and Payel is recognised by 11-year-old Sahana, Pulkit's daughter. She says, "If anyone faces any problem, they are able to understand what the person is going through and are very generous."

Deepak and his grandchildren share a very close relationship. Sahana even gives Deepak some swimming backstroke lessons, in the pool in their house. Sahana has followed her grandfather's passion for sports. She has won numerous medals for races at school. She loves her grandfather for having gone with her to buy her dog, Sparkle. She enjoys writing and has essayed an article on Deepak in her school magazine.

Time for Music, Movies and Books

In all the turbulence of travel and work, Deepak yet loves going back to music, movies and books, whenever possible. Sometimes, he can read a book or grab a movie only on flights. He enjoys listening to old Hindi Bollywood songs of the 1960s to the 1980s. His favourites songs are "Chaudavi Ka Chand Ho" from the 1960 film of the same name by Guru Dutt, "Pyar Kiya to Darna Kya" from the epic Indian movie Mughal-e-Azam" (1960), "Abhi Na Jao Chhod Kar" from the 1961 "Hum Dono", "Kabhi Kabhi Mere Dil Mein Khayal Aata Hai" from the 1976 movie "Kabhi Kabhi" and "Tu Meri Rani" from the 2016 movie "Tumhari Sulu".

Deepak enjoys a movie whenever he can. His favourite films which he can watch repeatedly with his family are the great musical "Sound of Music" starring Julie Andrews; the Indian blockbuster "Sholay" starring the three biggest Indian stars, Sanjeev Kumar, Dharmendra and Amitabh Bachchan; the "Godfather" trilogy which mesmerised the entire world and created three mega global stars Marlon Brando, Al Pacino and Robert de Niro; the "Gladiator" which became the crowning glory of Russell Crowe; and finally the iconic Indian move, "Dilwale Dulhania Le Jayenge" starring India's heartthrob and the world's richest actor Shah Rukh Khan. Of course, for laughs, Deepak can watch "Welcome" any number of times starring Anil Kapoor and Nana Patekar in unconventional mafia roles.

Like children across the world, Deepak enjoyed the books written by Enid Blyton as a child. As he grew older, he relished reading the P.G. Wodehouse books laced with British humour. Mystery books and detective books have continued to be his favourites. He yet enjoys reading books by Jeffrey Archer, Agatha Christie's Hercule Poirot mysteries and John Grisham's novels.

Time for Pets, Too

"So, you are leaving without meeting Sparkle, Angel and Biscuit?" asked Deepak of his friend Ramesh. There was pure hurt in Deepak's eyes.

Ramesh was a university classmate of Deepak, who now lived in Montreal. He had finished his visit to Delhi and was headed for the airport. He had not been to Deepak's home on this visit. However, Deepak was very upset. Ramesh was leaving Delhi without having met their pets Angel and Sparkle, of Maltese breed and Biscuit of Chihuahua breed. Deepak and Payel adore their pets. They are treated like family members.

Deepak, Payel and their two sons have always enjoyed having dogs in the family. There was Cutie, a Pomeranian; then Max, a German Shepard; later, Scotch and Rusty who were Golden Retrievers; there was Begum, a Great Dane; Blackie, a black retriever; and Fluffy, a Maltese breed. The Seth home is incomplete without pets.

Early morning, a large bird, an Australian Cockatoo, named Pearl, is brought to the lawns of Deepak's home. Then, Deepak talks to him and personally feeds him food grains.

Prayer Time

When Pallak and Pulkit were around five to seven years old, Deepak would take them every Sunday, to pray at the Malai Mandir (Temple), in R. K. Puram, near Vasant Vihar, in New Delhi. Deepak prays every morning. Sometimes, he gets too many calls in the morning. Then, he prays on the way to the office in the car.

Once he told his friend Ramesh who was travelling with him in his car in the morning, "Can you please give me few minutes? I need to pray."

“Deepak is a person with a large heart; the heart of a lion. He will do anything for a friend.
If you have a problem and telephone him, he will be the first person at your doorstep to help you. This is a very rare quality.”

- Pradeep Dinodia

***

In Latino countries like Brazil or Colombia, when you are invited to a friend’s house, the first sentence they say is, “My home is your home”.

Deepak and Payel have similar warmth in their hearts. They welcome their guests and friends with open hearts.

37
A Friend's Friend

Keshav was depressed. He was being bothered by his family for a loan that he had taken from them for a business, amounting to USD 1,00,000. He was Deepak's schoolmate. So, Deepak sat with him patiently circa 1980 and went through his assets and bank balances. He realised, that Keshav would have to give away everything he had to clear the loan. So, Deepak whispered quietly in Keshav's ear, "Look, just go and throw the money on their face. You are young. You will earn this type of money many times over in your life." Those 27 words hit Keshav like 27 bullets. He took quick action and cleared the debt within six weeks. He was a free man again. Keshav is grateful to Deepak, for life now. Deepak helps with the right words, at the right time. Even 27 words of encouragement, from a good friend can be life-changing.

Friends who need a bridge loan to buy a house or an office also approach Deepak for temporary financial support. Deepak always helps. He never charges any interest. He is just happy, that he could support a friend when he needed some assistance. "Pay, when able," he tells his friends. Deepak never asks for a friendly loan to be paid back to him. The friend can return the money in instalments, according to his convenience.

Kumar, another friend of Deepak was very miserable with his job in the corporate sector. He wanted to start a business, but did not have the capital to do so. Deepak told him, "Do not be so unhappy. You start your business. I will fund you completely. You can pay me back, whenever it is possible for you to do so. Pay, when able."

Deepak always takes time out for his friends, classmates and even business associates. If any of them need advice or support, he is a call away. If anyone ever approaches him for anything, the response invariably is, "Consider it done." Deepak works round-the-clock. Yet, no friend has to wait to talk to him or meet him. A call from a friend is answered immediately or on the same day. Deepak is the best friend, anyone can have. He is always happy to interact, entertain and party with his friends.

Deepak also supports his friends if they go to him with new business proposals, even in products in which he does not have expertise. Says a university friend, "I went to him with a proposal to establish a consumer products business. He trusts you completely. He empowers and supports you. All that he is interested in, is how large can we grow the business. He does not invest with any conditions. He just wants the new business to grow."

Deepak is always prodding his friends for new ideas or new projects. Some friend of Deepak, is always engaged in some feasibility study. If the project is viable, Deepak involves the friend in the joint venture. At various stages, Deepak has explored the feasibility of establishing a tea-bag business, a business school, a leather garments business, a travel business, etc.

Rakesh Kapoor recalls, "Deepak is unbelievably open and warm. It is difficult to make friends after a certain age. However, Deepak and I became friends in a very short period of time. He is an extraordinarily free spirited and generous person. People are rarely so giving in terms of emotional and mental help and time. It is a rare quality." Deepak always gives abundantly of his affection and time to his friends.

Humility

Deepak's friends admire his humility. "Deepak is a self-made businessman. He is very grounded, very real and a wonderful human being to spend time with," says a college classmate. He has not let his success impair his personality. His modesty and self-effacement have contributed immensely to his professional advancement.

Many of Deepak's directors have studied with him during his graduate and post-graduate days. The DS Group provides work to some of his classmates, who manage independent professional services companies. These classmates accord top priority to any work emanating from the Group. Deepak is very loyal to his friends. He builds relationships for life. He cares for his friends and their families. He tries to attend their wedding anniversaries and the marriages of their children.

Prior to finalising any date for an important celebration, Deepak consults his brothers and his close friends, to ensure that the date suits them. If he is having a three-day anniversary party in Turkey or in Singapore, he ensures that all his family members and friends are able to attend.

A friend of Deepak in the corporate sector, was hosting a party in Calcutta in 1995, for his Managing Director, who was retiring. Deepak and Payel both flew down for the evening to attend the dinner. It is not merely the happy occasions, that Deepak attends. When the mother of a close friend Gopal passed away in Bombay in 1993, Deepak flew down to comfort him. Later, Gopal was scheduled to visit Haridwar (religious town in north India), for some religious ceremonies. When Deepak realised that Gopal was travelling alone, he received him personally at Delhi airport and accompanied him for the journey of six hours, in his own car.

Best Adversity Friend

Deepak is the best adversity friend, anyone can have. Any person can go through a difficult situation in life like bankruptcy, loss of a job and breakdown of a marriage. This is the time, when many acquaintances shun the person or indulge in gossip. Not Deepak. When a person is going through a rough patch, Deepak will stand by him stalwartly. He will always stand by his friends, when they are battling odds heavily or are being victimised. He never laughs at anyone, going through a rough innings. On the contrary, his heart goes out to the person.

Deepak cares genuinely for his friends. If any of them, whether businessmen or professionals, have a glitch in their operations or careers, he is very supportive. He will not merely offer advice, he will also offer to speak to his contacts, if his intervention can help.

Many of Deepak's friends are corporate professionals. Deepak is a businessman. He is far richer than many of his classmates. Yet, he never displays his wealth. He is always humble and sensitive. His friends can trust him with any information. Deepak always keeps a confidence. He is very discreet. He was inspired by Rudyard Kipling's poem, "If....", which advises, "If you can talk with crowds and keep your virtue. Or walk with Kings—nor lose the common touch. Yours is the Earth and everything that's in it. And—which is more—you'll be a Man, my son!"

Similarly, Deepak helps many distant relatives with monthly contributions, but never ever talks about it. "Yes, I have helped lots of relatives over the years. I also try to donate to every appeal I get from people I know. Giving is very important for my peace of mind. God has been kind to me," says Deepak. He is even willing to help relatives to have a relaxed life. A distant uncle of his, enjoyed playing Rummy cards game over the weekends. However, as he grew older, he did not have the money to indulge in his passion. When Deepak learnt about it, he sent the relative some money every month, till the time the uncle passed away. Deepak believes that if you help anyone, it should be done silently and discreetly.

The qualities of being very fair and listening to everybody, endears Deepak to his friends and business associates. Friends always approach Deepak for advice and help to resolve family disputes, property issues or thorny business problems. They often ask him to be the sole arbitrator. Deepak provides the comfort to everybody, that their interests will be managed judiciously.

Now, mediating between people is time and energy consuming. It can also ruffle many feathers. All negotiations are a matter of give and take. Mediating can be emotionally exhausting. It can also be a thankless task. Sometimes, reaching a settlement can take days if not weeks or months. Frequently, Deepak has to travel two to three days, out of Delhi for meetings with all the concerned parties. Even when travelling to mediate between others, he will insist on paying all the expenses. Deepak gives his time, emotions and involvement to those, who seek his counsel. However, he also gives of himself.

He is always willing to contribute to deserving charities. Rakesh's wife Ritu was associated with an NGO called Pratham, doing charitable work in education. Ritu met Deepak to ask for a donation. Without a blink, Deepak issued a cheque.

Deepak loves breaking bread with his friends. Punjab state in India is renowned for good food. The best North Indian meals, snacks, spices, pickles and poppadums, (thin, crisp, Indian round flatbread, called "papads" locally), hail from Punjab. The state is also the granary of India, growing copious amounts of wheat, rice, maize, fresh fruits and vegetables, etc.

Most Punjabis love eating delicious food. They find delectable food irresistible. Deepak is no exception. He dines with his business associates, with élan at a seven-star hotel like the Emirates Palace in Abu Dhabi or in any of his favourite restaurants like Harry's Bar in London serving Italian cuisine. He also enjoys La Petite Maison in Nice, Italy, serving Mediterranean cuisine or the French seafood serving Le Bernardin in New York or El Bulli in Spain. Other favourites are the Japanese Zuma in Dubai or any of the three-star Michelin restaurants. Deepak looks forward to Japanese and Thai dishes like Japanese Yellow Tail, Tuna Tartare, Black Cod, Shrimp Tempura Sushi and Eel and crab.

However, Deepak is equally comfortable having a typical Indian dinner with his college buddies at a "dhaba" (wayside Indian eatery, serving local cuisine, normally heavily spiced and fried) like "Kesar Dhaba" in Amritsar (Punjab) or "Moti Mahal" in Daryaganj (Delhi) or "Puran Singh Dhaba" in Ambala (Haryana). He relishes "dal makhani" (black lentils cooked and simmered with home-made white butter) and "buttered nan bread" in a "dhaba".

Deepak relishes Indian savouries like "Chole bhature" or "aloo-tikkis" or "Punjabi samosas" with his school friends. He also relishes Indian sweets like "Rasgullas" or "Ras Malai" or "Jalebis". However, Payel's watchful eye prevents him from overindulging in these rich Indian foods.

Deepak's love of food, is inspiring him to consider establishing a vegetarian food restaurant in London. He is constantly meeting people and chefs in the restaurant business to understand how the business works. He is also scouting for the best location for the restaurant.

Pradeep Dinodia, a friend of Deepak comments, "He is a person with a large heart, the heart of a lion. He will do anything for a friend. If you have a problem and telephone Deepak, he will be the first person at your doorstep to help you. This is a very rare quality." Deepak never thinks twice before helping a friend in any way.

Fabulous Hostess and Host

In Latino countries like Brazil or Colombia, when you are invited to a friend's house, he and his wife greet you at the door. The first sentence they say is, "My home is your home." It is an honour, to be welcomed to a Latino home, with these five words. These five words make the guest feel special. Deepak and Payel have similar warmth in their hearts. They open the door of their house and tell you, "My home, is your home," to welcome you. Payel and Deepak welcome their guests and friends with open hearts.

Pulkit's wife, Shifalli is absolutely impressed with Deepak's hospitality. She says, "One of the things that I have learnt from him is "Atithi Devo Bhava" (A guest is God). There is never an empty glass or plate in anyone's hand, when people come for dinner parties to our house. If we have a house guest, no matter how late Papa has slept, he always gets up early to have breakfast with the person. Whosoever is at our home, he is always made to feel special. I think this is the trait, that has helped Papa to build very strong relationships over the years."

If any friend or classmate of Deepak is visiting Delhi, Deepak will send a car to collect him from the airport and invite him to his house. He will insist that his friend should stay at his house and not in a hotel. He will stop all his work and spend the day with him. After the visit, Deepak will also accompany the friend to the airport.

Whether Deepak is entertaining customers or industry colleagues, managers or friends, he makes efforts to make everyone feel at home. He does not leave the task of inviting to his staff. He personally telephones and invites every person. Then, he receives every guest personally.

He will introduce the various guests to each other. He keeps checking to ensure that everyone has a drink and that their plates are full. If the families are also invited, Deepak and Payel will speak to every member of the family. They welcome every member of the guest's family. When a guest is departing, Deepak will accompany the person to the car.

Being a gracious host, Deepak reviews the entire menu before any party. He studies all the dishes being served, to ensure that the guests are served food, which they will enjoy. There was a meeting at Pearl Academy, followed by a lunch. Deepak went through the menu and counselled the manager, that they should include boneless chicken in the menu. He felt that the chicken dish they had selected would not be relished. This miniscule attention to every dish being served at a party, ensures that the guests enjoy themselves.

Organising a Party

Payel and Deepak entertain buyers, office staff and friends very frequently at home. Sometimes, they have over 100 guests at a party. Organising a large party needs incredible advance planning. Payel and Deepak invite all the 100 guests personally. About eight days before the party, the house starts getting spruced up. The curtains are dry-cleaned. The carpets are vacuumed. The lawns are manicured. The marble floors are polished.

Then, by the third day, the crockery and cutlery have to be finalised and cleaned. The crystal and silver have to be polished. Flowers have to be ordered. The napkins have to be washed and pressed. If the food is being cooked at home, the menu has to be decided. The shopping has to be organised. The layout of the tables and the seating arrangement has to be finalised.

The cooking has to commence about 24 to 30 hours before the party. Each dish has to be checked and tasted before it goes to the dining tables. During the last 24 hours, the beverages have to be arranged with the various types of glasses.

Then, each guest has to be received personally and honoured. So, organising a party could mean going through a manual of check points. Payel and Deepak go through these chores, for they love entertaining their families and friends. "Increasingly," adds Payel, "Deepak loves to do a lot on his own. He even decides the menu and the dishes to be served. He enjoys it."

Best Pickles in the World

Payel and Deepak have built a wonderful team at their home to manage it. The staff has been with them for over three decades. So, they are familiar with the protocols.

Their chef, Ashok Chauan, has been with them for 35 years. He makes excellent pickles. No Indian meal is complete without spicy pickles. These are pieces of assorted vegetables and fruits like raw mangoes, lemons, onions, carrots, cauliflower and olives, cut and preserved in oils or vinegar. They are flavoured with Indian spices like chilli powder, turmeric and peppers. They last for 12 to 18 months.

Ashok can churn out about 35 varieties of spicy and sweet pickles, with assorted vegetables and fruits like lemons, raw mangoes, ginger, green chillies, cauliflowers, turnips, carrots and onions. He has mastered this art with guidance from Payel. The pickles at Payel's home are the tastiest and the most delectable in the world. Deepak also discussed with Ashok, the possibility of commercialising the pickles and launching a brand. The project may see the light of the day sometime.

Says Surender Dhillon, "Mr. Seth is a superb host. I give him 100 out of 100 marks as a gracious host. In July 2014, we had the Silver Jubilee celebratory lunch at the Delhi Club. It is a large venue. All the employees and their families had been invited. Mr. Seth made it a point to meet all the employees, their wives and children and talk to them." He spent some minutes with everyone, asking them, "How are you? How are the children?" Deepak even counselled many of the children about their future studies and careers.

Some of the professionals who work with Deepak, move on after some years to other ventures or to become entrepreneurs themselves. They continue to be friends with Deepak. At any party at his house or at the office, the ex-employees or the "Pearlites" are looked after as team members. Deepak and his family make everyone feel very special.

Deepak is a fine host who is thoughtful of every person. At any party, he ensures that the chauffeurs who have driven the guests are also served.

Deepak has a cardinal rule. He never discusses work when he is meeting anyone socially. In office, he maintains a very professional relationship with the managers and the staff. However, on social occasions, he is a very warm and hospitable person.

Unique Personality

Deepak sat alone in the hotel lobby in Manchester in 1985, nursing a beer. He was on a business trip and did not know many people in town. He was wondering where he would dine. From the corner of his eye, he noticed another Indian sitting at the bar. They smiled at each other spontaneously. This other Indian was Mr. Virender (Vindi) Uppal, owner of Richa Global Exports. He too was a garments exporter from India. When two exporters meet, they have a lot to discuss. So, the few beers they had together, stretched into a dinner, that night in Manchester. That chance meeting, has gradually elongated into a life-long personal and professional friendship. Now, 37 years later, Virender says, "Deepak is a gem of a friend."

Virender was celebrating his fiftieth birthday at Las Vegas in the USA, with his family. He had also invited his friends for the joyous occasion. Deepak kept telephoning him in his hotel, berating him for having chosen such a faraway location. Deepak also explained that he could not attend the celebration, because he was working in distant London. After a few minutes, the doorbell of Virender's room chimed. He was shocked to see Deepak standing there. Deepak had already travelled to Las Vegas to attend Virender's party. Virender was stunned and overjoyed. "He was the only friend who travelled all the way to be with me," he recalls.

Later at a family get-together in 2008, in Turkey, Deepak was to proclaim Virender as his reliable "Hanuman" (a Hindu deity, who always supported Lord Rama, in all his virtuous pursuits). Such is the bond of friendship between them.

Virender says "Deepak is a very open, true and honest person. He never has any hidden agenda and is very God fearing. Deepak believes in doing the right things, even if he suffers or loses in the process. He also cares very deeply and genuinely about people. He always builds relationships for life and always looks at the long term. As they say in Punjabi, he is a "Yaaran daa Yaar" (the best of buddies)."

There is no pride, pretentiousness or showmanship in Deepak. He helps his family, friends and associates selflessly. He is also very transparent. He never breaks his word. He always delivers on his promises. He is very open-hearted. Moreover, he helps people without any expectation.

All these qualities make Deepak a very adored family member, colleague and friend.

38
Pearl Academy: An Institution in Itself

Deepak and his three brothers Chand, Harish and Krishen were engrossed in a deep discussion, around their conference table at Rohit House in Delhi, in 1992. "It is critical we get more designers and merchandisers, if we are to execute all our orders," said Chand. "Yes, but from where, is the question. We only get raw graduates or school-certified students, who do not know anything about garment manufacturing or merchandising," commented Harish. The four brothers had a long discussion on how to source knowledgeable and trained staff. Deepak added, "Every time we train someone on the job, he gets lured by a slightly higher salary in the market."

In business, there is never a dull moment. As the business grew, Deepak and his brothers were confronted with a serious problem. It was simply impossible to source good quality professionals and skilled staff like merchandisers, designers and supervisors. They reasoned that instead of hunting for qualified staff, they should seize the initiative to establish their own school. They could then train youngsters in the manufacture and marketing of garments. This was their inspiration to establish a training school.

"The idea is good, but who will put all the bricks together?" asked Chand. "I guess it is our idea, so I will work on it to make it a reality," replied Deepak. He plunged into the project passionately.

It was a momentous decision. The fact that Pearl was willing to establish a fashion school to train youngsters, showed its long-term commitment to the garments business.

Deepak decided that the institute that they will build, would be a hands-on school with roots in the realities of business. He was inspired by his own post-graduate studies at the Jamnalal Bajaj Institute of Management Studies (JBIMS). The Institute was a business school, renowned for producing well-grounded, earthy MBAs.

Deepak called a meeting of the top garment exporters in Delhi and briefed them about the project. They were enthusiastic, as they too faced many challenges in sourcing qualified and trained staff for their operations. Deepak then sought their inputs on the type of training the students should be given at the institute. From these inputs, Deepak constructed the first syllabus of the Pearl Academy.

Search for Professional Staff

The garments industry in India was very competitive. To garner even a tiny share of the fiercely fought market, the exporter had to excel in providing seamless services to customers. Now, to provide impeccable services, a company needed high-quality professionals, staff and workers. However, there was a serious shortage of trained manpower and professionals in this nascent but growing industry. In 1986, the Government of India had established the National Institute of Fashion Technology (NIFT), the first fashion school in India. The graduates of NIFT serviced the needs of the growing garments industry. However, the supply of graduates was not adequate to meet the demand. This urgent need for professionals in the garments business, gave birth to the idea of setting up a fashion school.

Deepak had realised the potential of the garments industry as early as the late 1970s. He had also grasped, that the businesses would have to be managed by professional managers. Family members by themselves, would not be able to manage the growth beyond a certain stage. It was his vision, to build a training institute to groom professionals for the fashion and apparel manufacturing sectors.

A key strength of Deepak has been to pick up an abstract idea and transform it into a reality. It took him some months and a lot of midnight oil burning, to convert the concept of a training school into the Pearl Academy. He had to arrange a building, classrooms, desks, syllabus, a director and staff. It was painstaking and demanding. This mission of Deepak, was in addition to managing the ongoing business.

Deepak always had an eye for good quality professionals, who can deliver. He is a good judge of people, their character and calibre. He had heard about the reputation of Mr. A. K. G. Nair, a director in NIFT. So, he was amongst the first recruits. With his help, Deepak established the Pearl Academy in 1993. Mr. Nair's experience of working with NIFT helped the Pearl Academy during the foundation years. Mr. Nair led the Academy for around 20 years.

Practical Syllabus

Pearl Academy's wild success is due to the fact that its syllabus is dovetailed to the needs of the garments industry. When the institute was in its incubation stage, Deepak had numerous meetings with the exporters of garments to hammer out a syllabus. This paid rich dividends. The course content incorporated their assessment of the areas in which the graduates needed training. This dialogue between Deepak and the other exporters became a regular event. New and contemporary subjects were added to the syllabus every semester. Thus, when a student graduated from the Academy, he was well-equipped for the practical world.

A significant factor that has contributed to the success of the Pearl Academy is Deepak's focus on globalisation right from the commencement. He identified the best possible international associates and partners for the Academy. He forged strong relationships with them. He was a pioneer in building foreign partnerships for the Academy. One such partner was Nottingham Trent University in England. Its roots go back to 1843. It had established the Nottingham Government School of Design.

Over the decades, the Pearl Academy has evolved into a globally renowned institution of higher learning. The focus is on global practices and entrepreneurship. The Academy caters to the needs of the design, fashion and retail industries. It offers 57 courses, including 19 under-graduate courses, 20 post-graduate courses, two master's courses and 16 professional programmes. It offers four-year undergraduate and two-year post-graduate courses. The Pearl Academy enjoys almost 100 percent placements. The students get jobs even before they graduate.

The modest school which started in a simple building in Naraina, now has campuses in Delhi, Jaipur, Mumbai and Bengaluru. The Pearl Academy is now rated as one of the top fashion schools in India. It has a robust faculty of 400 professionals.

The Academy is India's leading institution in design and fashion. It is a catalytic force, contributing to the careers and success of students across creative industries, over the last three decades.

Deepak managed the Pearl Academy very professionally. He hired the best faculty and then let them do their jobs. Deepak always advised his team, "Do not compromise on quality. Do your best to help the students professionally. Do not favour anyone or pass him, just because I know him or his family."

Wide Range of Subjects

The Pearl Academy has about 5,000 students, of which about 40 percent are in the fashion space, studying design, styling, image design, etc.

The next important area of study is communication design, covering graphics, animation, interaction design, game design, interiors and product design. Media and creative industries also entice students.

Pearl Academy is the only school in India that teaches design, fashion, contemporary media and creative practices under one roof. Other institutes cover specific fields only. The National Institute of Fashion Technology (NIFT) focusses only on fashion. The Maharashtra Institute of Technology (MIT) specialises in design.

The under-graduate courses offer subjects like advertising and marketing, accessory design, animation and VFX, digital marketing and data analysis, fashion design, communication, fashion lifestyle, textile and jewellery design.

The post-graduate courses cover subjects like accessory design, costume design for film, TV and theatre, creative entrepreneurship, event management and experiential marketing and interior design.

The professional courses cover a range of areas like fashion buying and merchandising, digital filmmaking, advertising, graphics and celebrity and bridal hair and make-up.

Pearl Academy has alliances with many reputed partners like Adobe, Amazon, Fashion Design Council of India, Institute of Indian Interior Designers, Event and Entertainment Management Association (EEMA), Federation of Indian Chambers of Commerce and Industry (FICCI), Retailers Association of India (RAI), Indira Gandhi National Open University (IGNOU), Apparel, Made-ups & Home furnishing Sector Skill Council (AMHSSC), National Skill Development Corporation (NSDC), Gems and Jewellery Skill Council of India, Media and Entertainment Skill Council and National Skill Development Corporation (NSDC).

The Pearl Academy now has an alumnus of about 20,000 students. Some of them work in industry for some years and then join the faculty.

Global Recognition

The Academy's courses are well-recognised internationally. A student can study for three years at the Pearl Academy. Then, he can complete the final year at Manchester Metropolitan University or Nottingham Trent University and obtain a degree from there. The credits of Pearl Academy are accepted by many universities worldwide.

The Pearl Academy in Mumbai commenced in 2014. It has about 1,000 students. The Academy has earned a good reputation, nationally and globally.

Nandita Abraham, the President of Pearl Academy says, "Pearl has become a strong and trusted brand name. A lot of people aspire to send their children to this Academy. We have instances when three to four members of a family study with us. We often have the younger siblings coming to us, after the elder child has graduated."

Admissions time is very demanding on the selection committee. Parents of aspiring candidates bring references from the high and mighty of the land. People give references of the Prime Minster of India or the Chief Minister of Delhi or senior police officers, to secure admission. These references also emerge when a student is failing the exams. The Academy has learnt to soldier on despite these pressures. All selections and grades are purely on merit.

Pearl Academy has emerged as the industry leader. It has developed courses to cater to the needs of the industry. It supplies the fashion industry with professionals to drive growth and innovation.

Deepak is always ready to help the Academy at the drop of a hat, in any way he can. He deploys all his contacts in the industry, government and among his friends, if the Academy needs any help. He always attends the convocation ceremonies.

Whenever foreign retailers like JCPenney or Macy's visit India, Deepak invites them to lecture to the students. This provides the youngsters with first-hand and practical knowledge of how businesses operate. The DS Group (including PDS and PGIL), has operations in London, Hong Kong, New York, etc. Many of the Academy students intern in these businesses abroad. They get practical hands-on training.

Becoming a Star in the Industry

Deepak realised that garment business is akin to making a movie. When you go to see a movie like "Godfather", you go to a comfortable theatre. You come out and you remember Marlon Brando or Al Pacino or Robert de Niro. You do not remember the 1,500 to 2,000 persons who work as technicians, musicians, location facilitators, public relations staff, marketing personnel, etc. They are among the many who are also actively involved in making the movie, behind the scenes. Without all these professionals and staff, the movie would not get made. Without them, we would not remember Marlon Brando or Al Pacino, as we do.

Similarly, when we visit an Armani store to buy a suit, we remember the store and the fashionable suit. We do not even know the 100 plus persons who have worked to produce the suit. They are the designers, merchandisers, tailors, fabric manufacturers, button manufacturers and zip manufacturers. They also include laundry staff, pressing staff, logistics and transport staff, etc. Without all these people, there would be no sartorial suit.

Similarly, people remember the Armani store from where they bought an elegant suit. They also remember 007 James Bond, Daniel Craig, if he modelled a suit. People do not know who designed and tailored the suit. So, the garments business involves working in the shadows and not on the stage. The manufacturer could not be a star. The star would be Armani or James Bond.

The success of the Pearl Academy, made Deepak a star in the apparel industry. He gained widespread recognition and respect in India and abroad, for furthering the cause of education and generating jobs in the fashion industry.

Dr. Rajiv Kumar, Vice Chairman, NITI Aayog, Government of India, extols Deepak's pioneering work in establishing the Pearl Academy. He comments, "Deepak always tries to contribute to society. The Pearl Academy has trained many young people in the art of designing, marketing and logistics of the garment industry. This is a very big contribution to the industry and to Indian society. Deepak has no financial interest in the Academy. He is simply a social-minded person. The social spirit is a very valuable part of Deepak's and Pearl's operating philosophy."

Bright and sprightly, Nandita Abraham joined the Academy in 2001 as a faculty member. She has risen to the position of the President of the Academy. She worked her way up diligently as course leader, head of the department, operations manager, etc. She thinks that Deepak is a fine human being and a sharp and intuitive problem solver. He is well networked and a no-nonsense professional. These strengths have contributed to building the Pearl Academy. Nandita adds, "Deepak never ever told us to select any student or pass him. There are always pressures from various sources at the time of admissions. However, Deepak and his family have never interfered with the admissions process."

Nandita thinks that Pearl is a very special place. She adds, "A lot of people who are working here, get very lucrative offers from other universities. However, they do not leave us. Some, who do leave, always want to come back. This is because Pearl Academy cares about people. Pearl Academy provides youngsters with the opportunities to experiment, learn and grow. It cares for its staff and the students. Last year, we were certified as 'A great place to work.' It is the only design institute in the world with this certification." There are many faculty and staff members, who have worked for 20 to 25 years in the Pearl Academy.

Success Stories of Alumni

The success of Pearl Academy is evident from the achievements of its students and their success stories.

Jayati Gupta studied Interior Architecture & Design, between 2011 and 2015. She co-founded Lifestyle Dessein in 2014, with Abhinav Gupta. The multi-disciplinary firm draws inspiration from their expertise in the areas of design, art and architecture. Jayati has been published in the Insite magazine as an 'emerging designer' in 2017. She also has a passion for designing art and light installations; her design was shortlisted for the Borealis Light Festival in 2019.

She received the award for 'The most Innovative design' for her thesis project at Pearl Academy, a re-design for "Dilli Haat" in 2015. Her educational background includes studies in Interior Design from Parsons and the New School, New York, 2018. She has worked in New York and gained industry experience with Rottet Studio, New York. Her project, which focusses on Foster Care Interior Design in Harlem, was exhibited at NY+11 exhibition in New York, 2017.

Sreeked studied Jewellery Design, between 2009 and 2013. He is the founder and creative head of a company, Poetry of Gems. Sreeked hails from the city of Kochi in India and is a graduate in Jewellery Designing from Pearl Academy, Jaipur. He has experience in working in companies such as VNM diamonds, Malabar Gold & Diamonds and Gitanjali Brands Pvt. Ltd. in India. He has done an internship with Vacheron Constantin in Geneva (Switzerland), where he designed a swan pair watch for the company.

After the Internship with Vacheron Constantin, he joined Royal Insignia as a Design Executive. Royal Insignia is a luxury house based in Singapore, designing and manufacturing medals, fine jewellery and gifts for the world's Royal families, etc. The highlights of his work with Royal insignia include designing jewellery for the royal family of Malaysia in 2017, championship rings for a football team owned by a prince of Malaysia and the Arabian Gulf Super Cup Trophy in 2018.

In the quest to express his love for jewellery and design, he founded the brand, "Poetry of Gems" in August 2020. "Poetry of Gems" offers remote freelance designing services for clients across the world. It provides designing solutions with concepts, sketches, 3D modelling, product animation, etc.

Designer Vaishali Shadangule completed the Post Graduate Fashion Design at Pearl Academy. She built an eponymous brand, "Vaishali S". The brand is committed to handloom weavers. It has worked with over 900 weavers and explored 14 different techniques of weaving from various Indian states. "We consciously choose to work with female artisans and weavers across the country. They get empowered. They can make informed choices that enrich their lives. Eighty percent of our weavers are females," says Vaishali.

In 2011, the Vaishali S label debuted at Mumbai's Lakme Fashion Week. She displayed garments made from Chanderi and Paithani handwoven fabrics. Since then, she has launched several collections through New York and Milan fashion weeks, during the last five years. Her brand has also forayed into home décor. She continues to reinvent the use of hand-woven textiles and techniques, to create unique and contemporary products.

Guarav Khanijo studied Fashion Design & Technology, between 2002-2005. He is the CEO and founder of a company, Khanijo. Khanijo is a luxury brand founded in 2014. The eponymous label by Gaurav Khanijo, started with exhibiting his fine tailoring skills. Now, the label is often seen on both men and women. The label correlates fashion and anthropology, while preserving the craft of native artisans.

Kriti Tula studied Fashion Design between 2006 and 2010. She is the co-founder of Doodlage. At Doodlage, factory waste is used to make short limited-edition collections of garments. They recycle waste and convert scraps into new fabrics, to create season-less garments. Their fabrics are manufactured on ethical production units. The packaging is plastic free. "As a kid raised in the 90s in India, upcycling was a deeply rooted tradition in most middle and upper-middle class families. Every garment was cherished and every piece lasted more than we hoped. We were simply prudent. Everything was less disposable. Everyone had less money to spend. It was a good time for the earth," says Kriti.

Commitment to Excellence

The above examples of brilliance and success, show how Deepak through the Pearl Academy, has transformed the lives of thousands of youngsters, across India. He has provided avenues for them, to fulfil their dreams. He has provided a purpose to countless young people and also enriched the fashion and garments industry through them.

Dr. Sakthivel, Chairman of AEPC comments, "Deepak made a foray into the educational sector by starting the Pearl Academy of Fashion. It has been of great service to the exporters. Pearl Academy has opened new avenues for youngsters in textiles, fashion, etc. It is now a very successful and internationally recognised institution."

A college friend of Deepak opines, "It was his heart's pure desire that the Academy should impart education and skills to youngsters. This has enabled them to make a living. It also provides useful resources to the industry."

Pearl Academy is committed to maintaining its excellence in academic standards and improving the quality of the teaching.

"Pearl Academy has trained many youngsters in the art of designing, marketing and logistics of the garment industry. This is a very big contribution to industry and to Indian society.

Deepak has no financial interest in the Academy. He is simply a social-minded person. Deepak always tries to contribute to society.

The social spirit is a very valuable part of Deepak's and Pearl Group's operating philosophy."

- Dr. Rajiv Kumar, Vice Chairman,
NITI Aayog, Government of India

"Deepak and Payel's initiatives in "Arpan", Little Pearls, is pure service. There is no financial angle. They are trying to give children a good education. These are children who cannot afford to go to a school.

Instead of just giving them money, they are educating them, so that they can earn money on their own, in their lives.

This is a service to humanity."

- Pradeep Dinodia, schoolmate

39
"Little Pearls": Building Beautiful Minds

The 25 chirping children, all aged between four to five years, from different nationalities ran joyously inside the school building. They took turns to hug Payel Seth and Dr. Ekta Sharma. They were chatting with each other constantly, laughing and enjoying themselves. However, each time a child spotted Payel Seth or Dr. Ekta Sharma, he or she would embrace them spontaneously with a shout of sheer joy. Then, the child returned to chatting with the others. These were children attending a day school, in Delhi.

There was four-year-old John from London, whose dad worked with a British multinational in Delhi. There was three-year-old Phillipa from Amsterdam, whose father worked in the Dutch Embassy. There was three-year-old Joseph from Kenya, whose father worked in the Kenyan Embassy. There were about 25 children from 16 different countries and cultures, all bonding and twittering ceaselessly. The colour of their skins and their countries did not matter. What mattered to them, was that they were playing and chitchatting constantly. They were rejoicing their time together.

The venue of this multinational, global fraternity amongst children aged from three to five years, was the Little Pearls School, at Vasant Vihar in Delhi.

Deepak's father, Mr. M. L. Seth was an ardent believer in the value of education. He was delighted that Deepak had established the Pearl Academy to impart skills in fashion and design. He was ruminating for some time, about starting a creative school for children. It could enable kids to develop their imaginative faculties at very early stages.

Around the same time, Deepak had bought a plot of land in Vasant Vihar. Mr. M. L. Seth shared his vision with Deepak and Payel. Thus, was born the concept of “Little Pearls”, a play school for children with focus on ingenuity. Payel enjoyed a good relationship with the principal of a renowned school, who advised her on the project. Ms. Jyoti Titus was the first principal of the Little Pearls School.

The school became the personal passion and mission of Mr. M. L. Seth and Payel. Mr. Seth had retired from DCM. His sons were leading businesses on their own. His grandchildren were studying in schools and colleges in India and the USA. He missed his wife Minaji very much. Managing Little Pearls gave him joy and fulfilment. Every day, he visited the school with Payel and reviewed the progress.

Little Pearls School opened its doors to the children in 1994. The vision was to provide an environment to children, where they felt loved, comfortable and accepted. They would also have the freedom to explore and fall in love with learning.

Goals of the School

The goal of the school is to provide a happy and hygienic pre-school experience for kids between the ages of 14 months to six years. Little Pearls follows an international curriculum of Early Years Learning Framework (EYLF), used in the UK and Australia. It caters to children from different nationalities.

The motto of Little Pearls is love, laughter and learning. Children are always looking for the freedom to explore and to be happy. The entire philosophy of opening Little Pearls was to provide a place for children, to learn without any effort. Learning should never become a chore.

The toddler programme develops the child's fine movement skills, coordination and concentration, through sensorial experiences. A stimulating environment helps the children to understand the world through their senses.

Creative Options

The playgroup learning exercises, focus on hands-on learning experiences. Exploration, free play, pretend play, story time, art and music are some activities planned for the children. Interaction with the other children, communication skills and all-round personality development are encouraged.

The pre-nursery programme provides opportunities and materials to support a child's creative expression of ideas through music and movement. Children in the nursery are exposed to a variety of experiences which enable them to become independent learners. The focus of this programme is to encourage problem-solving skills at a very early stage.

Learning in kindergarten is focussed on building a strong foundation in reading, writing and numeracy skills. The effort is to encourage independent and creative learning. Thus, the children acquire self-confidence.

A Global School

Little Pearls is now a place of learning in a warm, comfortable and vibrant environment. The children are cared for by a team of experts and experienced teachers and nannies. With over 25 years of experience, the school is the first choice of many.

Little Pearls has students of different nationalities. The school has an international curriculum, to meet the needs of the expatriate children. Foreign children constitute about 40 percent of its total strength. Little Pearls School is the officially assigned school for the children of many foreign embassies in India. It is now the recommended day school of embassies like Lithuania and China. The diversity of nationalities, cultures and foods becomes a unique educational experience, for the children and even the faculty.

Researches have confirmed that a child's brain develops from the time of birth till the age of six years. The experiences in these years, provide the base for the mind's development and functioning. This is the time for building a child's personality. The maximum amount of attention should be given to a child at this stage. Says Ms. Kalpana Garg, principal of Little Pearls, "We do not have to work on a child's intelligence and personality in the early years. We just have to provide them with positive, happy and varied experiences. It is like creating lots of dots on paper, which can be connected later to form lines and structures." Thus, a child with exposures to joyful and creative experiences in the early years, will blossom into a successful personality later.

Sometimes, busy parents think that they can develop their children, as they grow up. However, children need the maximum inputs and support, from the time of birth till the age of six years. At Little Pearls, the child is exposed to various creative activities to develop the personality.

An open-door policy is practiced. Parents are welcome to observe their children at school for the first few days. This builds a bond between the school and the parents. The teachers devote a lot of time to get to know the children and their families. This creates a trustworthy environment. The school takes away many parental worries, as the children are managed with affection. The love showered by the entire school team, makes Little Pearls, a child's "home, away from home".

"Arpan" Initiative

Payel assumed full leadership of managing Little Pearls, when Mr. M. L. Seth passed away in 2005. It was a decade since Little Pearls had started. Payel took on herself to modernise the facilities, revamp the syllabus and introduce new amenities. She recruited Mrs. Madhulika Bhupatkar as Director in 2006, to assist her in the redevelopment of the school.

Little Pearls also started an NGO, Arpan, through which education, remedial help and development of underprivileged children are fostered. Arpan was started on 6 January 2006 in memory of Mr. M. L. Seth who had contributed to Little Pearls from 1994 till he passed away in 2005. Every year, about 150 underprivileged children are taken under the Arpan umbrella. These children are in the age range of four to 12 years. They start with kindergarten and are with Arpan until the eighth standard.

Arpan helps underprivileged children to cope with their school work and also develop all-round personalities. The goal of the programme is clear from its Mission, "We sometimes think that poverty is being hungry, naked and homeless. However, being uneducated is the greatest poverty. Arpan works towards eradicating educational poverty."

Arpan operates as a tuition service for the underprivileged children. The children are taught various subjects for an hour daily, after school during the weekdays. They are also provided with a nutritious snack. Vocational guidance is provided to children of 12 years, so that they can support their education independently, after the age of 14 years. Scholarships are given to students who perform well academically, by paying for their tuition fees and books. Children are also taken on educational excursions. Regular medical check-ups are organised for the children.

"Deepak and Payel's Arpan initiative in Little Pearls is pure service. There is no financial angle. They are trying to give children a good education. These are children who cannot afford to go to a school. Instead of just giving them money, they are educating them so that they can earn money on their own, in their lives. This is a service to humanity," says Pradeep Dinodia, a schoolmate of Deepak.

Day-Care Facilities

Little Pearls started day-care facilities in 2013, whereby personal attention is given to children for their all-round development. Dr. Ekta Sharma, a former Principal says, "We developed a world-class infrastructure and a quality programme for children from the ages of one to ten years. The day-care programme caters to the needs of all working parents, who need a home away from home, for their child." The facility was also started for employees of the company, to provide quality education to their children.

Nutritious and well-balanced meals are provided to the children attending the preschool. Breakfast, lunch and fruits are served. The food served to the children is cooked by in-house cooks in the school itself, to ensure safety and hygiene. There are two kitchens and many in-house cooks, who have been with the school for around 12 to 15 years. The modern kitchen in the school is hygienic and monitored through CCTV cameras.

The children eat a variety of foods and thoroughly enjoy mealtimes with their friends. The playschool's menu is shared with the parents on a monthly basis, to address any concerns that they may have. Parents of the children are free to visit the kitchen before the admissions, to reassure themselves. The day care has 50 children. A total of 270 children benefit from Little Pearls.

"Peekaboo" Kids Club

Delhi has an increasing number of nuclear families, with working parents. When the children go home they have no person to play with, as the parents are at work. Moreover, Delhi has three months of extreme summer and three months of extreme winter. So, the children cannot go outdoors to play. Payel conceived the idea of an activity club for children. "Peekaboo Kids Club" was established in 2014 at Vasant Vihar. Peekaboo is a creative club for children. It provides a place where the kids can spend the entire day creatively, in air-conditioned comfort.

The Peekaboo Club is based on membership and the focus is on learning, hygiene and fun. In 2015, an adventure zone was added to Peekaboo, to provide more involvement for the young boys. Sometimes, children look for an adventurous and healthy play environment. Then, the Adventure Room has just what they need, with its play centre made of safe and sustainable materials.

The Adventure zone includes rock walls, aerial walkway and rope bridge, for climbing and learning how to balance. All these activities are supported with soft landings, to protect the children. There are many other amenities at Adventure zone like air hockey and gymnastics. The child could spend the entire day here and be exhilarated with all the experiences.

Caring, Experienced Staff

Little Pearls is managed by qualified and experienced staff. There are 40 teachers in the school, supported by 40 support staff. The parents of children are concerned about the safety and security of their children. Moreover, the children are very young. Thus, there is extra support staff like cleaners, maids, nannies, guards and drivers. Furthermore, the entire school is covered by 32 CCTV cameras. All nooks and corners of the school are observed constantly. The screens are monitored in the offices of the principal and the administrator.

During the last 25 years, Little Pearls has added initiatives to reinvent and transform itself. To cater to the needs of the children and the parents, Little Pearls now offers a play school, day-care facilities, "Peekaboo Kids" club, etc. The school serves as a one-stop destination for children from the ages of six months to 10 years. Every effort is made to ensure that the child's education is playful, stress free and happy.

The congenial environment and coaching leads to significant behavioural changes among children. Seven-year-old John would throw tantrums during the snack time, when he joined. He now sits appropriately in a chair and eats by himself. Kids who had snags in languages, gradually enjoy communicating with their friends and teachers, using Hindi and English languages. Parents notice a significant improvement in the communication skills of their children, within four to five months of joining Little Pearls.

Safety and Hygiene

Little Pearls has been the top ranked school in Delhi in safety and hygiene. The school has received numerous awards for its contributions and maintenance.

The concern for the safety of children is reflected in the infrastructure, classroom designs and furniture. The books provided in each classroom are age-appropriate and changed monthly. Children learn how to handle books and keep them back on the shelves after reading. The bright, spacious classrooms are elegant and have areas for free play, work stations and reading for the children.

All classrooms and common areas are equipped with air conditioners and air purifiers for the comfort of the children. The air quality reading is taken on a daily basis and updated on the school website. The school is maintained surgically clean. Little Pearls is for children; hence, hygiene and safety are paramount. All areas of the preschool are sanitised regularly to eliminate any chances of contamination or breeding of germs. Regular pest control and cleaning practices are followed, ensuring the highest standards of hygiene.

The school's playground is equipped with outdoor toys like tricycles, toy cars, seesaws, swings, slides and a trampoline.

Little Pearls now has an infrastructure of international standards. It has spacious and well-maintained classrooms and activity areas. It has a safe and hygienic environment; above all, it has qualified and experienced staff.

A new educational theme is selected every month, to enthuse the children. Various activities are planned around it like, stories, pictures and even a puppet show. The themes are selected keeping in view the growth needs of the children. The themes could revolve around fruits, vegetables, animals, transport modes, family, seasons, earth, solar system, etc. These exercises create excitement among the children and also ensure that they understand a concept intrinsically.

All the activities are part of the well-planned curriculum. The goal is to bring out the best in all the children and let their talents flower. The passion of the children is infectious and has to be seen to be believed.

Children as Family

Payel is very caring and thoughtful of all the children at Little Pearls. They are part of her extended family. She studies every microscopic detail at the school. She always thinks of how to protect the children and enhance their learning experiences. She checked the table edges in the school. She thought a child could hurt himself due to the table corners. So, the table corners were covered. Payel reviews how all the doors open, to ensure that no child gets hurt. Payel studies the seats of the chairs of the children, to ensure comfort.

Over 25 years, Mr. M. L. Seth, Payel and Deepak have built a remarkable institution to serve children of all ages. Little Pearls day-care caters to children from the ages of six months to 10 years. The preschool programme is for children from the ages of 14 months to six years. Arpan accepts children between the ages of four to 12 years. Finally, the Peekaboo Club thrills children in the age range of one to seven years.

"The best part of my job is the affection and joy on the faces of the children, when they greet me daily. They make my day," says Dr. Ekta Sharma, an educational psychologist. She was on the faculty of the Lady Irwin College and joined Little Pearls in 2000. Dr. Ekta Sharma is a Child Development Specialist with a double Masters in Child Development and Education. She has a passion to connect with children and has also completed her Ph.D. in Educational Psychology. She has developed a Psychological Test on Emotional Intelligence, which is used in many schools and colleges. In addition, she has a Diploma in Early Childhood Education and a Certificate in Training and Assessment from Australia.

Dr. Sharma adds, "When you are with children, you forget all your problems. They give you the purest form of love. They are so innocent. There is great satisfaction in working at building the minds and the personalities of so many children."

Little Pearl organises an Annual Day, involving the parents and their children. It becomes a platform for unity in diversity. The children and their parents participate in performances, highlighting the culture and customs of their countries.

The Silver Jubilee celebrations of Little Pearls on 25th October 2019, brought together the past and present students. Their parents, the current and past faculty members also joined the celebrations. It was a joyous reunion.

Payel told the guests that love, learning and laughter are the three pillars of the school. "Little Pearls School has always ensured that the first step in a child's education is playful, stress free and full of smiles. I am delighted that we have been able to fulfil the needs of the expatriate and Indian parents," she added. About 45 ex-students of Little Pearls attended the Silver Jubilee celebrations. An ex-student from the first batch of Little Pearls had married. It was celebrated at the school. Another alumna of Little Pearls has now become an actress in India.

The play school ensures a smooth transition between the home and formal school, thus playing a catalytic role in the child's formative years. Parents and children are comfortable in the loving atmosphere of Little Pearls. They are reassured that their child is in the best hands.

Payel defines her personal mission as, "To ensure that the children at Little Pearls do not miss the warmth and security of their homes. Their physical, social and emotional needs should be catered to."

Awards and Accolades

The Little Pearls play school and day care have received several awards from reputed institutes like EducationWorld, Brainfeed and ASSOCHAM. The school has been ranked as the Best Institute in New Delhi and seventh best pre-school in India by Education Today, during the School Merit Awards, 2015-16. Little Pearls was recognised as the Asia's Fastest Growing Education Institute, in 2014-15.

The school has garnered awards for Innovative Teaching, Parental Involvement, etc. It has been the recipient of the Jury's Choice Awards for exemplary contributions in the educational field. It has also been designated as the Most

Preferred Playschool of the Year, by ASSOCHAM during the EduShine Excellence Awards, 2019.

The school has received an Award for Establishing Quality Benchmarks in imparting child-centric education. It is also appreciated for igniting young minds with the spark of knowledge and lifelong learning, by Brainfeed, School Excellence Awards, 2018-19.

Parents' Comments

The parents of many children have sent beautiful tributes to Little Pearls and the faculty. Some of them are reproduced below.

1. *For us as foreigners, Little Pearls has been a great experience for Nach. It was his very first school when he joined in 2017. The Principal, Teachers, Assistants and general staff always have been very caring and loving with us. He really has had a wonderful time in Little Pearls. He wakes up every morning happy to go to school. Thanks a lot.*

   Mother of Ignacio,
   Embassy of Guatemala.

2. *We have been very pleased to have our Tyyne with you this spring. She didn't speak any English when she came, but now she speaks some and understands more. Most importantly she has had a safe and loving place to be during daytime. God Bless You All!!*

   Minna Holappa (Mother of Tyyne)
   Embassy of Finland.

3. *When settling down in New Delhi in September 2015, we could not have found a better school for our kids than Little Pearls. The warm welcome we experienced since the moment we entered the school, has continuously made us feel really special. High education standards, combined with individual approach to children, a wide range of creative activities and the most welcoming and kind attitude from the entire Little Pearls staff, is what makes this school so special and distinguishes it among other play-schools.*

   My heartiest thanks to the Little Pearls team for all the efforts and hard work they are doing on a daily basis to educate and bring up our children and help them become intelligent, compassionate, responsible and self-confident young adults.

   And many congratulations on the well-deserved Award as No. 1 pre-school in Delhi, for the second year in a row! May you keep up the positive spirit and high standards that make this school so special!

   Regards
   Ms. Stella Ankrava
   First Secretary
   Embassy of the Republic of Latvia.

4. *I would like to express our gratitude to Little Pearls. All the teachers are professional and thoughtful to children, including foreigners like my daughter Nodoka. She had some difficulties, especially in language when she started her school life at Little Pearls, but now, she enjoys communicating with her friends and teachers using both Hindi and English. That was a really nice experience for*

her second home in India. Thank you very much for all your assistance in two and a half years.

Regards
Mr. Shinichi and Mrs. Tomoka Ichinohe
Embassy of Japan.

5. *We are very happy that our son Dulmeth had the opportunity to undergo an enjoyable learning experience at the Little Pearls playschool. We got to know about Little Pearls when we were in Sri Lanka from the parents of an ex-student. We were impressed by the friendly and accommodating approach of the school. Apart from its well balanced, rich curriculum, Little Pearls offers a relaxed, supportive and safe environment for the children. Further, its diverse student community provides a wonderful global perspective for the children, making Little Pearls a memorable experience.*

   Mr. Senarath Dissanayake & Mrs. Shamilka Abeyratne
   Minister, High Commission of Sri Lanka.

6. *I am from a family of armed forces, both me and my husband are doctors in the army. Our search for a wonderful playschool for our twin daughters Akira & Alaina brought me to Little Pearls play school.*

   All apprehensions vanished when I met the friendly engaging and dedicated teachers. As soon as you enter Little Pearls each day, you are greeted with great warmth and affection. The teachers dedicate a lot of time to know the children and their families, to achieve a natural comfortable environment. All the children are treated with kindness and respect which makes them feel so valued and important. The big hugs and the warm hearts make our kids jump with joy. The affection of the entire team makes Little Pearls a child's "Home away from home".

Never in my dreams I thought that my daughters will be so happy going to school. They go with big smiles and come back with bigger ones, that's the most satisfying feeling. Participating in the multiple activities of the school stage performances has increased my daughter's confidence, communication skills and interpersonal relationships.

At last, I would like to especially thank Mrs. Shreyashee, my kid's class teacher for all the hard work, love and affection, she has put in her golden pearls and congratulate the principal Mrs. Ekta Sharma, for leaving no stone unturned to make Little Pearls school an unparallel destination for kids.

I recommend Little Pearls play school, in the highest of terms.

Regards
Major Sonia Datta (Mother of Akira & Alaina Rao).

PHOTOGRAPHS

56. Little Pearls School.

57. Entrance lobby of the Little Pearls School.

58. Deepak and Payel Seth lighting candles at a School event.

59. Science Lab at Little Pearls School.

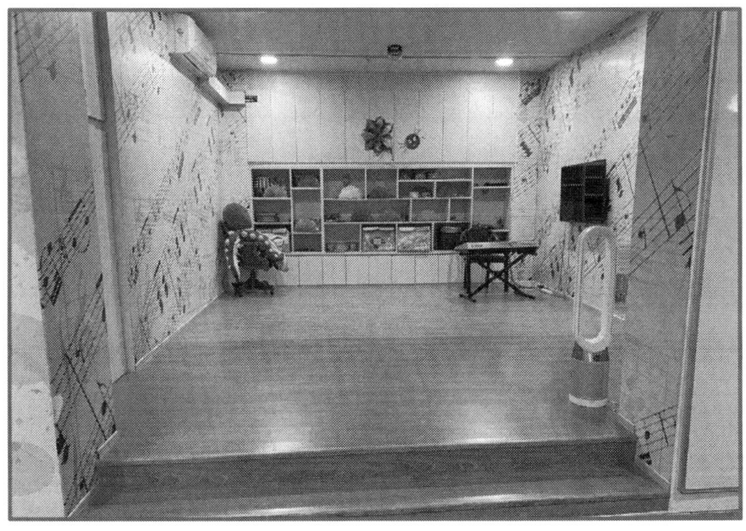

60. Music and Activity Room at Little Pearls School.

61. Indoor play zone at Little Pearls School.

62. Children playing in the outdoor play zone at Little Pearls School.

63. Playroom for girls, Little Pearls School.

64. Happy children playing at Little Pearls School.

65. Children at Little Pearls School.

66. Children learning at Little Pearls School.

40
Best Business Practices and Legacies

1. The Values

i. Integrity and Ethics in Business

The DS Group (Deepak Seth Group, including PDS and PGIL), adheres to all laws of the land, in every country it operates in. It maintains a high level of ethics in its dealings with all the stakeholders, including governments, customers, vendors, employees and shareholders.

The Group values its reputation. It maintains integrity in all its operations. It believes in absolute honesty in all its relationships. These principles constitute the foundation of the Group.

Within the DS Group, it is very clear to all employees, that a genuine mistake resulting in a loss of a million dollars will be excused. However, the company has zero tolerance for any lapse in integrity.

ii. Code of Conduct for All Employees

All Group units are governed by a Code of Conduct, wherein no abuse of any type is acceptable. All staff members are expected to abide by the laws of their countries and respect fellow employees. They are expected to be exemplary in their behaviour and conduct. The Group has a written Code of Conduct.

Every employee is expected to read and sign acceptance.

iii. Transparency and Trust

Trust is the glue which binds people and businesses together, in long-term relationships. The business maintains complete transparency in all its dealings with partners, vendors and employees. It has an array of partnerships and associations in all the countries, in which it operates. The Group aims at building long-term relationships with all its partners. It ensures that it is fair in all its dealings.

iv. Love and Care for Employees

The DS Group does not merely care for its employees. It loves them. The business has 30,000 employees now. Many employees have been with the company for around 30 years. Deepak treats every employee like a family member. The Group pays all employee dues like salaries and provident fund on schedule. There has never been a strike in any unit.

Deepak Seth has a reputation among his employees of being warm and hospitable. An employee was permitted unlimited leave with full pay, as he was suffering from cancer. Deepak has built a company with a heart and soul.

v. Philanthropy

The Group gives back to society, the goodwill it receives. So, every year, it undertakes activities which benefit the employees and the underprivileged sections of society. Some of the key initiatives are: a) Women empowerment, b) Worker training, c) Rural youth skill enhancement, d) Mina Seth Clinic, where economically weak sections of society can get free medicines, e) Pearl Academy of Fashion, f) Little Pearls School, g) Arpan, free education for children living in the slums, etc.

2. The Business Model

i. Having a Vision

Deepak wanted to clothe the world. He wanted to build a global business with first-rate customer service. He was the first Indian garment exporter to set up import offices abroad to service his customers. He also pioneered in providing design services to his customers abroad. Then, he took the lead in establishing manufacturing units in Bangladesh, UAE, Indonesia, Sri Lanka, Vietnam, etc. The Group also initiated a profit-sharing model, providing ownership and incentives to all the CEOs.

ii. Building a Brand

The Seth brothers have built the brand name "Pearl" to be synonymous with the family surname, "Seths". Deepak's mother used to fondly describe her sons as "pearls". In the early 1970s, the Seth brothers selected the word "Pearl" as their umbrella brand name. The brand name "Pearl" appears in many of the names of the companies started by the Seth family.

In the garment export companies launched or managed by Deepak, the brands PDS and PGIL have pride of place.

The Seth brothers have ensured that the brand name given to them by their mother, remains respected in business.

iii. Global Business, Customers

Deepak and his sons, Pallak and Pulkit, have built a global business. The Group has developed a robust network of global customers from Brazil and Chile, all the way to Australia and New Zealand. All the top retailers in the world are the Group's business associates. Having customers across continents is advantageous to the business. If any region faces a recession or crisis of any type, the Group can garner business from other regions.

iv. Services at the Doorsteps of the Customer

Robert Woodruff was the president of the Coca-Cola Company, from 1923 to 1985. He had promised to put a bottle of Coke "within arm's reach of desire" of everyone across the world. He did it.

Deepak's vision was similar. He wanted every large retailer customer to feel that he was just across the street to render service. The DS Group has its own offices in the USA, UK, Germany, Hong Kong, Dubai, etc. Earlier, it had established offices in Russia, UAE and Canada also. This has given the Group the opportunity to offer quick and quality services, to its customers abroad. The dedicated service, builds loyal customers.

v. Value-Added Design Services

Customers love value-added services. The Group has established Design departments in all its offices. They offer valuable design services to the customers. About 60 percent of PDS's orders emanate from designs offered by them to their customers.

vi. Factories Across the World

Deepak has established 22 garment factories in India, Bangladesh, Sri Lanka, Indonesia, Vietnam, etc. This gives the company immense production flexibilities. These factories are established after studying the costs of production, logistics, availability of raw materials, duties, investment, policies, etc. So, the Group can deliver any order from any customer, from its own factories.

In addition, the Group has operational relationships with about 200 third-party partner factories, who manufacture for it.

vii. One Hundred Percent Compliant Factories

Large retailers and customers source garments from factories, which comply with international ethical and social responsibilities. They prefer to deal with factories which are compliant in the areas of environment, sustainability and corporate governance (ESG). The Group has 100 percent complaint factories.

It has a clear policy to be fully compliant, irrespective of costs.

viii. Sustainable Growth

Customers insist that suppliers focus on sustainability. The DS Group factories are LEED (Leadership in Energy and Environmental Design) certified. The Group generates solar energy, ensures zero discharge, has effluent treatment plants, etc. It buys organic cotton. The factories strive for Green ratings from leading global buyers.

ix. Entrepreneurial Profit-Sharing Model

The CEOs' and Business Heads of the Group, have a share in the profits of the business units that they manage. This gives them an ownership of the results. They manage the operation with commitment. It fosters an entrepreneurial spirit. The DS Group is now, a "Company of Entrepreneurs."

x. Professionals to the Fore

Professionals are the backbone of any business. Deepak realised very early, that he could not be present personally in multi-locations. A family business cannot expand indefinitely, without recruiting professionals and empowering them. Deepak believes in hiring the best professionals for the business. He cares for them, pays them well and incentivises them. They can reach out to him through an e-mail, message or WhatsApp for any guidance.

xi. Company-wise Profit Centres

Each business in the DS Group is an independent profit centre. It has to be profitable on its own without any subsidies from the head office. All the companies are free to buy from any vendor, who offers the best price and quality. For instance, the Group sourcing office in Hong Kong, does not have to buy from a Group factory in Vietnam, if the price is not competitive. This keeps all the companies sharp and on their toes. It makes them competitive and cost-effective.

xii. Core Business: Stick to Knitting

The Group has adhered to its core business of garments, over the decades. Deepak understood fabrics, threads, buttons, garments, etc. So, he stayed with garments. Deepak did venture into the leather and the retailing businesses. However, he realised, it is best to grow in the fundamental business which he understands.

xiii. Constant Addition of Customers

The DS Group supplies garments to all the top retailers and customers across the world, like Marks & Spencer, Zara, Gap, Banana Republic, Walmart and Tesco. Over the decades, the Group has ensured that its customer base grows continuously. It has over 200 global customers. Deepak started the business with an order for 6,000 shirts from an importer. Now, all the top retailers in the world are direct customers of the Group.

xiv. Outsourcing Model: Scalable

The business has also developed an "Outsourcing Model", wherein it has third-party factories manufacturing for it. The production is supervised by the DS Group's local teams. This "Outsourcing Model" is highly scalable and has propelled growth.

xv. Hedging Future Risks

Deepak, Pallak and Pulkit are always mapping the future and taking proactive steps, to grow the business. In India, the Group has factories in metropolitan towns like Chennai, Bengaluru and Gurugram. The costs of production in these towns are rising due to escalation in rentals, labour costs, overheads, etc. The Group is therefore considering establishing factories in the interior regions, in states like Telangana and Andhra Pradesh, where operating costs are lower and there are investment incentives.

xvi. Cut your Losses, Move On

As a businessman, Deepak does not cry over spilt milk. If a business does not deliver results in about three years, he is quite open to shutting it and cutting the losses.

xvii. Succession Planning

Deepak Seth has planned the future of the business and his sons methodically. He sent his sons to study in the top universities in the USA. Then, he inducted them into the business via the Hong Kong operations. Later, he positioned Pallak in London to manage PDS.

Pulkit manages the PGIL operation from the USA and India.

Deepak trained them personally. He guides them regularly. He facilitated the demerger of the business in two parts, so that each son had a separate business to manage. He continues to be the Chairman of both the businesses and mentors all the teams.

3. Business Practices

i. Ahead of the Curve

A businessman has to stay ahead of the business curve to survive and grow. He has to keep abreast of business trends and monitor the political and economic environment constantly. Deepak, Pallak and Pulkit scan the global political and economic ecosystems constantly. They and their teams also monitor developments in the fashion industry closely. They are therefore always ahead of the industry in opening new offices, factories and recruiting new talent.

Deepak has mastered the art of reading the global markets in advance. He is thus prepared for changes in market dynamics.

ii. IT Practices, Measures

The Group has been a pioneer in introducing IT systems and processes in all its business units. Implementing SAP-ERP has interwoven all the production and sourcing offices. The use of barcodes helps to track a garment from stitching to packing.

This has improved inventory management in the factories. Use of RFID chips by larger units like the PT Pinnacle in Indonesia, improves production control. Introduction of other measures like the Net Contribution Concept in the ERP application, help to monitor financial performance. Line Planning, enables optimum utilisation of all the production capacities.

iii. Managing Cannibalisation

PDS comprises of 45 companies on its Platform. Many of the companies compete for the same set of customers. To eliminate the risks of cannibalisation, the firm has developed frameworks. There is the "Boundary System" to decide the best team to deal with the customer, based on select criteria. The "Collaborative Framework" ensures that the company which introduces a customer and the company which executes the order, share the profits.

iv. Risk Management

The DS Group manages risks by generating options. Each Group company has two to three vendors for every raw material. The maximum business with any vendor is 20 percent of the aggregate. This is simply to hedge risks.

The Group always has two or three bankers for each business. It has also built numerous factories to ensure seamless supplies. The Group has also created a basket of more than 200 customers. It has strong internal controls and regulations to ensure continuous operations.

v. Zero Stock Risks

A perpetual concern in the apparel business is the risk of unsold stocks. If an order is delayed or there is a change in fashion, the retailer or vendor could be left with unsold inventories. The Group does not take stock risks. It buys raw materials only after receiving confirmed orders. This helps to leverage effectively with banks, to get adequate working capital.

vi. Controlling Costs

The Group manages a tight cost-effectiveness programme. Every new order is rigorously costed. Operating costs are reined in line with budgets. The garment business operates on thin profit margins. Labour is a major cost. Globally, costs of labour, raw materials, infrastructure etc., are escalating due to inflation. So, the Group ensures that there is no overtime, orders are despatched on schedule by ship, etc., to guard the bottom line.

vii. Keeping Employees Motivated

Deepak and his teams, ensure that the staff is always motivated, by participating in a range of training programmes and self-development activities. The Group believes in internal promotions. It provides skills development training to its employees and has developed mobile applications like "WE" (Worker's Engagement), etc., to involve the staff.

viii. Happy and Loyal Vendors

The DS Group builds trust with all the stakeholders. It treats them as valued business partners. The Group builds strong and long-term relationships with all its vendors and suppliers. It makes all payments on schedule. Deepak believes in being fair with everyone.

ix. Execution Skills

The Group has acquired distinct expertise in brilliant and seamless execution. Whether it is transforming an idea into a factory or metamorphosing an idea into a new sourcing office abroad, the teams are very swift and efficient.

Despite being very effective in execution, Deepak does not ever rock the boat. He tries to ensure that there are no ruptured relations, in the execution of a project. The Group has built a top-notch team, which can deliver results expeditiously. Deepak himself, has the reputation of being a dazzling executioner.

x. Quick Decision-Making

Deepak is known for taking speedy decisions. He is always ready with a decision for any issue or problem that surfaces. All his team members extol him for his swift decisions, which contribute to immediate action. This propensity for prompt decisions and action, has percolated to the senior management team also, transforming the business into an energetic and vibrant organisation.

xi. Empowered Business Heads

The CEOs of the business offices and the factories, are profit-sharing partners in the enterprise. Deepak ensures that they have complete autonomy to manage their operations. They are empowered to manage their units independently. This, motivates them. Thus, the Group cements long-term bonds with its partners. Many of the business heads have worked in the Group for 20 to 30 years.

xii. Open to Suggestions

The Group is always open to suggestions for improving the organisation, irrespective of the level of the person making them. Hierarchy, does not determine the quality of a suggestion. Moreover, Deepak keeps an "Open Door Policy" so that any employee who wishes to speak to him, can just walk into his room, without an appointment.

xiii. Boots on the Ground

Deepak and his sons Pallak and Pulkit travel 10 to 20 days every month, visiting their customers, sourcing offices and factories. This helps them to get direct feedback from their customers and keeps them grounded. In business, despite all the information reports that flow in, there is no substitute for meeting people in the markets, offices and factories and talking to them.

The sights and sounds in the markets, provide the best clues to innovations and future growth.

xiv. Disciplines – Punctuality

Deepak is ruthlessly punctual for every meeting. He respects time. Time perishes. An hour wasted, is an hour gone forever. It can never be reclaimed. Deepak respects the time of others too. He will seek a postponement sufficiently in advance, if he is going to be late.

This respect for time, has percolated amongst his team members also and has become a part of the operating culture of the company.

41
Deepak Seth's Lessons for The Young

1. Sustained Work and Discipline

Dedicated work is a religion for Deepak. There is no substitute for sheer, sustained work. Deepak works round the clock. He works all seven days of the week. He sleeps with his mobile phone next to him. He attends to telephone calls from business associates, even in the middle of the night. He clears all messages and e-mails daily, before leaving his office.

Deepak does take holidays with his family. However, he continues to manage the business through his phone and laptop, wherever he is.

As a teenager, Deepak had observed his father work 12 to 14 hours a day, seven days a week. He had seen his dad rise from a humble chemist to Executive Director, in the prestigious DCM Group Company, DCM Chemicals. From his father, he imbibed the values of honesty, rigorous discipline, and unremitting work. These values got entrenched in him. They are the keys to success in any endeavour.

2. Importance of Family and Relationships

Deepak learnt the importance of family and relationships from his mother Mrs. Mina Seth. She maintained cordial and warm relations with everyone. Deepak is credited by his brothers for bonding the entire family together. He maintains excellent relationships within his own family and the extended family. The entire family stands together like a steel wall, all the time. This is a great family asset. Maintaining robust family relationships is very important for a productive and successful life. A stable and happy home contributes to success, outside the house.

3. Respect for Elders

Deepak has always had immense respect and love for his parents. He worships them. Respect for the elders in the family, is a unique Indian family characteristic. Deepak has immense respect for his elder brothers and heeds their advice. He consults his eldest brother Chand, on all the business plans. He also holds his mother-in-law in great esteem. The respect that Deepak has shown to his elders, makes him a role model for the younger family members.

4. Burning Desire to be Number One

From school onwards, Deepak wanted to be the best at whatever he did. Be it sports, athletics, academics, or business, he had the burning desire to succeed. He had a passion for everything and wanted to be at the top of the heap in every activity.

He always excelled in sports and academics. He garnered 14 trophies in his final school year in events like 100 metres, 200 metres, 400 metres, 800 metres, etc.

Throughout his career, he was never content to be a No. 2 or No. 3 in any business activity. He always wanted to be

No. 1, the best and the biggest. In 1976, he started business with an order for 6,000 shirts, without even having a factory. Now, Deepak has built the Group to become a global apparel fashion business. The DS Group (including PDS and PGIL), ships over 400 million garments annually, which is over a million pieces daily.

5. Never Give Up

Deepak never gives up. He fights adversity with effortless grit. He had fractured his leg and was on crutches in 1976 when he was starting business. Yet, he was the first to leave the home every day and the last to return. A broken leg did not deter him from working 12 to 14 hours a day. It was an ordeal for Deepak to complete the first order for 6,000 shirts, when he did not have a factory or staff. He deployed the drivers and the maids, to pack the shirts in the garage of his home. He delivered.

The path to success is often paved with failure and heartbreak. However, if a person is tenacious and does not give up, he fulfils his destiny.

Deepak aimed to build a global business with offices in the USA and Europe to service the customers. He wanted to build a network of factories in South Asia and Southeast Asia, to feed his customers. He did it. Single-minded pursuit of goals, leads to success.

6. Health, the Real Wealth

Wealth and success are utterly meaningless without excellent health. At school, Deepak learnt wrestling and athletics. He also played cricket and football. Now, Deepak exercises seven days a week for a minimum of an hour. It is a "must-do" homework for him. Then, he drinks about half a litre of bitter gourd juice, as an anti-acidic.

He is always ready for a game of cricket or golf. Deepak attended the alumni meeting of his business school classmates, in Goa in 2020. Every morning, he was the first person out for a brisk walk on the beach or into the swimming pool. Every few months or years, Deepak and Payel attend a detoxing health clinic in some part of the world.

In his youthful days, Deepak smoked about 20 cigarettes a day. Then one day, he decided to quit smoking. He just did it. "It does not do any good for me," he commented.

Deepak is yet open to an arm-wrestling bout, even with youngsters half his age. His palms with which he pulverised bricks in his school days, are yet as hard as steel plates.

7. Fight for the Weak

During his school days, Deepak was a bodybuilder and practiced weight lifting. He woke up daily at 4 am daily, to train at a wrestling ring. He was the strongest student in his school and would pick up the gauntlet for the weaker students. He was against any type of bullying of new students, particularly the girls.

The characteristic of helping others in need, got ingrained in him. Deepak never disappoints anybody who approaches him for any guidance or assistance. He is always there with a helping hand.

8. Tireless Innovations

Deepak's first project after joining the family business, was to establish a market for a bubble film, which their company was producing. It was a new product concept, being launched as a film wrapping, for electronic items. His dedication to ensure success inspired him to innovate new uses of the film, like table mats and bottle covers. It was a tough business; his creative ideas helped.

Deepak has shown the same enterprise in introducing design departments across the businesses abroad. Retailers and customers adore the designs being pioneered by the Group's designers. Deepak also innovated the CEO-entrepreneurial model and the scalable outsourcing model in the business.

9. Will and Way

When Deepak received the first order for 6,000 shirts, he knew nothing about the garments business. He got the fabric from wholesalers on cash. He got the hand embroidery done through teams of women, working overnight in their homes. Then, came the buttoning, washing and pressing. Finally, the shirts were packed in the garage at home. At 2 am, the shirts were on a flight to the USA. This is how the first order was executed. The rest is history. Thus, if there is a will, there is a way.

Deepak and his teams always find a way to get the job done. Failure is never an option.

10. Dedication and Commitment

In the initial years, Deepak carried garment samples to potential customers, on his Lambretta scooter. Fifteen years later, Deepak dragged suitcases of samples through the streets of London and Amsterdam, whilst visiting customers. He was Chairman of the company, but had no hesitation in carting samples to woo customers. The rides on Lambrettas and local trains, finally led to a Rolls Royce Phantom, in his parking lot.

Consistent dedication and commitment, are essential for success in any business.

11. Crisp Details, No Papers

Deepak works on his business 24 by 7. He has developed a razor-sharp memory and instantly recollects figures and previous discussions of 20 years ago. Since he is always focussed, he has developed a high grasping power. Some colleagues describe him as a walking-talking, high-speed computer.

Deepak is always short of time. He likes crisp discussions. He wants only relevant details tabled to him. He is a patient person, but has no time for stories. There are no mounds of papers on his table. He talks to a person and takes a decision. Issue resolved. No essays or papers. His table is always clean. Literally.

12. Being Fair – A Religion

Deepak has a penchant for being very fair in all his professional or personal dealings. He is very particular about this. Deepak nurtures all his relationships. He realises that fairness is the foundation of any long-term association. He never lets anyone down. He always stands by his word.

13. Decision-Making Skills

A critical quality in an entrepreneur, is the ability to grasp any situation quickly and take expeditious decisions. Deepak is a quick thinker and decision maker. He does not have lingering doubts. He takes a decision. If it turns out incorrect, there are fallouts. Then, Deepak deals with them expeditiously.

14. Grasping and Art of Listening

Deepak is very humble. He is a great listener. He is very sharp, too. So very often, when a person is talking to him, after the first few words or sentences, he grasps what the person wants to say.

However, he maintains his silence. He will listen to the person completely. Only after that will he react. His message to young managers is, "In business, always listen carefully, before you speak."

15. Immediate Responses

Deepak responds to any message instantly, within minutes. If he is in a meeting or on a flight, the response will come within hours, but definitely on the same day. He does not procrastinate or protract.

16. Thank People

Deepak never forgets anybody, who does anything for the Group or for him. He always thanks people with a smile. He is a very gracious person. He never takes anything or anybody for granted.

17. Invest to Grow Rich

Money should always grow. To earn money and leave it in the bank reduces it to paper. So, a smart businessman will always invest his earnings in ventures, assets and financial instruments which will grow. The investments may be in real estate, the stock market or in other businesses. Deepak ensures that he is highly literate financially. He keeps in touch with markets across the world.

18. Goodwill: Best Asset in Bank of Life

Deepak does not make enemies. Good relationships are the oxygen of any business. He maintains all relations. He helps anybody in need, but only seeks the blessings of people in return. The goodwill a person garners in life by helping others, is the best asset in the bank of life. It lasts forever. It never depreciates. It only grows.

19. Managing Reorganisation Amicably

The family business was reorganised amicably in 1987 and everyone stayed glued together. The businesses could be managed separately, but the family remained forged. Deepak and his brothers consult each other constantly on business and personal matters.

20. Maintaining Work-Life Balance

Managing a growing business needs focus, time, and travel. Deepak travels for about 10 to 20 days every month. However, his top priority is to spend some time with the family at every opportunity. Besides the annual family holidays, he ensures that there are frequent dinners, whereby all the brothers and their families meet regularly. The Seth brothers had learnt from their mother, the importance of family and cordial relationships in life.

21. An Integrated Lifestyle

Deepak has managed to evolve an integrated lifestyle for himself. He is close to his family and his brothers and their children. He loves his children, grandchildren and all his nephews and nieces. They are his darlings. They too, adore him.

He is also very caring of his business associates. He keeps his friends with him. His classmates from school, college and management school are yet his buddies, even after 50 to 60 years. He has time for everybody. He has the skill to make everybody he meets, feel like a very “special person”.

22. Time for "Sparkle", "Angel" and "Biscuit"

With all their time pressures, Deepak and Payel find time for their pet dogs Sparkle, Angel and Biscuit. They have Maltese and Chihuahua breeds of dogs. Whenever Payel or Deepak leave for work, the dogs come to the door to see them off. In the evenings, they wait near the door for them to return. No family meeting, dinner or celebration is complete without Sparkle, Angel and Biscuit being present.

Every morning, Deepak personally feeds a large pet bird, an Australian Cockatoo, named Pearl.

23. Power of Prayer

Deepak prays regularly. He also encouraged Pallak and Pulkit to pray regularly even when they were children. Deepak and Payel have tended to their children like flowers.

42
Poem on Mr. Deepak Seth By Mr. Surender Dhillon

Deepak means Light, Seth means Glory

Deepak, you glow with brightness
You have also illuminated the lives of others.

Your achievements are recognised by all
Your talent is cherished by everyone.

You are endowed with the passion of achievement
You have proved the real meaning of success.

Your personality is loved by everyone
You have earned a fine name
You have also enriched the lives of others.

We love your sensitivity
We love your care and concern
Well done, Deepak Seth.

OTHER BOOKS BY RAJENDRA ANEJA

Printed in Great Britain
by Amazon

79680516R00301